ADVOCATES OF HUMANITY

CLARENDON STUDIES IN CRIMINOLOGY

Published under the auspices of the Institute of Criminology, University of Cambridge; the Mannheim Centre, London School of Economics; and the Centre for Criminology, University of Oxford.

RECENT TITLES IN THIS SERIES:

Respect and Criminal Justice
Watson

Respectable Citizens—Shady Practices: The Economic Morality of the Middle Classes
Farrall and Karstedt

Intimate Crimes: Kidnapping, Gangs, and Trust in Mexico City
Ochoa

Police Community Support Officers: Cultures and Identities within Pluralised Policing
O'Neill

Last Chance for Life: Clemency in Southeast Asian Death Penalty Cases
Pascoe

Police Unlimited: Policing, Migrants, and the Values of Bureaucracy
Mutsaers

Common Enemies: Crime, Policy, and Politics in Australia-Indonesia Relations
McKenzie

Embodying Punishment: Emotions, Identities, and Lived Experiences in Women's Prisons
Chamberlen

Advocates of Humanity

Human Rights NGOs in International Criminal Justice

KJERSTI LOHNE

OXFORD
UNIVERSITY PRESS

OXFORD
UNIVERSITY PRESS

Great Clarendon Street, Oxford, OX2 6DP,
United Kingdom

Oxford University Press is a department of the University of Oxford.
It furthers the University's objective of excellence in research, scholarship,
and education by publishing worldwide. Oxford is a registered trade mark of
Oxford University Press in the UK and in certain other countries

First Edition published in 2019

Impression: 2

Published in the United States of America by Oxford University Press
198 Madison Avenue, New York, NY 10016, United States of America

British Library Cataloguing in Publication Data

Data available

Library of Congress Control Number: 2019946542

ISBN 978–0–19–881874–8

Printed and bound by
CPI Group (UK) Ltd, Croydon, CR0 4YY

General Editors' Introduction

The Clarendon Studies in Criminology Series aims to provide a forum for outstanding theoretical and empirical work in all aspects of criminology and criminal justice, broadly understood. The Editors welcome submissions from established scholars, as well as excellent PhD work. The Series was inaugurated in 1994, with Roger Hood as its first General Editor, following discussions between Oxford University Press and the Oxford Centre for Criminology. It is edited under the auspices of the Institute of Criminology at the University of Cambridge, the Mannheim Centre for Criminology at the London School of Economics, and the Centre for Criminology at the University of Oxford. Each supplies members of the Editorial Board and, in turn, the Series Editor or Editors.

Kjersti Lohne's *Advocates of Humanity* provides an in-depth treatment of 'criminal justice gone global', turning a critical eye to the dynamic transnational framework of more local entities and their role in shaping the international discourse. Specifically, this book aims to detail how international human rights NGOs have influenced the meaning of punishment at a global level. It achieves this by conducting innovative ethnographic research across multiple nodes within a transnational advocacy network of NGOs which disperse ideas of global justice. These nodes lie at the hub of global justice–the International Criminal Court in The Hague–and across the Coalition for the ICC and its Steering Committee NGO network, spanning from European and Scandinavian to African nodes. It first explores the constellation of entities which forms the infrastructure of international criminal justice, and then examines how criminal justice emerges through their interconnections and interactions. Crucially, it maintains a critical eye on these processes, probing structural inequalities in who has access to global justice-making and therefore who controls the discourse. In doing so, *Advocates of Humanity* identifies those key players who are the 'advocates of humanity' and locates their perspectives on justice in the global North.

This book then explores notions of global justice, who controls the terms of the dialogue and the dominant moral order, and how this sits uneasily in some cases with local ideas of justice. This filters into conceptualizations of punishment, what is just, and the centrality of the victim's experience in international justice. Finally, it turns to consideration of discontents with the current state of affairs, identifies directions of resistance and scrutinizes their implications for the legitimacy of, in particular, the International Criminal Court.

Kjersti Lohne's critical eye allows her to explore these topics from various angles, drawing on her observations and the knowledge gathered through her research. This culminates in an intriguing assessment of the dynamics of global justice, the differential impact of a variety of local players, and the challenges this creates for unifying international approaches to punishment. As Editors, we feel *Advocates of Humanity* book makes a very welcome contribution to our understanding and appreciation of the contemporary phenomenon of global justice, and our consideration of how it may evolve in the future. This book should have wide appeal, with relevance to scholars of criminology, sociology, international relations, international law, and so forth. We therefore warmly welcome *Advocates of Humanity: Human Rights NGOs in International Criminal Justice* to the *Clarendon Studies in Criminology Series.*

Kyle Treiber and Loraine Gelsthorpe
University of Cambridge Institute of Criminology
September 2019

Acknowledgements

After a decade of thinking about this topic, these acknowledgements are the last words I write. Yet they too have incurred many thoughts, as no project like this can be carried out without debts of many kinds. Most of these cannot be repaid, but the least I can do is offer thanks. First, these go to the many individuals and informants that have given shape to this research by sharing their time, ideas, and insights. Any language that seeks to bring an end to violence and suffering is useful; similarly, the pursuit of justice is a virtuous one. It is therefore out of deepest respect that I now attempt to offer an understanding of this pursuit.

This book is an adaptation of my PhD thesis defended at the University of Oslo. To be able to spend my time thinking, travelling, and dwelling under the auspices of a PhD Fellowship at the University of Oslo is a position of profound privilege. It is a position very far from the violence with which this book is concerned, although not from the spaces from where justice is exported. Such global inequalities should never cease to stir up activism and reflection.

Two people have been the pillars of the research project, and have followed the trajectory of my interests and research for many years. I will forever be grateful for their intelligence, kindness, and unflagging faith in this project, and my ability to do it. Katja Franko's analytical, thoughtful, and thorough feedback has given me the courage without which this book could not have been written. That this project was conceived at all is in large part due to Kristin Bergtora Sandvik. She has taught me how to be a researcher and given me her forthright advice on this project and wider concerns. The support of these two women has inspired me to work harder and better.

I am also indebted to a number of individuals who have generously engaged with draft versions of sections and chapters that have found its way into this book. I would like to thank Chrisje Brants, Mikkel Jarle Christensen, Edme Dominguez, Mark Drumbl, Richard Georgi, Maj Grasten, Jakob v. H. Holterman, Astrid Kjelgaard-Pedersen, Mikael Rask Madsen, Jed Odermatt,

Ole Jacob Sending, and Achilles Skordas. Carolyn Hoyle, Rene van Scheveningen, and Ole Hammesvik provided critical, excellent comments in their roles as my PhD adjudication committee. Their insights have been essential to adapting the manuscript. Thank you!

I am likewise grateful to my colleagues at the Department of Criminology and Sociology of Law, and especially to Heidi Mork Lomell, Turid Eikvam, Eivind Roll, May-Len Skilbrei, and Per Jørgen Ystehede for administrative support throughout the years. Thomas Ugelvik managed to be a mentor and friend at the same time. Anette Bringedal Houge became a precious ally, not only in international criminology, but also in life. Both of them provided invaluable feedback throughout the research process and on earlier chapters of the manuscript. Special thanks also to Sigmund Book Mohn, Kjersti Ericsson, Liv Finstad, Sverre Flaatten, Elise Koppang Frøjd, Hedda Giertsen, Vidar Halvorsen, Synnøve Jahnsen, Nicolay B. Johansen, Jenny Maria Lundgaard, Thomas Mathiesen, Marte Rua, Sveinung Sandberg, Lill Scherdin, Peter Scharff Smith, and Ragnhild Sollund. I am also thankful to Nils Christie, whose teachings and thoughts inspired the first seeds of this intellectual project, and whose ideas continue to be a source of critical reflection.

I have benefited greatly from a number of other academic institutions, affiliations, and research networks. In 2013, I was a Visiting Research Fellow at the Center for International Criminal Justice at the Vrije Universiteit in Amsterdam. Thanks to Joris van Wijk for his hospitality, humour and knowledge—and for introducing me to Marieke de Hoon, Barbora Holá, Annika van Baar, and Maartje Weerdesteijn. In 2014, I was an Academic Visitor at the Centre for Criminology at Oxford University, which enabled me to write in one of the most intellectually inspiring places possible. In 2018, I was a Visiting Researcher at iCourts at the University of Copenhagen, where the entire centre generously contributed to a critical seminar on my draft manuscript. The Research School in Peace and Conflict at PRIO, and especially Kristoffer Lidén and Lynn Nygaard, deserve recognition for providing an early interdisciplinary haven for young and early career research vagabonds. Throughout the years, I have benefited from the feedback and intellectual engagements with numerous scholars from the European Society of Criminology (the working group on Atrocity Crimes and Transitional Justice especially), the International Studies Association, and the COST action on 'International Law between Constitutionalism and Fragmentation'. I would also like to extend my thanks to the OUP team and the Clarendon Studies in Criminology editors for their feedback and assistance throughout the publication process.

I have received generous support from a variety of Norwegian and international funds and fellowships: The Tokyo Foundation's Royichi Sasakawa Young Leaders Fellowship Fund, the Scandinavian Research Council for Criminology Travel Grant, *Den norske banks fond for det Juridiske fakultet ved Universitetet i Oslo, Borgermester Edvard Christies legat, Ingmund Kirkerud legat, Pastor Harald Kallevigs legat, Assessor L. W. Knagenhjelm og fru Knagenhjelms født Rolls legat, Det juridiske fakultets reisefond av 1973*, and the Research Group on International Law at the University of Oslo. PluriCourts funded my fieldwork in Uganda and deserves a special thank you, and especially Cecilie M. Bailliet, Sofie A.E. Høgestøl, Silje Aambø Langvatn, and Nobuo Hayashi. With the latter I also had entertaining conversations about international criminal law and justice over many years.

A number of other people have also helped and contributed, though I cannot name them all. However, Morten Bergsmo first put me onto the idea of a sociology of international criminal justice more than a decade ago, for which I owe him a great debt of thanks, and for further inspiring conversations since. I am also grateful for the thought-provoking conversations I had with Bert van Roermund while visiting Rwanda, and to Harriet Loum, Hege Rytter Jacobsen and Lone Jessen, who put me in touch with friends and family in Uganda. Henrik Werenskiold provided critical support at the end of the research project. Daphne Day cleaned up the language. Jakob, my love, has given me reason to finish.

The book has included work abroad and away, sometimes for lengthy periods, sometimes in places that might be considered volatile. Often I've been distant too. Therefore, this has at times been difficult for dear ones, and I am truly indebted to my family and my extraordinary friends for their support and patience. I cannot love you more, but I'll try to love you better. None of this would have been possible without the solid ground provided by my parents Gerd and Thor Otto Lohne, dearest Mariann, John Roald, Ian Emiil, and mormor. Finally, to Erik Baltzer Osvik, who spent his life fighting for the rights of others. The world might be unfair, but it stood a better chance with him in it. The book is dedicated to his memory.

Contents

Detailed Contents

List of Abbreviations

AI	Amnesty International
ARLPI	Acholi Religious Leaders Peace Initiative
ASP	Assembly of States Parties
AU	African Union
CAR	Central African Republic
CEPEJ	European Commission for the Efficiency of Justice
CICC	Coalition for the International Criminal Court
DRC	Democratic Republic of the Congo
ECOSOC	United Nations Economic and Social Council
FIDH	International Federation for Human Rights
HRW	Human Rights Watch
HURINET-U	Human Rights Network—Uganda
IBA	International Bar Association
ICC	International Criminal Court
ICJ	International Criminal Justice
ICL	International Criminal Law
ICRC	International Committee of the Red Cross
ICTR	International Criminal Tribunal for Rwanda
ICTY	International Criminal Tribunal for the former Yugoslavia
LRA	Lord's Resistance Army
MENA	Middle Eastern and North African
MICT	UN Mechanism for International Criminal Tribunals
NGO	Non-governmental organisation
NPWJ	No Peace Without Justice
NRC	Norwegian Refugee Council
OPCW	Organisation for the Prohibition of Chemical Weapons
OSJI	Open Society Justice Initiative
OTP	Office of The Prosecutor
PGA	Parliamentarians for Global Action
PSVI	Preventing Sexual Violence Initiative
SC	Security Council

SCSL	Special Court for Sierra Leone
SGBV	Sexual and Gender-Based Violence
TAN	Transnational Advocacy Networks
TFV	Trust Fund for Victims
UCICC	Ugandan Coalition for the International Criminal Court
UCP	Union of Congolese Patriots
UIA	Union of International Associations
UN	United Nations
UNSC	United Nations Security Council
VRWG	Victims' Rights Working Group
WFM-IGP	World Federalist Movement-Institute for Global Policy
WIGJ	Women's Initiative for Gender Justice

In contemporary societies, where inequalities have reached an unprecedented level, humanitarianism elicits the fantasy of a global moral community that may still be viable and the expectation that solidarity may have redeeming powers.

This secular imaginary of communion and redemption implies a sudden awareness of the fundament unequal human condition and an ethical necessity to not remain passive about it in the name of solidarity—however ephemeral this awareness is, and whatever limited impact this necessity has.

Humanitarianism has this remarkable capacity: it fugaciously and illusorily bridges the contradictions of our world, and makes the intolerableness of its injustices somewhat more bearable.

Didier Fassin

Humanitarian Reason (2012: xii)

The universal offers us the chance to participate in the global stream of humanity.

We can't turn it down.

Anna Lowenhaupt Tsing

Friction (2005: 1)

1

Locating International Criminal Justice

Connections, Forces, Imaginations

We're mingling over canapés and drinks as a jazz trio plays in the background—diplomats, legal practitioners from the International Criminal Court (ICC), and representatives from non-governmental organizations (NGOs). As the trio finish their set, the Convener for the NGO Coalition for the International Criminal Court (CICC), William (Bill) Pace, steps onto the podium. As we gather around him, he reminds us of the responsibilities resting on our shoulders: 'History will write in awe about the achievements of international justice—unless we fail!' The other host of the night, the Mayor of The Hague, Jozias van Aartsen, follows him, declaring that 'the ICC represents the best of what the international community has achieved'. At this moment in time however, he says it is ever more important to defend the idea of the Court, highlighting the role of the city of The Hague as a worldwide knowledge hub for international criminal justice, and the significance of NGOs in this pursuit.

According to their homepage, the CICC—a 'global civil society network of over 2,500 member organizations'—'led the successful campaign to set up the International Criminal Court for war crimes, crimes against humanity, and genocide … [and are] continuing to fight for global justice through national courts and the now well-established ICC'.[1] From its seat in The Hague, in the Netherlands, the ICC began its work in 2002, and has indeed jurisdiction over crimes against humanity, genocide, and war crimes on the territories and over the citizens of states that have ratified

[1] http://www.coalitionfortheicc.org/about-coalition-0 (accessed 11 April 2018).

Advocates of Humanity. Kjersti Lohne, Oxford University Press (2019). © Kjersti Lohne.
DOI: 10.1093/oso/9780198818748.003.0001

its founding Rome Statute.[2] Today, 123 states are members of the Court, and with that have given up some of their monopoly of the use of force. Criminal punishment has 'gone global'.

This book is about this development, and more specifically about the signification of the relationship between a purported 'global civil society' with global criminal justice-making. What does it mean when it is said that the ICC is a 'global civil society achievement' (e.g. Glasius, 2006)—who are these actors, how do they imagine global justice through the ICC, and what do these connections imply for the meaning and social functions of punishment at the global level of analysis? To this end, the book offers an analysis of transnational networks in their mobilization for global justice through the ICC.

NGOs fulfil a number of functions in international criminal justice that, arguably, would be inconceivable at the national level of criminal justice (see Tomczak, 2016). In addition to their 'traditional' roles of advocacy and agenda-setting, NGOs identify and represent victims to the Court; they provide evidence and *amicus curia* briefs; do 'outreach' vis-à-vis affected communities; lobby states for financial and political support of the Court; and draft penal codes and promote their implementation in domestic systems of criminal justice—to give but a few examples. Yet more than just functioning as 'judicial institution builders' (Haddad, 2012), NGOs are presumed to provide the field of international criminal justice with moral authority (Dixon and Tenove, 2013). By speaking on behalf of victims 'everywhere', human rights NGOs produce moral outrage at distant suffering while asserting cosmopolitan notions of solidarity and justice in an ultimately state-centric international order. As such, their embrace of international criminal justice is considered part of the advance towards a more 'people-empowering' international rule of law (Glasius, 2002)—a global criminal order created by and for 'humanity' rather than the interests of nation states.

To discern the social organization of this connection, I have approached the transnational networks of NGOs advocating for the ICC as an ethnographic object, albeit a messy and multi-sited one. A central objective is to explore how connections are made, and how forces and imaginations of global (criminal) justice travel.

[2] Since 17 July 2018, the ICC also has jurisdiction over states that have ratified the amendment to the Rome Statute on the crime of aggression (see Kreß, 2018).

How do NGOs 'connect' for justice, and what are the aspects of global social organization that enable these linkages and ruptures? Ideas of global (criminal) justice travel with and across people, organizations, and the internet. Likewise, the work of international criminal justice is multi-sited. Conflict and mass violence in one part of the world are transported into the courtrooms in another; here they are rendered intelligible through law and legal experts who, with reason and logic, search for justice in the form of individual accountability. This trajectory of global justice-making is imagined to come full circle once the deliberations are over, when blame has been attributed, and 'justice' is dispersed back to the site of conflict and mass violence. The multi-sited materiality of the ICC, and of the field of international criminal justice generally, is thus symptomatic of the 'unbundling' of the local as a container of the social (Sassen, 2007). 'Traditional' ethnographic approaches that equate social phenomena with limited and bounded localities no longer suffice (Burawoy, 2000; Anders, 2007; Faubion and Marcus, 2009).

While research has spanned the nations of Belgium, the Netherlands, Norway, Rwanda, Uganda, and the UK, The Hague—as the centre of global justice-making—has been the primary perspective in research and analysis. There, multiple locations make up analytical sites; from the ICC and other courts in the city, the ICC Assembly of States Parties (ASP) diplomatic meetings in the World Forum, NGO headquarters and satellite offices, to the plethora of research institutes and informal sites of restaurants, pubs, and cafés around the city. The description of the CICC and The Hague Municipality's reception demonstrates the potential of such an approach. To further reflect the field's (dis) connections, I traced the network structure of the CICC, focusing on their Secretariat in The Hague; their core group of Steering Committee NGO members—most of whom had permanent representation in The Hague (or Brussels or London); and one case of centre-periphery relations, tracing its regional networks to Africa, its national networks to Uganda, and finally to its local network in Gulu in northern Uganda—one of the sites of mass violence that is the object of global justice-making at the ICC. Analytically, this approach involved a shift from an ethnographic focus on 'site' to the study of international criminal justice as 'field', meaning the *relation* between sites enables insights into the connections and disconnections of the whole (Burawoy, 2001).

Research Aims

The research for this book had already begun during my postgraduate work on the ICC's intervention in northern Uganda, a region tormented by a protracted violent conflict between the Ugandan government and the Lord's Resistance Army (LRA)—with the civilian Acholi population in the midst of it. As peace talks between the Ugandan government and the LRA were progressing, the ICC issued arrest warrants for five of the top commanders of the LRA. However, the ICC indictments turned out to be a major obstacle to achieving peace and security in the region, as the LRA refused to lay down arms and continue peace negotiations with the threat of arrests hanging over their heads. The situation in northern Uganda thus came to be, in the words of a contemporary observer, 'something of a battleground between those who have been promoting the immediate application of mechanisms of retributive justice, and those who feel that this particular way of pursuing justice substantially jeopardises the prospects of peace' (Okello, 2007: 1). When I explored the different conceptualizations of justice that characterized this 'battleground', the role of international human rights NGOs as carriers of discourses on justice emerged as a principal finding—and one that suggested further research. International human rights NGOs represented and promoted specific modes of thinking about justice and punishment, and a core objective of this research has been to unpack what these mentalities and sensibilities consist of. Questions of values and meanings attributed to international criminal justice has thus guided this research, particularly as regards its role as an expression of 'the international' will to punish. To whom is it meaningful, and why?

To this end, the central aim of this book is to explore how the role of international human rights NGOs in international criminal justice yields empirical insight into the meaning of punishment at the global level of analysis. This overarching objective has been guided by way of three separate yet interrelated sets of analytic questions:

1. What are the roles of NGOs in international criminal justice?
2. What characterizes punishment 'gone global'?
3. How is international criminal justice constituted by and of 'the global'?

1. What are the roles of NGOs in international criminal justice?

International law is no longer just about states. Triggered by globalization processes and a dispersion of political power in the wake of the Cold War, non-state actors began to feature more prominently in international treaty-making in the 1990s. The first act of what commentators coined the 'new diplomacy' (Davenport, 2002)—the cooperation of NGOs and middle-sized liberal democracies—created the Mine Ban Treaty during the Ottowa Convention in 1997. The second act followed the year after, in Rome during the summer of 1998, where the Rome Statute for the ICC was drafted at the United Nations Diplomatic Conference of Plenipotentiaries on the Establishment of an International Criminal Court. Much has been written about the success of NGOs—and human rights NGOs in particular—in Rome, and the celebration of a global and permanent international criminal court as a 'global civil society achievement' (Glasius, 2006) or even, an 'achievement of the masses organized' (Cakmak, 2008: 373; see also Barrow, 2004; Pearson, 2006; Watkins and Welch, 2011). Much less is known, however, about the continued significance of NGOs upon the Rome Statute system of justice (but see Haddad, 2013; De Silva, 2017) and for the development and dynamics embedded in the project of international criminal justice generally. What do they do for the 'fight against impunity' today? What exactly do they mean when they call for the ICC to do 'global justice'? What are the social conditions that facilitate or hamper their participation in global justice-making? Who are they? This book discerns the manner of NGO organization for international criminal justice as well as the ideas and values that underpin their engagement, with a view to how such an empirical inquiry yields insight into the sociological understanding of the field of international criminal justice. As such, the book continues the story of the purported 'global civil society' influence upon the Rome Statute system of justice.

2. What characterizes punishment 'gone global'?

Reflecting disciplinary divisions created by the increasingly slippery distinction between the international and the national, scholars of international law and international relations dominate the study of international criminal justice. There is a conspicuous neglect of this field by sociology of punishment (but see Lohne, 2018b; Savelsberg, 2018), in spite of the fact that international criminal justice fundamentally upsets the truism in criminological thought that the power to punish prevails in the nation state (Zedner, 2016). However, a question must be asked about the meanings, morals, and values that inform criminal punishment as the practical solution to global disorder, once the judicial mandate to punish is transferred from the nation state to the 'international community'. Who and what animate penal policy and punishment when it is 'disembedded' from the nation state? The lack of scholarship on the meaning of international punishment, and its signification for the making of global social order, is a disconnect that is also reflected in the field of global justice-making itself. Later chapters will show that while international human rights NGOs are indispensable advocates of the international criminal justice project, there is a lack of thinking about the role of punishment. This is all the more curious as punishment in global justice-making takes on a different character by being somewhat disconnected from the legitimacy of the nation state, and, not least by being expected to address harm of a significantly graver scale than is generally the case with domestic criminal justice. This book is thus the first of its kind to approach international criminal justice from the perspective of sociology of punishment, and, by extension, offer an interpretation of international criminal justice's significance for understanding the traits and characteristics of penal power under the global condition.

3. How is international criminal justice constituted by and of the global?

The ICC is a global institution, both in the sense that it has a global reach and because it concerns and connects global processes: contexts of conflict and violence are subject to judicial deliberation thousands of miles away, spanning territory, jurisdiction, and sovereignty. As such, a central aim of approaching international criminal justice in social and cultural terms is to situate the study of punishment at the heart of an inquiry into global social organization and pursuit of global order. Paraphrasing David Garland (1990b: 20), such an approach avoids the absurdity of thinking of international criminal justice as if it had nothing to do with international crimes, without falling into the trap of thinking of it solely as a 'fight against impunity' for such harms. This book is thus a study of global (dis)connections, forces, and imaginations: imaginations of global justice seized through the connections of transnational networks, and driven by the force of universals—of law, of human rights, and of the notion of humanity.

In approaching the global as the scale of analysis, some assumptions must be accounted for. First, the global is often framed in opposition to the national, as if the two were mutually exclusive entities. These are generally assumed to belong to scalar hierarchies, where the global is imagined as 'above' the national (Sassen, 2007). With these scalar hierarchies follows another set of assumptions: the global is associated with relevance 'beyond' the bounded and limited, singular and particular. In this manner, the global invokes the work of the universal. As examples of global forces, one speaks of *universal* human rights and crimes against *humanity,* notions of absolute and abstract truths that are unquestionable by nature of their own unidentified essence (Douzinas, 2007b). The ICC was set up to protect these universals, enabled by globalization's forging of people and ideas across space: a mobilization for universals realized through global connections. Tsing (2005: 7) however, poses an unsettling question: 'How can universals be so effective in forging global connections if they posit an already united world in which the work of connection is unnecessary?' If justice, human rights, and humanity are self-evident categorical truths, why do they need delineation, implementation, and intervention? Why is there a need for experts and legal professionals—or even *advocates of humanity*—to recognize that which is universal? Letting go of the universal as an abstract and self-fulfilling truth enables attention to specific situations, and to see invocation of the universal as aspirations, as always unfinished achievements, instead of articulations of what is already 'out there'—of pre-formed law. Then, one may observe how universal aspirations travel, in time and across distances, sometimes without effort, sometimes with friction. I take this travel to be my ethnographic object (Tsing, 2005: 1–2, 7). In recognizing the invocation of the universal as a global force, the global is, thus, always unfinished (Urry, 2002; Aas, 2013). In this manner, my concern is with the making of the global.

International Criminal Justice in Context

The creation of the international military tribunals in Nuremberg and Tokyo following the Second World War marks the birth of the international criminal justice system. This was when Justice Robert H. Jackson, in his opening statement at the Military Tribunal at Nuremberg, declared that 'four great nations, flushed with victory and stung with injury stay the hands of vengeance and voluntarily submit their captive enemies to the judgment of the law is one of the most significant tributes that Power has ever paid to Reason'. Power, however, would almost immediately come to triumph over the international reason to which Justice Jackson referred, as the Cold War paralysed whatever efforts made towards the realization of an international criminal justice. In the following four decades the idea remained dormant and hidden in various UN commissions. Yet, as the Cold War came to an end, at a time when Europe faced another genocide, international criminal justice would again begin to take shape (for historical orgins, see Bassiouni, 1998; Bergsmo et al., 2014). Since then, another seven international criminal courts have been established, including the International Criminal Tribunal for the former Yugoslavia (ICTY) and the International Criminal Tribunal for Rwanda (ICTR) set up by the UN in 1993 and 1994, respectively (for an empirical overview, see Smeulers et al., 2013). As ad hoc institutions, they have recently both closed down, although the UN Mechanism for International Criminal Justice maintains essential functions such as tracking fugitives, appeals, supervision of sentences, and protection of victims and witnesses.[3] In contrast to the ICTY and the ICTR, the Special Court for Sierra Leone, the Special Panels of Dili in East Timor, the Extraordinary Chambers in the Courts of Cambodia and the Special Tribunal for Lebanon are all, to varying degrees, 'hybrid', or 'mixed' courts, meaning they contain elements of both domestic and international criminal law, are staffed by international and domestic personnel, and are usually located within the target state (for an introduction to international criminal law, see Van Schaack and Slye, 2010).

The ICC is the first permanent international criminal court. Since 2002, the Court has opened twenty-six cases—all against

[3] See https://www.irmct.org/en (accessed 4 August 2019).

African nationals—in eleven situations under investigation. At the time of research, the ICC had opened investigations in nine situations and states: Côte D'Ivoire, Central African Republic (CAR), Democratic Republic of Congo (DRC), Kenya, Libya, Mali, Sudan, Uganda, and CAR II. Since then, the Court has also opened investigations into the situation in Georgia and Burundi. There have been three convictions and three acquittals.[4] Most of the defendants remain at large, or have had their charges vacated, withdrawn, or not confirmed by the Pre-Trial Chambers because of, among other things, lack of access to evidence or due to their passing.

The book discusses the situations and cases at the ICC in various levels of detail, focusing on the situations in East Africa rather than those in the central and northern territories of the African continent. This has a practical dimension—giving full details of all the situations before the Court would probably not only cause data overload, but also fail to give more than a cursory overview of the issues at stake. The variation also has an empirical dimension. During the research, the situations in the territories of East Africa were given more attention in the field than

[4] Thomas Lubanga Dyilo (Lubanga) was found guilty on 14 March 2012 for charges of the war crimes of enlisting and conscripting child soldiers in DRC. He was sentenced to fourteen years of imprisonment. On 7 March 2014, Germain Katanga (Katanga) was found guilty of one count of crime against humanity (murder) and four counts of war crimes (attacking a civilian population, destruction of property, murder, and pillaging) during the February 2003 attack on Bogoro village in eastern DRC. He was sentenced to twelve years' imprisonment. Pleading guilty, Ahmad Al Faqi Al Mahdi (Al Mahdi) was found guilty on 27 September 2016 of the war crime of intentionally directing attacks against historic monuments and buildings dedicated to religion in June and July 2012 in Mali. He was sentenced to nine years' imprisonment. Mathieu Ngudjolo Chui (Ngudjolo Chui) was acquitted of charges of war crimes and crimes against humanity allegedly committed in DRC on 18 December 2012, in a verdict upheld by the Appeals Chamber. The Appeals Chamber acquitted Jean-Pierre Bemba Gombo (Bemba) on 8 June 2018 in a reversal of Trial Chamber III's decision of guilt on charges of war crimes (murder, rape, and pillaging) and crimes against humanity (murder and rape) allegedly committed under Bemba's command in CAR in 2002 and 2003. In connection with his case, he and others were found guilty for offences against the administration of justice, for which sentences have been served. Charles Blé Goudé and Laurent Gbagbo were acquitted in January 2019 of all charges of crimes against humanity allegedly committed in Côte d'Ivoire in 2010 and 2011. The Prosecutor may still appeal this decision. See ICC case information sheets on https://www.icc-cpi.int/Pages/cases.aspx (accessed 20 June 2019).

the other situations. Indeed, the 'NGOization' of the DRC, Kenya, and Uganda is an important backdrop for understanding how already established international materialities are reflected in global justice-making (Mutua, 2009b).

The Ugandan situation was the first ever referral by a State Party to the ICC, and at first glance, a seemingly uncomplicated case for the Court. The scale of violence inflicted on the Acholi population in northern Uganda and their suffering had begun to figure on the international agenda, particularly once the UN Under Secretary-General for Humanitarian Affairs, Jan Egeland, had described the situation as the 'biggest forgotten, neglected humanitarian emergency in the world' and an 'epicentre of terror'.[5] In the course of the more than twenty-year-long conflict, the LRA abducted an estimated 30,000 children who were forced to become soldiers or sex slaves. Such children became their only source of conscripts (as this policy fed discontent), and at the height of the conflict (2001–2004), over 90 per cent of its troops were abducted children, some of them as young as seven or eight years old. To bind them permanently to the group, they were forced to commit atrocities against their own families or each other. While the violence perpetrated by the LRA under the command of Joseph Kony in most accounts are rendered bizarre, incomprehensible and as (yet) another instance of African inhumanity, the 'official discourse' on what was a *de facto* civil war has significantly whitewashed government violence (Finnström, 2008; see also Mamdani, 2010). Besides reports of overt physical violence—murder, rape, torture—the government policy of forced displacement of nearly the entire Acholi population into so-called protected villages has been paralleled to concentration camps, 'given that internment is an explicit government policy that targets the Acholi as a group and has led to tens, or even hundreds, of thousands of deaths and to the slow destruction of an entire ethnic group' (Branch, 2007: 182).

In a joint press conference in London in January 2004, the then Prosecutor Luis Moreno-Ocampo of the ICC and President Yoweri Museveni of Uganda made public the latter's referral of the 'situation concerning the Lord's Resistance Army' to the ICC (ICC, 2004). In July the same year, the Office of the Prosecutor (OTP)

[5] See https://www.aljazeera.com/archive/2003/11/2008410151518420888.html and http://www.irinnews.org/report/58638/uganda-northern-conflict-an-epicentre-of- terror-egeland (accessed 7 November 2018).

opened an investigation into the situation in northern Uganda (and not exclusively into the crimes of the LRA as Museveni's referral somewhat awkwardly and erroneously did). In October 2005, the ICC unsealed its first ever arrest warrants for what it considered the five top commanders of the LRA: Joseph Kony, Vincent Otti, Okot Odhiambo, Dominic Ongwen, and Raske Lukwiya. At the time of research, all men were at large, except for Lukwiya who was confirmed deceased in 2006. Since then, the proceedings against Odhiambo have also been terminated due to his death, and, crucially, Ongwen has been apprehended and is currently facing trial in The Hague.[6]

A sort of peace has come to the region today. Yet it is the sort of peace limited to the absence of violence rather than the presence of what enables society's integration (Galtung, 1964). Although the scars of violence are far from healed, northern Uganda is described as a *post* conflict society (Branch, 2013). The LRA has left Uganda and are scattered across the borders of DRC, CAR, and South Sudan. As was mentioned by way of introduction, the ICC's intervention in Uganda has thus proved to be far from an 'easy first case'. Instead, it has come to illustrate many of the predicaments of international criminal justice, including the fact that local civil society favoured a peaceful resolution to the conflict, and opted for amnesties to be part of this endeavour—contrary to the views of major international human rights NGOs. For those who seek an analysis of the conflict in Uganda or the ICC's intervention in it, this book will not do it justice (see generally Allen, 2006; Finnström, 2008; Allen and Vlassenroot, 2010; Baines, 2009; Branch, 2011). Instead, the analysis in coming chapters applies a view from Uganda to contextualize connections and frictions in global justice-making, and of the ICC as its flagship manifestation.

[6] Kony is charged with twelve counts of crimes against humanity (including murder, enslavement, sexual enslavement, rape and inhumane acts of inflicting serious bodily injury and suffering) and twenty-one counts of war crimes (also including murder and inducing rape, cruel treatment of civilians, intentionally directed attacks against civilians, pillaging, and forced enlistment of children). See https://www.icc-cpi.int/Pages/cases.aspx (accessed 7 November 2018). The remains of Vincent Otti, the LRA's second-in-command, rumoured to be dead since 2007/2008 after a fall-out with Joseph Kony, were allegedly found and identified by Ugandan forces in April 2015.

Crucially, the ICC is no 'ordinary' court. In contrast to criminal justice institutions in established democracies, international criminal justice is not as readily subject to the checks and balances of democratic processes involving parliamentary committees, a critical media, and academic scrutiny—in short, to a democratic and public constituency. This is all the more significant as institutional power is more concentrated in international criminal justice than is the case with its domestic counterparts. Where the latter is composed of a state institutional patchwork comprising several state institutions—police, courts, correctional services, health care, etc.—the ICC is not merely expected to adjudicate international crimes, but to investigate and detain, do outreach to a variety of communities, provide protection and reparations to victims and witnesses, among other things. This all in the context of international politics, intervening—in more times than not—in the midst of ongoing armed conflicts (Kersten 2016).

The ICC is composed of four 'organs': the OTP, the Judicial Division, the Presidency, and the Registry. The OTP is arguably the most visible organ of the Court, and carries out investigations and prosecutions. It is headed by Chief Prosecutor Fatou Bensouda from the Gambia, who took office after being Deputy Prosecutor under the ICC's first Chief Prosecutor, the Argentinean Luis Moreno-Ocampo. Although independent of the Court, there are three other offices under the administration of the Registry. These semi-autonomous offices are the Office of Public Counsel for Victims, the Office of Public Counsel for Defence, and the Trust Fund for Victims (TFV), whose mandate is to provide reparations to victims of international crimes. At the time of research, the Court had a staff of 688 people in established posts and 171 people on general temporary assistance contracts, in addition to a number of interns (ICC-ASP, 2014), and whose significance for the field of international criminal justice is elaborated on in Chapter 4.

While the diversity of the activities carried out by the ICC complicates perceptions of the ICC, as different sections of the Court have different functions, it also exposes and complicates the question of what type of justice the Court and the field of international criminal justice 'stand for', that is, the *substance* of justice. The opening up of retributive and prosecutorial goals to a host of other justice 'deliverables'—victims' justice, gender justice, restorative justice, transformative justice—has led to a 'contested justice making process' (Hoyle and Ullrich, 2014: 684) where different actors pull in different directions; the role of human rights NGOs being one of them. Hence, international criminal justice is frequently depicted as in a state of identity crisis (Robinson, 2008), with several diagnoses offered of its 'acute ontological anxiety' (Vasiliev, 2015: 705; Mégret, 2016a). One diagnosis offered suggests that the field is oversaturated as legal practice, having peaked in terms of institution-building last decade, and is now slowly shrinking (Christensen, 2015b), as illustrated by the recent closure of the ICTR and ICTY. As coming chapters aim to help explicate, the current condition also speaks to broader notions about the 'identity' of the international criminal justice project, about what it 'is' compared to other systems of justice-making, and to a strained self-image due to recurrent criticism about the gaps between its promises and the realities of what it can (be expected to) deliver.

Following a period of initial enthusiasm and support for the ICC to 'end impunity' for 'the most serious crimes of international concern' (the Rome Statute's Preamble), the ICC is now subject to widespread and increasing criticism. Culminating in the threat of a mass exodus of African member states from the Court in late 2016, the most potent point of critique has been accusations of the Court 'targeting Africa'. Charged as it is with colonialism and imperialism (Clarke et al., 2016), the legitimacy crisis for the Court must be seen alongside a shifting geopolitical landscape. The 'transformationist rhetoric about "post-Westphalia"' (Hurrell, 2007: 9) has lost traction in the face of the emerging multipolar world order, that is, 'a world of renewed sovereignty, resurgent religion, globalized markets, and the stagnation or rollback of universal norms about human rights' (Hopgood, 2013: 166). By focusing on the imaginations of justice-making that animate international criminal justice, and the structural inequalities that give shape to its materialization, this book seeks to identify trends, characteristics, and dynamics of the field that explicate a lack of authority in global justice-making, and offer sociological explanation to the legitimacy challenge that international criminal justice is currently facing.

On balance, however, the research for this book was conducted at a time when faith in international criminal justice was strong but waning among actors in the field. No doubt also reflecting the maturing of myself as a researcher, critical voices towards the project of international criminal justice were less present and welcome during my postgraduate and early doctoral years (2007–2012) than is the case today. At the present time, it has become somewhat of a joke among fellow scholars that there is no one left inside the church (of international criminal justice). These days, a standard critique of international criminal justice is to find some lofty ideal of the ICC, easily found in The Rome Statute's Preamble or in celebratory speeches by representatives of the Court, State Parties, or the NGO community, and demonstrate how the ICC is unsuccessful in achieving such objectives. In response, ICC advocates, academics, and practitioners' enthusiasm for an expanding international legal regime is now frequently replaced by the need to 'manage' expectations. The analysis presented in this book can therefore be read as an interpretation of how such inflated ambitions on the part of the international criminal justice project arose, given the push by human rights NGOs to accredit international criminal justice with wider socio-political goals beyond its adjudicative functions, and to increasingly equate the fight against impunity with a fight for global justice (Engle et al., 2016).

Moreover, the dynamism in the field is also reflected in jurisdictional 'preferences', as there is an increasing focus on domestic and regional prosecutions of international crimes, the crimes of concern here being crimes against humanity, genocide, and war crimes.[7] There are three basic types of prosecutions for holding individuals criminally responsible for international crimes. First, there is *international* jurisdiction brought to bear by international courts such as the ICC. Second, there is *universal* jurisdiction, which comes into play when a domestic court takes legal action against an individual from another state; and finally, there are *domestic* prosecutions of international crimes. The focus in this analysis is on *international* prosecutions and punishment rather than *transnational* prosecutions, such as those undertaken under the principle of universal jurisdiction, or *national* prosecutions. However, as may already have been observed, I refer to the project of international criminal justice as *global* criminal justice-making because it not only has universal ambitions, and as such, seek to

[7] These were the crimes that the ICC had jurisdiction over at the time of research. Piracy, slavery, torture, terrorism crimes against the peace, or crimes of aggression, are examples of other acts that may also be referred to as international crimes.

expand, but also because it is embedding within the national. The ICC is a 'court of last resort'. What this means is that a situation or case is only admissible to the Court if a member state is 'unwilling or unable genuinely' to carry out investigations and prosecutions itself (Article 17, the Rome Statute). Whether or not national proceedings meet the threshold of 'genuine', is subject to review by the Court's chambers. This is the Principle of Complementarity, which is an essential part of the 'Rome Statute system of justice', enabling it to reach beyond the institution in The Hague and into national justice systems worldwide. As is discussed in Chapter 7, and while originally perceived as a sovereign shield for the larger powers, complementarity issues are high on the NGO agenda, as it is viewed as a tool for rule of law promotion in states with 'underdeveloped' criminal justice systems. The objectives of the ICC project is thus to ensure the universal prosecution and punishment of international crimes, first and primarily through the domestic criminal justice system, and if this is either 'unable or unwilling', that is, if national justice fails, the ICC represents an international recourse—a court of last resort. In this way, international criminal justice as materialized in the Rome Statute system of justice signifies not only the Court in The Hague but also efforts to implement or mainstream the Rome Statute system at the national level, including socio-political aims beyond criminal adjudication. In this manner, the 'fight against impunity' for international crimes has become the pursuit of global justice.

Theoretical Orientations for a Sociology of Punishment for International Criminal Justice

The establishment of certain crimes as issues to be addressed at the global level is a relatively new development within the discipline of criminology.[8] Reflectingthe increasingly 'artificial distinction between the domestic and the international' (Loader and Percy, 2012: 213), international crimes and criminal justice have long been the disciplinary domain of international law and international relations. In a similar vein, transitional justice scholarship

[8] However, the international exchange of penological ideas have been part of the criminological discipline as both theory and practice since the birth of the prison. On the historical emergence and institutionalization of crime as an international issue, see Knepper (2010); (2011).

has grappled with debates on 'exceptionalism'—of whether transitional justice is 'normal' and 'ordinary' justice too, or if its pursuit is a special kind of justice with its own distinctive sets of expertise, justifications, and rationalities (Posner and Vermeule, 2004).[9] A related division of labour characterizes the sociology of punishment, equating the boundaries of sociological analysis alongside nation state borders by being almost exclusively concerned with *state* punishment and *national* society (e.g. Lacey, 1988; Garland, 1990b; Smith, 2008; Valverde, 2012). However, under processes of globalization, criminal justice has 'not only expanded but changed its effect and, at least in part, its justification' (Bosworth 2012: 125). This is the theoretical point of departure for this book, which engages social explanation as to how crime, punishment, and ultimately justice have now also become matters of common responsibility in a 'perceived shared space of humanitarian consciousness' (Aas, 2013: 219). In doing so, the book ventures into international criminal justice as relatively new criminological territory, exploring, perhaps, an unfamiliar penal 'culture'; yet, with a conceptual toolbox that is familiar to scholars of sociology of punishment.

Specifically, the book approaches international criminal justice as a particular site of penality, the term referring to the 'whole of the penal complex' (Garland, 2013: 476, fn. 472), including its institutions, laws, and practices, but also its discourses, representations, and symbols. As a penal field detached from the nation state, and as driven by cosmopolitan sensibilities and justifications transcending the state-centred view on crime, justice, and society, what I attempt to describe, understand and explicate in coming chapters I refer to as a 'cosmopolitan penality', cosmopolitanism being the ethical, philosophical, and scientific world view transcending a nation-state outlook on society. This approach enables a view of international criminal justice as a penal field embedded in social structures and cultural meaning, but also as part of a general structuring of society under the global condition. In other words, taking a sociological approach to international criminal justice not only engages the study of society to make sense of international criminal justice, but also, crucially,

[9] The substantive literature on the ordinariness of extraordinary violence, or the 'banality of evil', parallel these debates (Arendt, 2006).

uses international criminal justice to understand society (see also Lohne, forthcoming).

As is characteristic of 'punishment and society' scholarship generally (Simon and Sparks, 2013), I draw on a number of theoretical orientations to inform a sociology of punishment approach to international criminal justice. Generally, these orientations draw on disciplinary insights from international law, international relations, and criminological scholarship generally. The following section sets out the major strengths and contributions of these three different disciplines to the object of study, and how they inform my approach. With great respect, their blind spots also animate the value of moving towards a sociology of punishment for international criminal justice.

As an amalgam of different legal fields—criminal law, human rights law, and humanitarian law—there has emerged an abundance of international legal scholarship on international criminal law, ranging from theoretical and doctrinal studies to a proliferation of critical, empirical, and interdisciplinary studies in recent years (on the state of ICL scholarship, see Vasiliev, 2015). In particular, the body of work commonly referred to as critical approaches to international criminal law provides key pointers to the practices and representations of international criminal justice as a legal field as well as to its flaws and inconsistencies (e.g. Drumbl, 2007; Nouwen and Werner, 2010; Schwöbel, 2014; Mégret, 2016a). Drawing on critical international legal scholarship and especially the work of Koskenniemi (2001; 2005; see also Werner et al., 2017), and concerned with basic sociological questions of power and legitimacy, this literature is primarily concerned with international criminal law as a legal system. While indebted to its insights to substantiate my analysis, including doctrinal reasoning and institutional descriptions, my framework of analysis remains, however, sociological.

To understand the structures of social action and systems of power that international criminal justice is part of, there is a need for engagement with international studies too. In addition to understanding the *politics* in and around the field of international criminal law (Bass, 2000; Roach, 2009; Bosco, 2013), the constructivist strain of international relations theory has made substantial contribution to understanding norms and values in international society, and the role of non-state actors in their emergence, development, and diffusion (Adler, 1997; Wendt,

1999; Risse et al., 2013). Studies pioneered by Keck and Sikkink on *transnational advocacy networks* (TAN) (1998) have demonstrated their role as central infrastructures in transnational politics, and for advancing what Sikkink later labelled the 'justice cascade', referring to the 'shift in the legitimacy of the norm of individual criminal accountability for human rights violations and an increase in criminal prosecutions on behalf of that norm' (2011: 5). There are also a number of insightful institutional biographies on major international human rights organizations, such as Amnesty International (Clark, 2010; see also Hopgood, 2006) and Helsinki Watch (Snyder, 2011), as well as contributions that take a more collective or comprehensive perspective of the role of human rights NGOs in world politics (Welch, 2001). Generally, the efficacy of norm dispersion and TANs are sought in the attributes of the actors involved or the issues in question (see also Price, 1998; Carpenter, 2007). Despite its many virtues however, a more sociological and grounded approach to these processes facilitate attention to what is often downplayed in TAN approaches, namely the disconnections, frictions, and power differentials embedded in transnational networks. As studies of development NGOs (Nelson and Dorsey, 2008), humanitarian relief NGOs (Krause, 2014), and human rights NGOs in regional settings (Mutua, 2009b) demonstrate, attention to political opportunity structures, fields of practice, and the situatedness of norms and values, reveal the importance of a more structural approach to transnational networks.

Following the work of Pierre Bourdieu and others, recent years have thus seen an interdisciplinary strengthening of relational sociological approaches to *transnational* fields of practice (Dezalay and Garth, 1998; Madsen, 2006; Christensen, 2015a; Mégret, 2016b; Lohne and Sandvik, 2017). Particularly, studies of international relations and international law have 'thickened' the study of authority of and in global governance institutions and the international judiciary, focusing specifically on the politics of expertise (Sending, 2015) and transnational power elites (Kauppi and Madsen, 2013) in constituting and consolidating transnational fields. Crucial to an understanding of a cosmopolitan penality, adding a criminological dimension to the relational study of transnational networks enables insight into how these actors not only shape the participatory dynamics of international law and society, but also shape the substance of international criminal justice as a meaning-making enterprise and solution to global disorder.

As such, the book contributes to the burgeoning criminological engagement with 'supranational' crimes and transitional justice studies (Smeulers and Haveman, 2008), which generally addresses the nature of international crimes and their contexts, the nature of large scale victimization, and the plethora of institutional responses to this type of violence and suffering (see Parmentier, 2011). Perhaps it is of no surprise given the gravity and scale of injustice with which this research deals, much of it situates the criminological agenda on a par with international criminal law and the 'fight against impunity'. By doing so, the latter's claim to be universal, and to belong to a realm beyond politics, is left uncontested; its legal order and moral claims unconnected with history, geography, and power. However, much of criminology's distinctiveness is found in its critical engagement with notions of crime and justice, and its refutation of the claim to universality by domestic systems of justice; it is vital that these perspectives are also brought to bear on global universals. In Cohen's *Visions of Social Control* (1985), he describes how the criminal justice system spreads, or widens its net, through community-based social control mechanisms, frequently enforced in the name of the good, and as a more social, humanitarian form of assistance than the criminal justice system situated at the core of state power. Aas (2011: 407) takes Cohen's vision to the transnational and global, asking perceptively whether criminology is 'in danger of re-entering the complex and paradoxical terrain defined by terms such as "reform", "progress", "doing good", "benevolence" and "humanitarianism", only this time on the transnational level?' This book should be read as a reflection of this development, whereby the boundaries between private and public, punishment and humanitarianism, are blurring, so elements on either side of them becomes increasingly difficult to distinguish (Lohne, 2018b). Above all, I argue in this book that what characterizes the role of human rights NGOs in international criminal justice is their *embeddedness* in the field of international criminal justice, and thus in constituting a cosmopolitan penality.

This means that the aim of this book is not to contribute to the increasing fragmentation of criminology (Bosworth and Hoyle, 2011), but, quite the contrary: to understand how penality today is not only shaped by a new set of actors and institutions but also constituted within a transnational and global scale. In the classic sociology of punishment literature, '[c]hanges of laws and legal institutions were seen not only as precisely illuminating the process of modernization, but also as active forces that shaped the process itself' (Karstedt, 2007: 53). A sociology of punishment approach to international criminal justice is thus not only concerned with how it is a result of increased global connectedness but also how a cosmopolitan penality itself constitutes and shapes the global.

The Organization of the Book and its Relationship to the Research Strategy

One of the central ways of thinking about globalization is that it somehow alters the nature of space and time, and its relation to the social. A sociology of punishment for international criminal justice must thus necessarily be attentive to the configurations of space and time under the global condition. International criminal justice—and its increasing claim to global justice—is based on a set of assumptions, or imaginaries, of space and time. For starters, international criminal justice invokes the work of the universal, obscuring the fact of situatedness by implying a type of 'spaceless' justice—as if speaking to and from nowhere in particular. As the dimension of civilization, development, and progress, time, on the other hand, becomes a conspicuous element of international criminal justice. In the chapters to follow, I will critically examine these assumptions, and show that—despite claims to the contrary—global justice-making is both situated and situated in global hierarchies of power. This renders problematic the apparent 'spacelessness' of international criminal justice, and demonstrates the importance of a critical sociology of punishment gone global.

Before I describe the organization of the book however, I do want to point out the gains of having approached this research by way of ethnography. Albeit there are trade offs to any research method, the grounded and critical impulse of ethnography led me 'naturally' to engage with the question of boundaries—of the 'where', 'how', and 'who' of global criminal justice-making and global civil society. The following three chapters map out those interrogatives as a way of 'objectivizing' international criminal justice as a research object by identifying the structures and conditions of international criminal justice as a social field (Dezalay and Garth, 1998; Eslava, 2015), and through a process that does not uncritically reproduce the borders, discourses, and 'rules' of international criminal law and its professionals (Madsen, 2011). What emerges through ethnography is thus not merely a body of law regulating 'the most serious crimes of concern to the international community as a whole' (the Rome Statute's Preamble), or the inferred values upon its practice because of the embrace and mobilization of human rights NGOs. Rather, what comes into view is an expansive normative penal order at play, constituted through materialities of space, networks, and individuals.

Chapter 2 engages the space-time configurations of international criminal justice in more detail, showing, simply, *where* global justice-making takes place. Attentive to the relational positioning of places, events, and things, I demonstrate how international criminal justice takes place across scales, geographies, and sites. First I show how international criminal justice is visibly and materially located, recognizing The Hague as a hub in the global networks of global justice-making—a 'global city' (Sassen, 2013) of justice-making. Not only are many of the world's most important global institutions based there, but the city also brands itself as the 'city of peace and justice'. Yet, even though The Hague as the global city is the main production site for global justice-making, it is related to and depended on other spaces, such as those where the crimes were committed. Uganda is one of these sites. There however, 'justice' is almost invisible, and, from a view from The Hague, at a standstill. The disconnect between the metropole and periphery of global justice-making is also apparent in the virtual spaces of international criminal justice, as the chapter moves on to identify and discuss social media as a crucial space of global justice-making. While the internet is a major ground for debate, international criminal justice is promoted and legitimized globally through social media. Delinked from the nation state, I argue that social media is but one strategy of building constituency for international criminal justice. Another is the Assembly of States Parties (ASP) meetings that work as an annual ritual of international criminal justice invoking cosmopolitan images and justifications, yet in a space of increasing political friction. These three parts make up my analysis of how international criminal justice is spatially arranged, and which I see as material expressions of the cultural, social, and political relations that it works in and through.

Paraphrasing Massey (1994), while space is the dimension of materiality; of jurisdiction and territory—of the land out there; it is also the dimension that confronts us with the simultaneous existence of 'the other'. As such, space is the dimension of multiplicity, always imbued with power and always therefore social and political. An enquiry into how international criminal justice is spatially situated is therefore an inquiry into its geography of power. The chapter therefore brings out not only the new and informal spaces of international law but also situates transnational and non-state actors—human rights NGOs—as part of this geography of power. In doing so, it provides the necessary conceptual and empirical backdrop for exploring, as I do in Chapter 3, how networks of NGOs navigate within the transnational space of global justice-making.

A sociology of punishment concerned with globalizing society is necessarily informed by a conceptualization of the state, and of the 'penal state' (Garland, 2013), as a more loosely disaggregated unit than the institutionalized structure generally suggested in criminology, law, and political science (on the disaggregated state, see Slaughter, 2004). Networks are a dominant conceptualization of social organization since globalization became part of sociology's research agenda in the early 1990s (Castells, 1996). Facilitated by the technological paradigm, the 'network' is both a metaphor and a concept for thinking about patterns of social organization, and for making sense of how global society as an unbounded social system is constituted—as materializing this notion of 'the global' as abstract linkage. Moving from the 'where' to the 'how' in exploring the relationship between a purported 'global civil society' and global criminal justice-making, Chapter 3 analyses *how* the NGOs organize in order to promote the ICC, and in doing so, engages networks as an empirical and conceptual feature of what makes the global. In doing so, the grounded and contextualized method of ethnography enables recognition of 'friction' (Tsing, 2005), of awkward disconnection and unevenness in the transnational networks of global justice-making. Through a critical unpacking of the institutional organization and processes of the Coalition for the International Criminal Court (CICC), the literature on networks (and TANs in particular) is revealed to give too little weight to this friction, including internal conflicts and power differentials. Departing from the celebratory narrative of the ICC as a 'global civil society achievement' (Glasius, 2006), the first part of the chapter examines the networked structure of NGOs at the ICC, and the centrality of the CICC and its core member NGOs. Against the structural inequalities and disconnections of transnational networks, the second part shows how the CICC manages to claim a role as reflecting *the* global civil society in international criminal justice by largely controlling the 'who' and the 'what' of civil society participation in the politics around the ICC. At the same time, they stimulate the idea of the 'transnational' as a particular space for political engagement by operating as mediators between different geographical scales (local, national, regional, global), and by using law as the *lingua franca* between NGOs, states, and the ICC. Through representing 'humanity' in global justice-making, human rights NGOs serve an important role in international criminal justice as providers of moral authority. Animated by these claims to authority and representations, the final part of the chapter critically examines NGO participation against these claims, finding that they are too embedded in the field of international criminal justice to claim a position of being beyond that of externality, and of vested interest. Thus, having situated the NGOs within the cosmopolitan penal field through a macro-level analysis of space and a meso-level analysis of networks in global criminal justice-making, Chapter 4 narrows the unit of analysis to ask a key question: *who* are the individuals with access to global justice-making processes? Who are the advocates of humanity?

A sociology of punishment for international criminal justice enables attention to the norms, morals, and values at play in the motivational dynamics of penal reforms. At the same time, these cultural forces must be analysed against the background of social organization and structure, indeed, to what enables people to think and feel in certain ways and to promote policies in accordance with their sensibilities. As such, Chapter 4 explores international criminal justice as a field replete with cosmopolitan sensibilities, but also of lifestyles, qualifications, and restraints. Finding that international criminal justice is perceived as a cosmopolitan expression of social justice, the first part conceptualizes human rights NGOs working in international criminal justice as global moral entrepreneurs and shows how they use humanist discourses to promote global justice-making through law, turning them into advocates of international criminal justice. Balancing claims to authority in the field, the NGOs have to navigate between being 'insiders' as experts and 'outsiders' that can claim moral authority (Lohne 2017). In spite of the many contributions of mainstream network theories in identifying connections and consensus-building in transnational norm development, these diagnoses fall short of establishing how these networks are simultaneously structured by the social world. My analysis thus draws on scholarship inspired by Bourdieu and others and put to work on transnational fields, enabling attention to what is often downplayed in 'international legal practices, namely, social interest and ultimately class' (Madsen, 2014b: 51). As such, the chapter inquiries into *whose* imaginations of global justice become part of its materiality, finding that advocates of humanity predominantly belong to a class of transnational western professionals. In this way, norms and values, morals and sensibilities of global justice-making are 'located within the grid of social interests and positions in a way which reflects the complex realities of cultural life' (Garland, 1990b: 198).

By drawing on relational sociology to the study of transnational fields, the chapter stresses the importance of a 'double view' of social practice, or to what Garland has emphasized as a multi-dimensional approach to the study of penality, namely the interrelations between materialities and imaginaries, structures and agency, people and ideas (2006). As this book demonstrates, a critical issue concerns asking 'who' is to be at the centre of attempts to make a morally more acceptable and practical form of global social order, and how. Rather than accepting an opposition to a politics based on either presence or on ideas, it seems that insight and representation should aim precisely at the relationship between the two. As Phillips (1995: 25) observes, problems may quickly arise when a politics based on ideas and on presence are treated as exclusionary opposites, as is the case when ideas are set up as independent from those carrying them out, or when people dominate representation, without consideration of the ideas, policies, and values they stand for. A distinction of emphasis and not exclusion, chapters 2, 3, and 4 are primarily concerned with mapping the structural connections and disconnections embedded in global justice-making. Chapters 5, 6, and 7 focus more on the uncovering of assumptions, discourses, and imaginations, given that globalization 'is not just the production of (dis)connections, but simultaneously … the production of a *convincing ideology* that obscures the source of those (dis)connections and presents them as something natural and eternal' (Burawoy, 2001: 150). The domestic system of criminal justice is imagined to involve three embodied relations: the offender and the offence—who and what is punished; the offended against and the victimized—representing the harm that has been caused by the offender's offence; and the punishing authority, that is, the state. Chapters 5, 6, and 7, analyse this tripartite structure of criminal punishment as it operates in global criminal justice-making, examining, in brief, the mentalities and sensibilities at play in criminal justice when these are disembedded from the 'Westphalian' imaginary of political community. As such, the analysis identifies the cultural meaning of international criminal justice, and the cultural framework animating and structuring cosmopolitan penality more broadly.

Chapter 5 analyses the cosmopolitan penal imaginary building on western domestic penality, delving into the relationship between human rights sensibilities and criminal justice mentalities in the 'fight against impunity' for international crimes.[10] The study of humanitarian sentiments and humanism in relation to crime, punishment, and justice has mainly focused on how these sensibilities have 'humanized' or 'civilized' penality. Generally, these studies have either adopted a historical approach (Elias, 1978 [1939]; Garland, 1990b) or used human rights as a normative and legal framework from which to critique contemporary penal practices (e.g. van Zyl Smit, 2005; Murphy and Whitty, 2013). While non-punitive forces have a major place in the human rights sensibility; indeed, to the extent that the penal aspects of international criminal justice is given uncomfortably little weight, human rights have also become a force of punitivism, which is particularly apparent in human rights NGOs' approach to amnesties. In the fight against impunity, human rights NGOs are at the forefront of penal policies with global objectives and global capacities. Applying a sociology of punishment perspective to the field of international criminal justice, the chapter brings out the similarities and differences in 'penal imaginations' between domestic and international criminal justice. Crucially, international criminal justice is imagined and promoted by its advocates as a form of social justice, albeit on a cosmopolitan scale. I argue that

[10] The terms 'penal imagination' and 'penal imaginary' are used by Smith in *Punishment and Culture* (2008) where he outlines a cultural research approach to the study of punishment.

while international criminal justice relies upon retributive and expressive undertones, it makes no appeal to punitive sensibilities: a fact that can be understood in light of the close relation between international criminal justice and human rights NGOs. Through the fieldwork in Uganda and Rwanda, I describe how asymmetries and tensions emerge in international criminal justice, particularly between the national and the international, as international criminal justice both echoes the national and departs from it. For example, a lot of practical issues had simply not been 'thought of' when setting up the ICC, such as acquittals and asylum-seeking witnesses. Yet, human rights NGOs rely too strongly on punitive answers and amnesties can be just a matter of pragmatism in situations of profound violence. Thus, while the ICC has both punitive and reparative aims, the situation in northern Uganda demonstrates how international criminal justice became an impediment to peace because of its punitive and legalistic approach.

Chapter 6 focuses on one conclusion from Chapter 5, namely the centrality of the victim for global justice-making. The figure of the victim is the *sine qua non* of the fight against impunity for international crimes. Engaging the victimological imagination of international criminal justice,[11] the chapter shows how victims are represented, and how justice for victims is imagined. The first part of the chapter focuses on imaginations of 'justice for victims', and argues that the ICC represents a form of hybrid justice (Hoyle and Ullrich, 2014) by incorporating restorative and transformative rationales for justice. Unlike ordinary courts, the ICC incorporates what can be thought of as both 'punitive' and 'reparative' arms. Part of the latter is the Rome Statute's provisions for victims' rights to participation and reparation. However, a closer look at the implementation of these processes reveal a conspicuous discrepancy between ideologies and realities. For example, at the time of research only thirteen victims had appeared in court as direct participants, five of whose statements were dismissed as unreliable (Kendall and Nouwen 2014). The second part of the chapter situates victims as a source of moral authority, and one that is claimed in representational practices by both

[11] The term victimological imagination is used by McGarry and Walklate (2015) in their cultural approach to victimology. The notions of penal and victimological imaginations are references to Young's work on the criminological imagination (2011) and Mills's classic sociological imagination (1959).

human rights NGOs and international criminal justice generally. The chapter explores suffering as a type of 'currency', both on an individual level for victims' advocates, as their source of purpose, and on a broader cultural level as the source of global moral outcry. I argue that the victim is culturally represented through imaginations from the global North and becomes universalized as a symbol of humanity,[12] of which the gendered and racialized victim of sexual and gender-based violence provides particularly powerful victim imagery (Houge and Lohne, 2017). In this way, the image of the victim of international crimes is characterized by her essential 'otherness': she is humanity that suffers.

Having explored the cultural authority of the ICC, the NGOs' claim for advocacy of humanity, and the moral authority of victims, Chapter 7 addresses the pivotal question: who are 'we' who punish? To what extent can international criminal justice be understood to reflect bonds of common values and beliefs, tradition, and interest on the global scale? As apt for analysis that positions penality at the centre of social organization, the final analytic chapter cultivates a Durkheimian approach to global justice-making. The chapter argues that international criminal justice reinforces a social imaginary of cosmopolitan solidarity, embodied in the notion of humanity. Durkheim's emphasis on how solidarity in modern society is based around a notion of individualism, and of law and punishment as modes of social integration, make his insights particularly well equipped for a sociological analysis of the global as a site of crime, justice, and solidarity; in short, to the integrative functions of international criminal justice for the making of global social order. Being an early prototype of universal human rights discourse (Cotterrell, 2015), the moral individualism put forward in Durkheim's later work (interchangeably referred to as the 'cult of man' or 'religion of humanity') is one in which the 'religion of humanity' is not philosophical and transcendent, but, instead, 'a social institution like all known religions' (Durkheim and Lukes, 1969: 28). Seeing the criminal justice system as a communicative system where punishment functions to sustain society's moral and internal

[12] The terms 'global North' and 'global South' are used to emphasize relations between institutions and intellectuals in the metropole and periphery of the world—of authority, appropriation, and dominance, inclusion and exclusion—and not necessarily to specific states and societies (Connell, 2007: ix).

solidarity, impunity becomes a sign of weakness in the societal corpus—a desacralization of something sacred. Chapter 7 thus demonstrates how agents of international criminal justice argue their cases and punish in the name of humanity. However, rather than something 'given', the cosmopolitan moral order embodied by 'humanity' reflects a *dominant* moral order, and one that is actively constituted (for a reworking of Durkheim to make room for power, see Garland, 1990a; Smith, 2008). Using the Rome Statute as a 'crowbar' for penal aid and rule of law promotion in the global South, the chapter demonstrates how global justice-making through international criminal law is intertwined with the promotion of rule of law and penal aid in contexts of 'failed' justice, where cosmopolitan values—or more specifically the cosmopolitan penal imaginary—are supposed to spread through the notion of 'positive complementarity'. Global justice-making through international criminal justice is thus a multiscalar project, and one which, albeit solidarist, is coercively and deliberatively implemented. By getting away from the 'villains' and 'victims' of global violence, a sociology of punishment for international criminal justice reveals some of the ways in which moral, personal, and social order is constituted globally.

The final chapter situates some of the book's major findings within contemporary resistance towards international criminal justice as *global* justice. It addresses how current pushback against international criminal justice is not only part of the story of the breaking of the universal and the move towards a multipolar, or a multiregional system of international relations, but is a result of the unevenness, tensions, and disconnections as revealed in this analysis. Because criminal justice has materialized transnationally, with transnational agents and with ideas of criminal justice as part of a narrative of civilization circulating between borders, the book concludes by sketching out some key orientations for a sociology of punishment beyond the nation state.

A Multi-sited Network Ethnography

As part and parcel of the ethnographic research process, there have been paths of messiness and serendipity (Cottle, 2001). The contingencies of international criminal justice as an ethnographic research field, like any ethnographic research field, are nonetheless determined by the researcher's positionality. Two excerpts from my field notes may serve as an illustration.

Uganda, January 2014:

'For the Wicked, there will be no Mercy. For the Wicked, there will only be eternal, unquenchable fire. The Wicked will burn. This is the Will of the Lord, the Almighty.'

I pretend not to hear these words, pretend to sleep, avoid the preacher's gaze, turn my own eyes to the window and onto the changing landscape—from the dry, flat plain to the lush tropics as we approach the Nile and the north of Uganda.

I am on the post bus to Gulu. It takes longer than the regular buses—eight hours instead of six—but on these roads, slow is good. We drive past enough broken-down buses, cars and boda-bodas that are casualties of the combination of potholes, cracks and reckless driving—even a large truck overturned at the side of the road—for me to know this was the right move. I have plenty of water, fruit and nuts, and toilet paper. I just hadn't expected hellfire preaching, and I hadn't expected to so clearly excel at the list of Sins, and to so evidently top the list of the Wicked.

The preacher, a woman roughly my age, blessed the bus as we drove out of Kampala. Last Tuesday, a bus had not made it up north. Our journey was now in the hands of the Lord, may He have mercy on our souls. But after this blessing—for which many of my fellow passengers thanked her—she goes on. For an hour, an hour and a half maybe, she preaches as the Lord has instructed her to, and she condemns what I think—or hope—are all of us on the bus. At least then, I am not alone.

'There will be no mercy for homosexuals, or those that practice lesbianism. Homosexuality is not natural; it is not Ugandan. Men should only be with their wives, not infest their homes with diseases and sin. Women should marry; take care of their husbands, their families. They shouldn't wear trousers; they shouldn't dress like a man.'

I'm of course wearing trousers, thinking they were the most appropriate attire for a journey like this. I try to hide behind my fellow passenger, whose rolling of eyes gives me enormous comfort. I sink deeper into my bus seat as her preaching takes a geographic turn.

'People should stay where they are born, where their families are, where they belong, where the Lord intended for people to be. Blacks should be where blacks are; whites should be where whites are. This is the Will of the Lord, the Almighty.'

I am matter out of place.

The Hague, November 2012:

The name of the restaurant is Pangea. I've been here long enough to look up the word on my laptop—in any case, I'm trying to look busy, like the rest of them. The World Wide Web informs me Pangea is Ancient Greek, derived from pan, meaning all, entire, whole; and gaia, Mother Earth, or land. It's the name of the supercontinent that existed as long as 300 million years ago, before it broke down and was split, divided and fragmented. Pangea is the name of a world united.

It is a fitting name for a restaurant in the World Forum, the convention centre in The Hague where the ICC's 11th Assembly of States Parties meeting is being held. This is the place to be for 'events that shape the world', I read on signs in the entrance hall. Continuing its claim to global importance, the convention centre has given its floors and rooms geographical names—continents, mountains and rivers make up the centre in its assertion to 'hosting the world'.[13]

The only problem is I cannot get into it. I am sitting in Pangea—this historic imaginary of wholeness—because I cannot get past the security checkpoint into the continents, mountains and rivers of today's discussion on global justice. In contrast to those around me who meet in Pangea to devise plans and strategies for discussions on the inside, while they get some food (for thought), I'm not wearing an accreditation pass. I don't have access.

Notions of access and positionality, of inclusion and exclusion, proximity and distance featured prominently throughout the research process. What renders these processes relevant, beyond the challenges they put in the way of the conduct of this research, is how they also generated valuable data and stimulated reflection on how the research field operates. Who is allowed behind the security checkpoints at the World Forum? Who can claim to represent the global and the universal, the good and the just? How do imaginaries of global justice travel?

The two excerpts illustrate not only the travelling dimension of multi-sited ethnography, but also how I in many respects came to embody the very processes I was studying. In one site, I was outed as out of place; in the other, I was able to conduct covert observation behind a laptop and an espresso—both these situations resulting from my positionality in global social hierarchies. While I was able to some extent to blend into The Hague—both as a geographical location and as a site of global justice-making—I was unable to blend into Uganda. Yet, I also acquired an identity because of my physical appearance: when I was out with Ugandans,

[13] See the brochure for the convention centre: http://www.worldforum.nl/uploads/sfSympalBossMediaPlugin/document/9c2c1cb8bbc7e54809eb7245b8ad13cda0d4a56c.pdf (accessed 5 April 2015).

waiters would ask me to pay the bill; if I asked a taxi driver to take me somewhere with internet access, he would take me to a place 'mzungos' (white people) go, and so forth. As a young white woman, I was identified as being one of the other young white women in Uganda, most of whom work for an NGO (or an embassy), or are doing a PhD at a western university. Whether I research or practice international criminal justice—whether I do so descriptively or normatively, critically or policy-directed—is utterly irrelevant. The intention here is to draw attention to how my own body, personality, and social situation engendered various reactions in different sites of global justice-making. In all sites, I could pass for *being* one of my informants—an international criminal justice advocate. Thus, contrasts and tensions that I experienced while conducting a multi-sited research process, such as familiarity and unfamiliarity, indicate analytic pointers to what those who really are international criminal justice-makers might also encounter in these different sites. Importantly, however, a minority of my informants in The Hague travel to situation countries, yet what is important is that their work and networks spanned this journey—these are spaces across which imaginations of global criminal justice travel.

The following year, however, I wore an accreditation pass and was able to follow the ASP meetings' proceedings in The Hague from within.

The World Forum, November 2013:

I am early. The NGO strategy meeting doesn't start for another half an hour. People are sitting around the room, scattered in groups working, talking, laughing. The atmosphere is less tense today, people seem more settled. I talk to a guy who's interning with the Coalition. He is writing a PhD in Ireland. He's here for two weeks, he tells me, because he's unsure whether he'd like to work for the Coalition afterwards. I talk to two other interns, one Dutch the other Flemish. The latter is interning here for three months and wants to 'get into the EU', by which I can only assume she means working in one of its institutions rather than dwelling on its territory. I speak to Owen about what happened yesterday. Carolien comes over. They talk about wanting to set up a meeting between the Congolese, the NGOs and the delegates. Carolien tells Owen to talk to Ankit about this. I approach Sam, I have heard he's leaving for the US tomorrow and I want to talk to him before he heads out. He has already introduced his replacement. We sit in the NGO room and talk for a while. The strategy meeting starts and we go outside, finding ourselves a couch along the corridor. People move past as we sit and talk. One of the 'big guys' come over and talks to Sam for a little while. Paulien and Michelle, two academics, also walk past. They signal for me to meet them in the Delegate's Lounge afterwards. [14]

In order to research networks, I participated in networking; in order to research lobbyism, I participated in the merry-go-round of information on international criminal justice. This is yet another example of how I came to embody the very processes I have been studying, and to participate in the global connections of global justice-making. At the ASP meeting for example, I ran after NGOs in the same way they ran after state delegates. Everyone was busy and there was always someone somewhere else to talk to, and someone more important (see Gille and Riain, 2002). Importantly, these experiences yielded crucial insights into the internal working of the field, such as the field's volatility: it coalesces intensely and intricately before dispersing out to different corners of the world.

In many respects, then, I have been part of the very processes I have been studying. There is therefore also reason to question to what extent I am part of the problem. I am by no means the only white young woman researching post-conflict justice issues in East Africa, or on the ICC in Uganda for that matter. Similarly, talking to transitional justice researchers in the global North academe, we had mostly travelled to the same locations and in the same direction, following the beaten track of colonial relations. Nouwen (2014: 237) is one of those who did so before me, making the following remarks about the European female researcher:

> She cannot escape a sense of complicity in sustaining a post-colonial division of labour in the production of knowledge, even if this is one of the challenges that she, perhaps ambitiously, tries to overcome. Seen in this light, public reflexivity is not a narcissistic exercise or a performance of what Robert Meister calls 'feel[ing] good about feeling bad'; rather, it is the beginning of making visible the role of the researcher in the construction of the world.

To do this necessitates a globalized research imagination—not only in empirical but also in methodological, or epistemological, terms (Kenway and Fahey, 2008; see also Aas, 2013). Criminological theory has for a long time lacked reflection on

[14] For reasons of anonymity, names are fictitious.

its geographical applicability, and suffered from a corresponding tendency to conflate the metropole with the 'general', the 'transferable', and the 'universal' (but see Agozino, 2003; Carrington et al., 2015). This stands in sharp contrast to how universal claims are inaccessible to scholars and perspectives from the global South, which is defined by its particularity instead (Aas, 2012). Because of global inequalities, the metropole is constituted as the 'home of theory' (Connell, 2007: 106), or science generally, while the periphery becomes the space from which either metropolitan knowledge is applied or data collected. 'Instead of addressing the imagined universality of the global', Aas calls for criminological scholarship to decentre its parameters of knowledge production—epistemological and social: 'In place of unity of the global, we need systematically to explore its divisions and frictions' (2011: 416). What this entails is letting go of the universal as an inevitable truth and to approach global universals as objects of inquiry in their own right, thereby addressing how 'emerging forms of penal cosmopolitanism [are] infused with relations of power and global inequality' (Aas, 2011: 411).

Along with this goes the recognition that 'we' not only travel in the same direction, but also to similar locations, contributing to research fatigue in particular places and on particular issues. Across the board—from academics, donors, ICC missions, and civil society—Uganda has received substantially more attention than most other situations in which the ICC is involved. Referred to by Winston Churchill as the 'pearl of Africa', Uganda has been an international 'donor-darling' in the global aid regime since the late 1980s (Tangri and Mwenda, 2006; Fisher, 2013). As such, this research inscribes itself within the structural inequalities between the centre and periphery. However, as set out above and 'perhaps ambitiously' so, it is precisely the dismantling and rendering visible of global and transnational networks of power—of connections, forces and imaginations—that is the objective. Thus, the conditions of ethnographic research is similar, but the engagement is not (on global ethnography, see Burawoy, 2000).

From June 2011 to June 2013, I spent a total of nine months in the Netherlands, spread out over a summer course on international criminal law in The Hague, several shorter research trips in relation to 'events' such as conferences, seminars, and ASP meetings, and a visiting research stay at Vrije Universiteit in Amsterdam. During these stays I conducted interviews, observed trials at the ICC (and occasionally at the ICTY), went to as many debates and seminars on international justice as possible, to various Hague intern association events such as its General Assembly meeting and 'Thursday tribunal drinks', and socialized with people working—as academics, practitioners or advocates—in international criminal justice. In January 2014, I spent two weeks in Uganda, in the capital Kampala and in the northern town of Gulu, the centre of the conflict that had recently taken place. As will be discussed at length in Chapters 3 and 4, international criminal justice is a transnational field in which authority and expertise are less stable than in a national field. Academia occupies an important position within international criminal justice, not only because the field's participants are highly educated and thus rely on academic authority and credentials, but also because the lines between academics, advocates, and practitioners are blurred. Methodologically, this meant that I was also able to study international criminal justice as a participating academic, in seminars and conferences with participating donors, human rights activists, international court officials and other academics, and on research trips and research stays abroad. A study tour on transitional justice in Rwanda in March 2013 visiting various segments of Rwandan society dealing with transitional justice, and a study trip to Cyprus and the divided capital Nicosia were particularly insightful; so were research stays in European metropoles. For example, the central positionality of the University of Oxford in global structures of knowledge production meant that it was also empirically valuable: I met international criminal law practitioners here too, and talked to fieldwork researchers on transitional justice issues in East Africa.

As is usually the case with the ethnographic method, additional forms of data supplement observations. The empirical data consists of written text: a research diary including notes from my observations and interviews, interview transcripts, policy papers, websites, reports, statements, cases, legal texts etc. Formal semi-structured interviews were carried out with thirty-four people, lasting on average between one and two hours. I interviewed two people twice: one of these had switched jobs from the NGO sector to the ICC, and was interviewed in both capacities. Twenty-eight people participated in their capacities as NGO representatives, together with three from the ICC, three from the Norwegian Ministry of Foreign Affairs, and one doing an internship at an international criminal court in The Hague. Apart from the administration and finance officers, I interviewed all staff members of the Coalition's Secretariat Office in The Hague (seven people). I also interviewed the Coalition's Convenor and Executive Director of the World Federalist Movement, and representatives from two national coalitions (Uganda and the US), and one regional staff member of the Coalition (Africa). Two people who formerly had been central NGO actors were interviewed in their capacities as independent victims' rights experts, acting as consultants and experts on the ICC and victims' rights in particular. Moreover, I conducted interviews with informants working on international justice and the ICC in particular from the International Bar Association (IBA), Human Rights Watch (HRW), Open Society Justice Initiative (OSJI), Parliamentarians for Global Action (PGA), and REDRESS.[15] In Uganda, I conducted interviews with representatives from *Avocats sans Frontières*, Invisible Children, Human Rights Focus, Norwegian Refugee Council, Ugandan National Coalition for the ICC/HURINET, a former representative for the Ugandan Victim Foundation, and the Norwegian embassy's humanitarian sector.[16]

Importantly, fighting global injustice—making global justice—is a noble profession. Yet, nobility of aims do not confer exemption from either scrutiny or accountability for one's actions. This relates to me and my own conduct as a researcher as much as it does to the ramifications of my informants' actions. Throughout this research process, I have attempted to achieve a balance

[15] Although Human Rights Watch is based in Brussels and REDRESS in London, I will refer to these interviews as also having been conducted in The Hague for reasons of anonymity. I requested interviews with representatives from Amnesty International, the Women's Initiative for Gender Justice (WIGJ), the International Federation for Human Rights (FIDH), and No Peace Without Justice (NPWJ), which all belong to the core group of organizations advocating and lobbying for the ICC. Although I have been in touch and communicated with their representatives, I have not been able to formally interview them. However, I have had informal conversations with and about them, and observed and followed their work online and at the ASP meetings.

[16] I also contacted many more organizations—many of which would have been highly relevant—but unfortunately, some of my appointments fell through for various reasons. This is the great drawback of absolute time limitations in fieldwork, but I was nevertheless able to get an overview of NGOs concerned with ICC issues in Uganda and to supplement interviews and observations with written sources and reports once I returned to the office.

between gaining valuable data that enables critical scholarship of 'established truths' while simultaneously being sensitive and reflecting ethically over my informants' occupational and activist worldviews. What I have aspired to do is to recognize the phenomenon, to try to identify some of the driving and enabling connections and forces upon which the imagination of 'global justice' materializes. That is an analytical rather than a normative objective.

Even so, although my focus has not been on the crimes or their victims, the topic is—understandably—deeply troubling and emotional. Some of my informants have spoken about personal experiences, and the victimization of friends and family. During interviews and conversations in The Hague, I heard stories of childhoods destroyed by war, of lost family members, and of loss of hope of justice. When conducting fieldwork in Uganda, it is impossible *not* to talk with victims of the conflict, and the same is true in Rwanda. In my interaction with people that in some way or other live this issue—either as an advocate of justice, a practitioner, or someone who has experienced destruction first hand, I have been cautious. However, I been careful to not do so to the extent that I seem overly sensitive, compassionate and by extension, naïve. Although naivety may sometimes be a useful strategy that encourages informants to explain and elaborate on issues of interest, appearing oblivious to the 'real world' is not. In such circumstances, which have indeed arisen, I have been seen as someone from whom, as the recipient of a narrative, compassion and moral outrage are required. This has provided valuable data as to the 'genre' of the field—the importance of humanitarian sensibilities. When talking 'business' however, these layers of horror are left behind, though they always lurk beneath the surface, framing the discussion, such as when narratives of atrocities open and close seminars to remind participants of the seriousness of the debates, or when photographic images of victimized Africans fill the entrance hall where diplomatic meetings take place, reminding us what is at stake as we enter and leave the spaces of global justice-making. What emerged as important throughout this research process was thus to recognize compassion, which also includes being conscious of its clouding effects. It is difficult to be 'objective' or maintain what can be called academic distance regarding people and institutions that strive to do good, especially when one is confronted with representations of the suffering they are attempting to address and aspiring to put a stop to. Speaking on behalf of victims is a claim to moral authority, and one that is difficult to argue 'against'—whether in direct conversations with informants or as a global force. As such, this has been a critical pointer to the moral outrage on which international criminal justice depends, 'the morally driven, politically ambiguous, and deeply paradoxical strength of the weak' (Fassin, 2011: xii).

2

Spaces and Places of International Criminal Justice

One of the central philosophical dimensions of thinking about globalization processes concerns space and time, and how processes of globalization transform the nature of spatio-temporal phenomena as well as people's experiences of them. Facilitated by information and communications technology, global media and transportation, social relations in late modernity are increasingly 'stretched' and 'disembedded' (Giddens, 1990). The rise of global social movements and transnational networks are a prime example of the increasing global connectedness of social relations, wherein the 'global' and the 'transnational' have come to be regarded as particular sites of political engagement (Keck and Sikkink, 1998; Tarrow, 2005; Della Porta and Diani, 2006; Castells, 2012). As regards global justice-making, the increased presence and significance of non-state actors and NGOs are challenging the state-centric framework of international law, confronting powerful hierarchies of scale and space (Pearson, 2008). In order to think critically about how the global is constituted as a site of crime, justice, and community (McMillan, 2016), a sociology of punishment for international criminal justice is attentive to how globalization processes reconfigure not only temporal but also spatial relations.

Temporality is embedded in criminal justice as both theory and practice—of making right for the future some wrong of the past. One of the major objectives attributed to international criminal prosecutions and punishment is the trial as a ritual. Performed under the rule of law, the trial orchestrates a symbolic break from the violations of the past to the moral community of the future (Cassese, 1998; Robinson, 2003). However, what distinguishes global criminal justice-making further is the appeal to humanitarian progress: International criminal justice invokes a historic

Advocates of Humanity. Kjersti Lohne, Oxford University Press (2019). © Kjersti Lohne.
DOI: 10.1093/oso/9780198818748.003.0002

narrative, generally beginning with Nuremberg, continuing via ad hoc tribunals and national prosecutions of human rights violations to the present day International Criminal Court (ICC) and its founding Rome Statute, including its domestication in national justice systems. As expressed by one of the central human rights advocates in the field:

> There is a proliferation of proceedings, which vary greatly in quality, and what they are accomplishing, but it really is a phenomenon. There is not sufficient awareness, or each point in the constellation is being looked at in isolation, as opposed to realizing that we're witnessing this really exciting period of potentially having new ways to enforce the rule of law, and new ways to protect human rights.

There is a sense of history-making embedded in international criminal justice, an awareness and celebration of progress through history, and of being part of this progress (Lohne, 2018b). The celebratory narrative of progress through time is also reflected in core literature. In Sikkink's *The Justice Cascade* she argues for a shift in the 'legitimacy of the norm' of individual criminal accountability for mass violence by demonstrating a corresponding increase in criminal prosecution 'on behalf of that norm' (2011: 5). This development is, generally, seen in tandem with a 'humanization' of international law; what Teitel calls '"humanity law"—that is, the law of persons and peoples ... departing from the preexisting interstate regime' (2011: x). The development of a more 'people-empowering' law, and of a 'global civil society' able to advance such legal development, are considered interrelated: they 'feed and drive one another' (Glasius, 2002: 137). The dimension of time is thus explicit in international criminal justice, as the dimension of development and progress, and of *making* global justice.

By contrast, space becomes the dimension that is left behind; a 'flat' surface that global justice passes through. Although the ICC's jurisdiction and enforcement is rooted in the state system, its claims to universality imply a type of 'spaceless' justice, as if speaking to and from nowhere in particular (Pearson, 2008). However, rather than the 'flat' dimension that time cuts across, space is the dimension that confronts us with the simultaneous existence of 'the other'—of how we relate to one another in the same time. Spatial arrangements are social relations 'stretched out', and 'since social relations are inevitably and everywhere imbued with power and meaning and symbolism, this view of the spatial is an ever-shifting social geometry of power and signification' (Massey 1994: 2). Attuned to how globalization reconfigures spatial relations, this chapter analyses the world of places, events, and things in international criminal justice to demonstrate how it is comprised of multiple scales, geographies, and sites.

The Hague as the City of Global Justice

To the extent that there is a place to 'visit' international criminal justice, The Hague is it. The Hague hosts many of the world's most important global institutions. Over 160 international organizations are based in the city (City of The Hague, 2013). Besides the ICC, The Hague hosts the International Tribunal for the former Yugoslavia (ICTY), the Special Tribunal for Lebanon, The Hague office for the Special Court for Sierra Leone, and the UN Mechanism for International Criminal Tribunals (MICT), which deals with the residual functions of the now closed ICTY, and the International Criminal Tribunal for Rwanda (ICTR). Furthermore, the imposing Peace Palace (Vredespalais) is home to the primary institutions of international law: the International Court of Justice and the Permanent Court of Arbitration. The latter is therefore referred to as the 'seat of international law', and The Hague, accordingly, as the 'legal capital of the world'.

While the study of the city is central to sociological analysis of crime and social control (Park and Burgess, 1921), a *relational* approach to cities has become important for understanding how globalization impacts spatial, and thus also social and political, relations (Sassen, 1994; 2013; Massey, 2007). Global integration and spatial dispersion have generated new roles for major cities. What Sassen calls 'global cities' have come to function in four new ways: 'First, as highly concentrated command points in the organization of the world economy; second, as key locations for finance and for specialized service firms ... third, as sites of production, including the production of innovations, in these leading industries; and fourth, as markets for the products and innovations produced' (1998: 3–4). Instead of being a hub in the global networks of financial capital, I suggest that The Hague can be understood as a hub in the global networks of global justice-making.

The Hague's prominence for global justice is reflected in symbolic sculptures and monuments, and rows of flags decorating the streets outside 'global' buildings. One can enjoy the city's scenery while immersing oneself in its history on a peace and justice themed 'tram walk' through its *International Zone*, stopping by The Humanity House, The Peace Palace, the City Hall's film exhibition of the history of the city of peace and justice, and so on. For those visiting with children, there is a *Kids Tour* option.[1] In a report by the City of The Hague entitled The Hague International City of Peace and Justice, one is told:

> The Hague is proud to play her part in building a more peaceful and just world. A world where disagreements are battled out in court rather than in streets or trenches. The Hague works in service of a future world without chemical weapons, without ethnic cleansing, without the supremacy of the law of the jungle. A world where reason and truth combine in providing justice for all, and where those who attempt to disrespect international justice do so at their peril. They will face judgment—in The Hague. (City of The Hague: 14)

At the time of research, the ICC was located in Voorburg, in the southeastern part of The Hague. Rising tall and white against the sky, the Court shared its premises with EUROJUST (the European Union's judicial cooperation unit which seeks to 'reinforce the fight against serious organized crime' in the region), including the entrance, canteen, and smoking area.[2] Apart from the odd academic, a trial monitoring intern, or a visiting boyfriend, most visits to the Court were group visits, particularly school visits. Visitors went through a security checkpoint into an entrance hall decorated with pictures of judges and video installations of how the Court operates, and the construction process of its present and permanent premises. There were seating areas for waiting visitors, and racks of brochures—in Arabic, English, French and Spanish—that deal with the Court's composition, cases, situations, and so forth. Groups receive a brief introduction in the entrance hall from a Court official, see a film about the Court's creation and development, and have a follow up Q&A session with another Court official. If a trial was in progress, and it had not gone into 'private session', visitors could enter the public gallery and observe it from behind a glass wall.

[1] Brochure available at http://www.thehaguepeacejustice.com/peace-and-justice/topics/sightseeing.htm (accessed 4 June 2014).

[2] See http://www.eurojust.europa.eu/about/background/Pages/history.aspx (accessed 30 October 2014).

Occasionally, court proceedings attract public attention. Such was the case with the confirmation hearing of charges against the former President of Côte D'Ivoire, Laurent Gbagbo. The event attracted the pro-Gbagbo diaspora from all around Europe, who staged a protest in support of Gbagbo outside the Court's premises, and sat in the public galleries smiling at and waving to the man they considered a national hero. Usually however, court proceedings at the ICC seem, as court proceedings generally do—technical and mundane, foreign to the outsider because of all its legal jargon and technicalities. From the public gallery, it is difficult to imagine the chaos of war that is transported into the courtroom: here, with simultaneous interpretation into multiple languages, with computers in front of members of the Office of the Prosecutor (OTP), the Defence Counsel, the Judges, the Victims' Legal Representatives, and the Registry, there is a space of clinical modernity. Underlying the contrast between order and chaos created by the trial imagery is the physical distance between the Court and the locations in which it intervenes. The violence transported into the European heartland is the violence of the 'global borderlands'—the imagined geographical space of brutality and breakdown (Duffield, 2001).

To 'reflect the significance of the Court in the fight against impunity',[3] the new permanent premises are located in The Hague's 'International Zone', and thus in proximity to the Scheveningen prison hosting those detained by the ICC and the ICTY. Additionally, the International Zone is home to most of the other global institutions in the city, including The Hague World Forum, where the Assembly of States Parties (ASP) meetings take place when held in the city. Quite visibly and materially, The Hague has become an 'obvious' site of production for international (criminal) law.

One way to understand the embeddedness of global justice-making in The Hague is as part of the city's moral and political economy. While the notion of moral economy is often used to describe norms and habits informing market rationalities, it also refers to that lending legitimacy to the constitution of markets and the economy (Karstedt and Farrall, 2006). In The Hague, the

[3] Seehttp://www.icc-cpi.int/en_menus/icc/about%20the%20court/permanent%20premises/Pages/permanent%20premises.aspx (accessed 29 October 2014).

production of global justice seems to have become part of the city's moral economy. Branding The Hague as the 'city of peace and justice' has become an important claim and financial strategy of The Hague municipality, to the extent that the maxim *Vrede en Recht*, the 'vocation of the The Hague', has been added to the city's coat of arms (City of The Hague, 2013). On the municipal websites, one can learn that 'The Hague's economy is doing well thanks to the presence of the international organizations in and around the city,'[4] and in addition, that 'the municipality's efforts to brand The Hague as the international city of peace and justice are paying off' (City of The Hague and Decisio, 2011: 2). From 2004 to 2010, the international organizations' share in The Hague's contribution to the gross national product increased from 5.9 to 10.8 per cent. A municipal report informs that the 'employment level at the international organisations as well as employment which organisations create due to their purchasing behaviour and international staff's spending is worth 35,000 jobs. Each job at an international organisation means one job outside the organisation (City of The Hague and Decisio, 2011: 4).

In addition to the more than 100 embassies and consulates represented in the city, The Hague is not only the seat of international courts and tribunals, but also of numerous academic institutions specializing in peace and justice, as well as over a hundred NGOs, concerned with peace and justice, security, and development (and water management). In parallel to how Sassen observes how 'the key sector specifying the distinctive production advantages of global cities is the highly specialized and networked services sector' (2001: xx), it appears that the vast number of NGOs, consultancies, research centres, and institutions working on global criminal justice-making in The Hague serve a similar function vis-à-vis 'headquarters', that is, the courts and tribunals of international criminal justice.

'(A)s a venue for humanitarian concerns worldwide' (City of The Hague, 2013: 87), NGOs account for approximately 14 per cent of employment in international organizations in The Hague, and over a third of the city's total number of international organizations. In fact, NGOs constitute more than half (110/199)

[4] See http://www.denhaag.nl/en/residents/International-The-Hague/to/International-orgs-good-for-The-Hagues-economy.htm (accessed 4 June 2014). Please note that these websites are edited and updated.

of international organizations in The Hague (City of The Hague and Decisio, 2011). Part of the municipal strategy has been to attract NGOs to The Hague, by providing practical guidance and assistance on 'Starting an NGO in the Hague' (City of The Hague, 2012), and subsidizing office buildings accommodating the 'growing stream of NGOs that seek shelter in our city, from there to monitor the world' (City of The Hague and Decisio, 2011: 87).

This shows how notions of morality and justice-making have become central to The Hague's identity, including its economic interests. The point here is not to say that international criminal justice 'only' serves economic interests, nor that the location of international criminal courts and tribunals in The Hague 'merely' reproduces global economic arrangements. Yet when analysing The Hague as a global city for justice, it seems important to recognize the local economic, political, and social forces that animate such spaces. '[E]ven "purely economic" phenomena are always also cultural phenomena in so far as they depend on cultural understandings of what is to count as valuable or useful, as well as cultural understandings of what are effective and acceptable means to pursue these values' (Garland, 2006: 425). It seems the pursuit of global justice is a 'good' economy, in the dual sense of the world. However, a question may be asked for whom?

A familiar element of economic growth is the expansion of service and low-wage jobs. Yet as is the case with global cities, it appears that in The Hague too, 'growth' is related to spatial, social, and economic inequalities *within* the city. Just outside The Hague's city centre lies Schilderswijk, one of the Netherland's poorest neighbourhoods, and with a relatively high-density population of immigrants. Featured by right-wing politicians and media under politically scorning nicknames such as the 'Sharia triangle',[5] the district also gave rise to mass protests in 2015 following the death of Aruban Mitch Henriquez at the hands of the police, who have been accused of brutality and discrimination in the area.[6] A question may be asked about what it means for a city to be successful, and, one may add, 'global'. As Massey observes, 'the very characterization of cities as "global" is a strategy whereby the part

[5] https://www.irishtimes.com/news/world/europe/dutch-anxiety-over-sharia-triangle-police-no-go-area-in-the-hague-1.1404541 (accessed 18 July 2019).

[6] https://www.theguardian.com/world/2015/jul/03/the-hague-arrests-protest-death-police-custody-mitch-henriquez (accessed 18 July 2019).

stands in for the whole, where the city is defined by its elite and the rest is consigned to invisibility' (2007: 216).

In response to one third of The Hague's population of 500,000 consisting of immigrants and expats, the municipality launched *The Hague Bridge Project* in efforts to 'bridge' the social gap between 'high-skilled migrants' and its local population, the Hagenaars (City of The Hague, 2013). Arguably reflective of this gap, there is a particular 'international sociability' in The Hague consisting of transnational professionals, students, and interns. One of the Dutch nationals working in the NGO sector explained that 'everyone here is an expat so you tend to have a different social world constructed because you hang out with more expats. Then you tend to find people in your social group that have the same interest because you share the same field of work.' Besides having similar work in common, the internationals share similar backgrounds—even if they are not from similar countries, at least they are foreign to The Hague and the Netherlands. The 'Thursday Tribunal Drinks', for example, bring together international interns and young professionals working in international criminal justice—good for networking and finding opportunities for internships and job openings, as well as friendships. However, not everyone stays in The Hague very long. As one of my younger informants revealed, 'It's difficult right now because a good chunk of my friends have left, so I have like two friends here, and they're probably going to leave in a few months. So the amount of goodbyes to go through … it's exhausting!' But then, I am told, 'It's a small field. They're off to Cambodia for a bit, but they'll probably be back.' And if not, there is a better chance of running into familiar faces from the 'expat bubble' at another time and in a different space—perhaps another global metropolis—than of meeting one of the Hagenaars. These dynamics illustrate the embeddedness of global networks for the field of international criminal justice, yet, at the same time, indicate how transnational professionals are more globally than locally connected—more in tune with transnational encounters and global flows than locally embedded social life.

It is not only the physical location of the ICC, or of the other courts, or the constructions of international criminal law, that make The Hague a global justice city. The myriad academic research and policy centres of 'global justice' and 'international criminal law', along with the NGOs specializing in international justice in the city are likewise essential to understanding the role of The Hague for global justice-making, and above all its role as a strategic site in the production networks of global justice. The Hague disperses people and ideas on global justice to the periphery; it is from here that global justice becomes a global export, the city being where global justice is 'created, interpreted, maintained or transformed' (Pearson, 2008: 491).[7] In this manner, a geography of dependencies in international criminal justice emerges, revealing the power of some places over others.

Geographies of dependencies: international crimes before the ICC

From advocates and academics to diplomats and practitioners, The Hague is the connection site for people working and thinking about international criminal justice, its laws, and trials. However, The Hague is not the place where what international criminal justice deals with actually happens; it is not the site of mass violence and armed conflict, or that of the international crimes deliberated over in The Hague. Instead, these sites come into play through law, 'triggered' by the jurisdiction of the ICC in three ways. Here, space is understood as geography, as a flat surface, and in its relation to law, as a matter of territorial jurisdiction (Philippopoulos-Mihalopoulos, 2011).

First, the UN Security Council can refer a situation to the Court under Chapter VII of the UN Charter, that is, when considered a threat to international peace and security. From a legitimacy of punishment perspective, this trigger mechanism is the most contentious as it also includes states that have not signed and ratified the Rome Statute. It represents a continuation of the ad hoc tribunal model, as these too were created under a Chapter VII Resolution. Two situations before the Court have so far been triggered by a Security Council referral: Darfur in Sudan, and Libya. The situation of Darfur in Sudan was referred to the Court in March 2005, and seven individuals have so far been indicted, including Sudan's President Omar Al-Bashir, the first ever indictment against a sitting head of state for genocide charges. Despite

[7] As is the case with Sassen's 'global city' thesis, there is no such thing as one global city. New York, Brussels, and Geneva may likewise function as strategic nodes for global justice too.

the Security Council referral of the situation of Sudan to the Court, states have since been reluctant to cooperate with the Court in enforcing arrest warrants, and all of the indictees remain at large. Al-Bashir's visits to neighbouring and ICC signatory states, such as Chad and South Africa, are a continuous provocation of the Court, and reveal how toothless international criminal justice is without the support of states with the political will to enforce it.

The Security Council referred the situation of Libya to the ICC in late February 2011, just a few weeks before it also authorized the use of force to protect civilians. Warrants were issued in June 2011 for the arrest of Muammar Gaddafi, whose case soon terminated following his death in November, and of his son Saif Al-Islam Gaddafi, and security and intelligence chief Abdullah Al-Senussi. Debates on the admissibility of cases dominate the ICC's intervention in the Libyan conflict, as the case against Senussi was ruled inadmissible to the Court.[8]

The second trigger mechanisms is the *proprio motu* powers of the Prosecutor, meaning that they can pursue investigations based on their own independent initiative, subject to confirmation by the Chambers of the Court. The inclusion of *proprio motu* powers in the Rome Statute are held up as an example of concerted NGO efforts during the treaty negotiations in Rome (Glasius, 2006). Three situations before the Court have been triggered *proprio motu:* the situation of Côte d'Ivoire and Kenya—both at the initiative of former Chief Prosecutor Luis Moreno-Ocampo—and Georgia, initiated by current Chief Prosecutor Fatou Bensouda. As regards Côte d'Ivoire, Pre-Trial Chamber III authorized the Prosecutor to initiate investigations into the country in October 2011, following election violence in 2010 between supporters of Laurent Gbagbo and Alassane Ouattara. Charges have been brought against the former, including Gbagbo himself, his wife Simone Gbagbo (the first female to be indicted by the Court and who remains at large), and Charles Blé Goudé. Gbagbo and Blé Goudé were acquitted of all charges in January 2019. At the time of writing, it remains to be seen whether the Prosecutor will appeal this decision.

The first time the Prosecutor initiated his own investigation concerns the situation in Kenya. During most parts of my research,

[8] See https://www.icc-cpi.int/libya (accessed 20 September 2019). See also Kersten (2016).

Kenya was the 'hot topic', as put by an informant. The OTP had initiated an investigation in March 2010 following post-election violence in 2007/2008, in which an estimated 1,300 people were killed and a further 6,000–7,000 displaced. After the post-election violence, Kenyan authorities first appointed a commission of inquiry into the violence, known as the Waki Commission. Failure to proceed with prosecutions of high-level perpetrators led Kofi Annan, serving as an AU mandated peace negotiator, to turn over the Waki material to the ICC. In December 2010, the OTP requested Chambers to issue summonses to appear at court for six Kenyans allegedly responsible for crimes against humanity, including Uhuru Muigai Kenyatta and William Samoei Ruto, who would go on to become President and Vice President in Kenya following the 2013 elections.[9]Since then, the ICC's cases in Kenya have collapsed, largely due to the Kenyatta and Ruto's successful campaign to avoid prosecution by turning the ICC's intervention into a question of neo-colonialism, and, not surprisingly, by not cooperating with the Court. The analysis put forward in this book contributes sociological explanation to the legitimacy crisis that the Kenyan situation inflamed, by identifying characteristics and dynamics of international criminal justice that reveal a lack of authority at the level of global justice-making.

In December 2017, the ICC intervened for the first time in a situation outside Africa when the OTP was authorized to open *proprio motu* investigations into the situation in Georgia, following alleged crimes against humanity and war crimes committed in and around South Ossetia between 1 July and 10 October 2008. This is also the first full investigation implicating a major power, Russia. The OTP's request for authorization to investigate the situation linked to the armed conflict in Afghanistan, which would most likely have implicated another great power, the US, was rejected by Chambers in a controversial decision that it was not in the 'interest of justice', as they found state cooperation to be unlikely.[10]

By the third trigger mechanism of the ICC's jurisdiction, a State Party can refer a situation on its territory to the Court, as has been the case with Uganda, the Democratic Republic of the Congo

[9] See https://www.icc-cpi.int/kenya (accessed 23 September 2019).

[10] https://www.icc-cpi.int/Pages/item.aspx?name=pr1448 (accessed 20 June 2019). The OTP may appeal this decision.

(DRC), the Central African Republic (CAR), and Mali. In April 2004, the DRC referred crimes committed within its territory to the ICC, and the OTP opened investigations in the country two months later. Charges were since brought against six individuals, three of whom have been tried. The case of the DRC is thus the one that has involved the most judicial activity of the situations before the Court, and will accordingly be discussed throughout the book. The case against Thomas Lubanga was the ICC's first case and ended in a conviction: he was sentenced to fourteen years' imprisonment for enlisting and conscripting child soldiers, a war crime. In the ICC's second verdict, Mathieu Ngudjolo Chui, charged with crimes against humanity and war crimes, was acquitted and released from detention. Germain Katanga was sentenced to a total of twelve years' imprisonment for crimes against humanity and war crimes, and the trial against Bosco Ntaganda, who voluntarily surrendered to the Court, is currently ongoing in The Hague. The situation of the CAR was referred to the Court in January 2005, and the OTP started its investigations in May 2007. Jean-Pierre Bemba Gombo, a DRC national and military commander was found guilty in 2016, and he was sentenced to eighteen years in prison for war crimes and crimes against humanity. In June 2018, however, the Appeals Chamber acquitted Bemba of all charges (see also Chapter 1, note 4). In September 2014 the OTP announced the opening of a second investigation in the CAR, also at the government's request. In July 2012, the government of Mali referred the situation to the ICC, who opened investigations in January 2013. Pleading guilty, Ahmad Al Faqi Al Mahdi was found guilty on 27 September 2016 of the war crime of intentionally directing attacks against historic monuments and buildings dedicated to religion in June and July 2012 in Mali. He was sentenced to nine years' imprisonment. In January 2004, President Museveni of Uganda referred the situation 'concerning the Lord's Resistance Army' (LRA) to the ICC.

Before the Ugandan situation is considered in more detail, this brief overview shows where and how the ICC has become involved in global criminal justice-making throughout the world. It also describes how the materiality of the ICC is coupled with law. While The Hague remains a stable site of the ICC's materiality, other sites come into play *through* law, demonstrating the specific and central position of The Hague in global justice-making in relation to other sites. Moreover, because the ICC does not have its own enforcement powers but ultimately relies upon state cooperation for security and the enforcement of arrests, especially the third trigger mechanism, illustrates a certain bias in favour of state power in international criminal justice, as evidenced by Kenya. In all but two situations before the Court (Kenya and Sudan), the ICC has not explicitly confronted state power by indicting state officials; rather, it has pursued actors challenging state power, such as the LRA in Uganda.

Uganda as a site of global justice-making

When President Museveni referred the situation to the ICC, Uganda became part of the ICC's materiality. Today, however, the LRA has left the northern territories of Uganda and is scattered across the borders of CAR, DRC, and South Sudan. The mass violence that prompted the global justice-making process has ended, yet the delivery of 'global justice' has remained out of reach, as at the time of research, all of the ICC indictees remained at large.

While the ICC's premises in The Hague are celebrated for its grandness—because, as put by former ICC President Song, 'an institution of global significance deserves a world class premises' (ICC, 2013)—the ICC's 'field office' in Uganda hid behind a fortified compound located on Nakasero Hill, an upmarket, embassy district in Kampala, Uganda's capital. The inside of the compound comprised two buildings, apart from the watchtowers on either side of the gate, and a small parking space for the land cruisers. How can we understand this celebratory visibility of global justice in The Hague, compared to its conspicuous invisibility in Uganda?

The fortified compound is a familiar construction of 'bordered international space' in the global borderlands (Duffield, 2010: 456). But even in Kampala, which Lonely Planet calls 'safe as far as capitals in Africa go',[11] defensive living in the form of 'bunkerization' and gated communities is common, with hotels, upscale restaurants, embassies, and NGOs sheltered behind reinforced gates and security personnel. This is a potent reminder of the need for criminological analysis to look beyond the geographies of the West; here, it is clear that barriers and gated communities serve as indicators of social exclusion on the global scale,

[11] See http://www.lonelyplanet.com/uganda/kampala/essential-information (accessed 19 April 2015).

separating both physically and metaphorically 'insiders' from 'outsiders' (Low, 2003; Aas, 2013). As much as the fortified compound 'highlights the exclusivity of the international space of flows and its unequal relationship with the surrounding environment', they also form an uneven yet distinguishable 'archipelago of international flows'—as physical signs of 'the international' (Duffield, 2010: 456–7, 469). In Kampala and in Gulu too, entering a compound to meet with informants became an indicator of whether I was meeting with international and foreign entities, as opposed to local and national informants, because it represented a form of international materiality. It shows how space continues to matter, also for those at 'home' in the transnational 'space of flows' (Aas, 2013: 74).

During my fieldwork in February 2014, it became evident that the ICC field office in Kampala had been substantially scaled down. It was composed of merely a dozen people including the OTP, the Registry, and the Trust Fund for Victims (TFV), which at that moment was by far the most active ICC unit in the country. Only one person staffed the outreach unit, which initially comprised five people. He identified the lack of personnel as the office's biggest challenge, saying 'I've been on leave since November, and there's no one here to cover for me.' The reason, he explained, was the lack of judicial development.

> When there is lack of judicial development, what can you do? Nothing! Our strategy now is just called a maintenance strategy. The Court is not going to leave today or tomorrow, so our strategy is just to maintain a presence in order to draw on these networks and pull them back when there is judicial development.[12]

Most of the international staff had relocated to more urgent places, neighbouring Nairobi in particular. Some of the local staff, however, had 'relocated' to the NGO sector, such as a former outreach officer at the time working for the Ugandan NGO Coalition for the ICC.

[12] Despite the lack of resources, Uganda was the situation country in which the ICC conducted the second highest number of outreach activities in 2013 (ICC-Registry, 2013). This says more about the situations in which the ICC intervenes than the Court's activities in Uganda, as the security situation elsewhere to a significant extent prevents the ICC from interacting more with affected communities (see Lohne, 2018b).

The Ugandan Coalition for the ICC is the sub-national network of NGOs—part of the transnational advocacy network represented in The Hague. The Ugandan Coalition is hosted by Human Rights Network-Uganda (HURINET-U), which was based in another part of town, north east of the city centre in what appeared to be an 'NGO neighbourhood'. Old Kiira Road had innumerable signposts to organizations fighting for rights and justice across a variety of issues, or offering their assistance and services out of humanitarian or religious convictions. The Ugandan Coalition's office was also inside a compound. When I visited, a smiling security guard welcomed me. As was the case with the ICC, my ride had to wait for me outside. A representative from the Ugandan Coalition told me that this was not a very busy period for them, and that they mainly worked on applying for funding. 'I don't interact with The Hague much,' she said, indicating that for her, 'The Hague' was not so much a geographical place on the European continent but rather the signification of international criminal justice. The MacArthur Foundation, which was the major donor for funding international justice in Uganda, had not renewed their funding. Thus, the Ugandan Coalition was working on changing their mandate to become more cross-cutting—diversifying into 'transitional justice', 'early warning', 'prevention of genocide'—in order to attract funding from alternative donors.

Due to the lack of judicial progress, it was not only the ICC that was receding, but also NGO donors, illustrating an interesting dynamic within the flows of global justice-making. In this case, NGO advocacy on the ICC was more or less dependent on the ICC being involved, as that is when funding appears. Rather than agenda-setting, it seemed more like momentum-building: assisting global justice-making by mobilizing civil society through funding flows.

At the time of research, Uganda was, in other words, 'standing still' as concerns international criminal justice. It had become a peculiar 'non-site' to the ICC. To the extent Uganda was talked about in The Hague, the focus was on the Court's (lack of) exit strategies and legacy (see discussion on victim reparations in Chapter 6). Meanwhile, in Uganda, there was 'progress' in other domains of justice-making. In 2013, the Ugandan Justice, Law and Order Sector launched a draft policy on transitional justice, which was what many of the Ugandan-based NGOs have turned their attention towards (e.g. JRP and Ederu, 2013). Uganda was, thus, not standing still as concerns justice-making at all, but from a view from The Hague, that is how it seemed. There, it was as if justice in Uganda only had one future, namely the one represented by the Rome Statute system of justice, resembling one of Massey's central arguments about globalization's 'evasive imaginations': that of turning 'space into time, geography into history' by conceptualizing spatial difference as temporal sequence (2006: 90). It was as if they were saying that there is no alternative. However, while The Hague stands for one kind of future, there are also others (see also Massey, 2007: 7).

As expressed by the ICC outreach officer, the intention was to pull back networks when, and if, there was judicial development. However, most of the Ugandan-based NGOs were no longer working with the ICC and the international NGOs seemed to have withdrawn *en masse* from northern Uganda. When the LRA left and Gulu Town, the centre of the conflict, became safe and accessible, the international aid community descended upon Gulu—to the extent of suffering from NGO obesity (see also Lie, 2014). When I was there, however, the NGOs that had not already left seemed to be packing up. The Norwegian Refugee Council (NRC), which had been the largest humanitarian actor in the town and in the region generally, was impatiently waiting for permission to cross the border into South Sudan or to relocate further north. After all, Gulu Town was by then classified as being in a 'development phase', and the NRC's mandate is not for development but for humanitarian assistance; as we spoke, the representative I met with was acutely aware that, a few kilometres to the north, massacres were occurring in neighbouring South Sudan, and large numbers of refugees were already fleeing the violence.

While international engagement is in many ways intentionally transient, operating, so to speak, in the temporality of emergency (Fassin and Pandolfi, 2010), as a moral economy, it nonetheless becomes an important source of employment and income at the local level. As the exodus of NGOs from Gulu shows, this is ultimately a temporary opportunity: local jobs cease with the departure of international NGOs. It illustrated the vulnerability of the moral economy generated in northern Uganda by international justice-making and other humanitarian efforts (see also Branch, 2013). As the place of injustice and violence that fed global criminal justice-making in The Hague, Gulu was losing its relevance and hence also its materiality for the ICC.

However, the absence, or lack, of materiality of international criminal justice in Uganda was conspicuous altogether. The ICC has never actually had permanent representation in Gulu, so there was no door to knock on, or guardhouse to approach that connected the makers and the potential beneficiaries of global justice. Instead, the ICC travelled up north from its base in Kampala. When the Court got involved in Uganda, the conflict in the north was still ongoing. While the forcible detention of four staff members of the Court in 2012 by the Libyan government underscores the need for the ICC to take precautions when carrying out its work, and to ensure the safety of its staff,[13] a local human rights activist in Gulu expressed disappointment with how this affected the Court's involvement and its perception of the conflict. He contended, 'I don't expect people to risk being killed in order to work with human rights. I understand, but still! The ICC stayed in Kampala and read the newspapers—they based their understanding of the conflict on news they believed was independent of the government.' Even after the LRA left, the ICC kept its field office in Kampala. It makes one wonder whether it is more important for the ICC to remain linked to the global networks and space-of-flows offered by the capital, than to be connected to the space-of-place of mass violence (Castells, 1996). Without commenting on the investigative methods of the ICC, the comment above illustrates a sense of disconnection. The ICC was not there. Rather, 'it was represented at best by an ephemeral presence in the localities and lives of those in whose name justice is pursued' (Lohne, 2018b: 9).

Global Justice and Social Media

In 2011, the LRA and the conflict in Uganda quickly rose to the top of the global agenda as 'KONY2012', a video campaign launched by the US-based NGO Invisible Children, went viral. Almost overnight, the 30-minute long video became a worldwide success, generating approximately 1 billion views on YouTube. It demonstrated the power of the internet, and the potential of social networks animated by emotional filmmaking to make a 'self-sustaining, citizen-propelled tidal wave of messaging' (Beckett,

[13] See https://www.icc-cpi.int/Pages/item.aspx?name=pr820&ln=en (accessed 12 November 2018).

2012: 7). A representative from Invisible Children's Gulu-based office explained that 'The intention was to make Kony famous. That was it. To raise awareness in the world about what was going on,' invoking the widespread premise of humanitarian advocacy that knowing about suffering generates action by others (Givoni, 2014).

In response to the sudden and massive attention to the international crimes of the LRA, the then Chief Prosecutor Moreno-Ocampo asserted that Invisible Children would—and no less—'produce the arrest of Joseph Kony this year' (quoted in Slosson, 2012). Another representative from the OTP elaborated on the matter:

> The KONY2012 campaign was very good for us because we have had an arrest warrant out for Kony since 2005 and nobody was talking about it. Then comes Invisible Children. They do this whole campaign in the US, and they manage to pass a bill in the US congress to allow for a hundred US military advisors to go to the region to advise Ugandan forces on how to arrest Kony ... Kony is also now in the 'Rewards for Justice' program in the US.[14] This is a big thing for us—now we have ICC people on that list. That is a result of what the Invisible Children did.

Whether or not the increased military efforts by the US were indeed a result of Invisible Children's campaign—the representative from their NGO's office in Gulu was much more cautious about asserting a causal effect—their campaign certainly added legitimacy to the ICC's intervention in the conflict. It is a striking example of the power of social media, not only to produce moral outrage on behalf of distant others (Boltanski, 1999), but to gain support for global justice-making generally.

Using technology as an instrument of social change is by no means a novelty, and much has been written on the transnational mobilization of 'networks of outrage and hope' facilitated by the spread of internet access (Castells, 2012). The internet and its social media platforms not only connect otherwise physically distant actors and agendas, but also offer novel ways of *doing* advocacy (Guo and Saxton, 2014). However, as a space of law, the role of social media remains relatively unexplored (Barberá et al., 2018).

[14] http://www.rewardsforjustice.net/ (accessed 8 January 2015).

The Coalition for the ICC has a range of social media accounts: Twitter, Flickr, YouTube, as well as a Facebook profile and a blog entitled #globaljustice. The same is true of many of its member organizations such as Amnesty International and Human Rights Watch. What is perhaps more interesting is that international criminal courts have also recognized the importance of social media in their communication with external audiences: The ICC too has Twitter, Flickr, and YouTube accounts. To a considerable extent, international criminal justice takes place on virtual sites. As a particular space of global justice-making, it calls for further analysis.

NGO advocacy on international criminal justice relies on arousing moral outrage by researching, monitoring, and reporting on global human suffering, and by disseminating these messages to a wider audience. KONY2012 is an example of how social media enable images of global violence and justice to be imagined, in this case, for instance, presenting the conflict in northern Uganda within a familiar narrative of African violence and helpless victims in need of western intervention and rescue (Mutua, 2001; see generally Taub, 2012).

However, technology is not neutral. Rather than society passively adopting and adapting to technology, technology and society engage in a mutually constitutive relationship (MacKenzie and Wajcman, 1999). As Hayward argues, 'digital technologies create what one might describe as porous *spaces of subjectivity* in which moves made via the rhizomic, hyperlinked internet appear materially or spatially insignificant, but, in reality, have tangible consequences'; communication technologies change 'the way we experience the sense of *being* in an environment' (2012: 457). This is important for understanding the role of social media in international criminal justice, particularly regarding mobilization and support, as it can be understood as part of building a *constituency* for international criminal justice as a whole. Compared with domestic criminal justice systems whose constituency follows the relation between State and citizen, the constituency of international criminal justice is much less clear. I therefore suggest that one of the major functions of NGOs in international criminal justice is to *create* constituency, social media being a crucial space upon which constituency-building takes place.

However, a distinction is made between different kinds of audiences, or constituencies. One of the Coalition representatives explained that their use of social media platforms depended on who they are trying to reach, and what 'conversation' they are trying to participate in: 'On Facebook we're very much trying to build that kind of community of people who have a passing interest in our work. We post things that are more accessible and interesting for the wider public, and who definitely are not as knowledgeable about the ICC.' He explained that their engagement on Facebook is about creating a community of awareness about the fight against impunity, and that they post images and videos for their followers to 'like' and 'share'. In this way, individuals are able to express their moral outrage over distant suffering, to join groups with different social and political agendas, support this or that cause, and to express their opinion from their own living room sofas (Douzinas, 2007a: chapter 3).

When considering digital expressions of solidarity and contemporary humanitarian sensibilities, there is, thus, reason to pause with the turn to self-expression.

> The process of technologization is, in this context, no longer simply a matter of the media platforms that carry the message but also a matter of what Foucault calls the 'technologies of the self' that the publics of solidarity are invited to engage with—that is the practices of feeling, thinking and acting that these publics are mundanely socialized in so as to become certain types of citizens rather than others. (Chouliaraki, 2013: 17, 19–20)

Clicking 'like' on the Coalition's Facebook updates, 'sharing' the KONY2012 video, or 'retweeting' an update from the ICC communicates something about 'us'. The digital expression of solidarity is at the same time an expression of cosmopolitan dispositions, of humanitarian sensibilities towards distant and vulnerable others, 'strangers we will never meet, without the anticipation of reciprocation' (Chouliaraki, 2013: 3). In this manner, social media contributes to create 'global justice subjectivities', and hence, a constituency for international criminal justice.

However, whereas Facebook and similar social media platforms address a 'generalized' audience, it appears that Twitter is being used for a more specialized and expert audience; as explained by the representative from the Coalition, Twitter is 'where the policy makers are':

> There will be an engaged constituency on Twitter who are all always talking about the ICC, like 'Did you see what happened in this case?'

They will be very much involved. Usually, they are academics or journalists or NGO people, or people working at the courts. So more and more we are trying to engage in that conversation. In recent weeks, we have encouraged all of our staff to be on Twitter and identify themselves as staff, so that they can really be at the conversations when it's happening.

Twitter is recognized as a space where international criminal justice is 'happening'. Due to the vast physical distances between engaged individuals and participants in global justice-making, spanning regions, countries, and continents, the significance of social media as a space of international criminal justice is easily understood. Social media *connects* these different geographies, bringing global justice into the space-of-flows. It was therefore interesting to observe how at the ASP meetings, which is the foremost forum for different actors in international criminal justice to come together physically in the space-of-place, the conversation was still to a significant extent 'happening' on Twitter and other social media platforms. During plenary debates, NGO representatives were sitting listening in, and while in immediate proximity to one another, tweeted and re-tweeted each other's tweets. This not only underscores the use of social media as a space of law and global justice-making, but also indicates how international criminal justice operates in so-called 'hybrid spaces', that is, 'mobile spaces, created by the constant movement of users who carry portable devices continuously connected to the Internet and to other users'(de Souza e Silva, 2006: 262). What gives pause for thought with international criminal justice as a hybrid space however, is that it requires the 'possibility of an "always-on" connection' (de Souza e Silva, 2006: 262). As put by a Coalition representative:

Websites, social media, online strategies, social media strategy—it is an up-and-coming field that I think has been overlooked in this field. There has not been the expertise or the recognition of the power of these tools ... For us in the Western hemisphere, it is unavoidable. But if you are in the Central African Republic, it is a different story altogether.

From the Zapatista movement's globalization of local plights to the 'digital' revolutions of the Arab Spring, internet and communication technologies enable globalization from below by elevating and distributing local struggles to global networks. However, most of the alleged crimes under investigation and prosecution by the Court have taken place in remote rural settings with radically different infrastructures, including those of education and communication technology, which, as shown here, is a crucial space in which interaction in international criminal justice takes place. The internet is not only the space of networks but also the space of deliberations. This is where drafts are circulated, opinions exchanged and decisions made, in the space-of-flows rather that in the space-of-place. Online communication is the *modus operandi* of global mobilization, but without access to and know-how about the internet, one remains globally disconnected. A victim's advocate in Kampala explained that as concerns civil society participation in ICC debates, there have been 'internal debates online for a very long time. But also here,' he says, 'the international ones are the most active'. I asked him to elaborate:

> On the ground, there is ICC reluctance; there is not as much ICC enthusiasm. The (international) staff are very technical, and you will not find that in the local organizations, so besides accessibility, there are a number of other challenges that contribute to the lack of participation. Also, you won't find that these organizations have lawyers. And like me, being a lawyer and having access to the internet, one might think that I should travel around and involve local organizations, but then this needs funding, funding that there is not, so this of course affects participation in local communities.

In this way, global justice-making has a hard time bridging the digital divide in terms of access and technical competency in local settings in situation countries (see Selwyn, 2004; on humanitarian technology, see Sandvik et al., 2014). Even if views of local civil society organizations are reflected in advocacy on global justice making in The Hague, these views are *collected* from the ground—they are not *connected*.

Global Connections: The Assembly of States Parties Meeting

The Assembly of States Parties (ASP) is the oversight and legislative body of the ICC, convening annually for two weeks in either The Hague or New York. The ASP meetings represent one of the primary forums bringing together a diverse set of actors and participants in international criminal justice-making in the same space-of-place (Castells, 1996). For two weeks, actors who are often thousands of miles apart come together in the same physical location. In addition to delegates from States Parties to the

Court, the ASP meetings are attended by a number of other actors, including observer states, ICC staff, academics, practitioners, journalists and, not least, NGOs. Aside from the general debate and other formal plenary sessions, where significant time is devoted to the budget and other managerial aspects of the Court, there are stocktaking sessions, formal and informal working group meetings, and side events. As a global connection of law and politics, the ASP meeting makes possible a view of global relations on the basis of social space (De Hoon and Lohne, 2019).

Focusing on its spatial arrangements and its symbolic expressions, I suggest that, like social media, the ASP meetings serve to build a constituency for international criminal justice; in this case pursued through the invocation of cosmopolitan imagery. Calling to mind the Rome Conference that established the Statute of the ICC, the ASP meetings can be seen as annual rituals reiterating consensus on global criminal justice-making. However, the ASP meetings are also the setting for political battles. International criminal justice is contested and resisted; the 'justice cascade' (Sikkink, 2011) is now stacked up against its undercurrents. Within these spaces of friction, human rights NGOs have come to serve a significant role as expressions of the ICC's value system as embodiments of liberal cosmopolitan frames of justice.

Constituency building

As an annual event, the ASP draws upon the legacy and success of the Rome Conference in establishing agreement on a common moral order, and attempts to recreate what many refer to as 'a unique moment in time'—where everyone is a friend, conjoined in a mutual campaign against atrocity crimes on behalf of humanity. This illustrates my earlier point concerning the prominence of the temporal dimension in global justice-making. Rather than emphasizing politics at a diplomatic conference, this sort of narrative emphasizes global criminal justice-making as part of a single linear history, rather than as being the result of political struggles and social relations. A lot of work at the ASP meetings, therefore, goes into emphasizing consensus rather than conflict, this being what Mathiesen refers to as the 'compliance norm' of UN conventions (1986). Cosmopolitanism—rather than a nationalist and state-centric outlook on justice—is the underlying value system that is invoked, and in this way, the work of the universal is at play in the diplomatic conference.

One way in which this is expressed is through the spatial arrangements and symbolic materiality at the ASP meeting (De Hoon and Lohne, 2019). When walking through the entrance to the World Forum, the venue for the ASP meetings, the slogan 'events that shape the world' fill the entrance hall. Designed for high-level international conferences, the World Forum is located in the middle of The Hague's international zone, vis-à-vis the building hosting the residual mechanism for the UN ad hoc tribunals (MICT) and what was previously the ICTY. With a capacity for five thousand participants, the World Forums' floors, meeting rooms, and recreational rooms have geographical names. Continents mark the ground floor, mountains loom over the second and top floors, rivers flow on the first floor and oceans run in the basement. The ASP plenary sessions take place in the auditorium—the World Forum Theatre—while most of the working group meetings are held on the ground floor, that is, in rooms named after the world's separation into distinguishable continents. The NGOs meet in 'Africa'. Every morning, the Coalition hosted an NGO strategy meeting to prepare for the day to come. When they did not host a side event, interns, and representatives from various NGOs congregated in 'Africa' throughout the day, bending over laptops. In such manners, the spatial imagery at the ASP is reminiscent of the ICC—not only due to the dominance of NGOs in Africa, but also because it draws upon notions of the cosmopolitan—it invokes world connections. However, crucially, not everyone is allowed to enter the space where 'events that have a bearing on the entire world' take place.[15] The emphasis on importance is coupled with exclusivity (Mathiesen, 1986).

Should one find oneself in the World Forum however, and wanting a souvenir of the experience, one can take away a little bit of the ICC and the ASP when returning to the real world. I bought a t-shirt emblazoned with the Rome Statute Preamble; my colleague bought an ICC mug. Should one *not* be within the World Forum however, and be restricted to the entrance hall, one can nonetheless take in the ICC's multimedia exhibition 'Justice

[15] See the World Forum Brochure, p. 2. Available at: http://www.worldforum.nl/accueil-en (accessed 8 June 2014).

Matters', which is also available as a temporary loan (or in a pdf version) to take the exhibition back home.

The ICC exhibit Justice Matters uses intimate portraits and videos to explore how justice is crucial to survivors of the world's most heinous crimes, and how it matters to the world as we strive together to achieve lasting peace. It also illustrates the daily matters of justice, inside the ICC Courtroom and behind the scenes, to show exactly what it takes to make justice happen.[16]

Referred to as an educational tool by the ICC, it is all the more interesting to note the imagery that the ICC makes use of in building constituency: pictures of African victims whose suffering is relieved by the delivery of ICC justice. What purposes do transportable materialities of international criminal justice serve, and how can we understand the way the ICC commodifies itself in this manner, presenting itself as a brand and an export? I would like to suggest seeing this as being a type of humanitarian communication, and thus a way of building an engaged constituency for its undertaking.

For NGOs working on international criminal justice, the ASP meeting is the most important lobbying event of the year. Continuing the success of the 'new diplomacy' in Rome, NGOs, and especially the Coalition, perform a number of critical functions at the ASP meetings. For example, NGOs provide background reports and position papers, including research and legal analysis. This is particularly useful for state delegations that do not have the resources to keep up-to-date on relevant issues. Likewise, they produce daily summaries of events, programme development, and the position of negotiations. NGOs host and organize side events and receptions, bringing together diplomats, practitioners, and experts (often themselves); they host and organize strategy and working group meetings amongst themselves, between NGOs and regional states and on issues of particular relevance. They also provide translation, lunch packages, and photograph events, and as mentioned, tweet, and report extensively online about what is going on at the meetings (and also among themselves to share information). Importantly, they are also allowed to address the plenary, giving prepared statements and admonitions on what is

[16] See http://www.icc-cpi.int/en_menus/icc/educational-resources/justice-matters/Pages/default.aspx (accessed 31 October 2014).

really at stake in the ASP negotiations: 'humanity's determined quest for peace and justice throughout the world', represented by: 'This great Treaty, the Court, and the Assembly' (Pace, 2013).

Aside from the NGOs' valuable service and advocacy functions at the ASP meetings, the role of NGOs at the meeting can largely be understood as being embodiments of cosmopolitanism. In an ultimately state-centric site—the Assembly of *States* Parties meeting—NGOs stand for what is 'above' state interests, claiming representation as 'global civil society' (see Chapter 3), and as such, material symbols of 'the idea of abstract linkage' constitutive of the global (Connell, 2007: 59). Rather than the singularity of interest and (state) politics, NGOs invoke concepts of 'networks' and 'connectivity' between peoples and sites, across borders and boundaries. Moreover, in contrast to state delegations at the ASP, the NGOs' source of authority is moral rather than political. And as much as moral authority stems from their claim to speak on behalf of victims, it is also fundamentally dependent on a perception of their being 'outsiders', as actors external to the process and thus beyond political interests (Hopgood, 2006; 2009). Instead, their commitments are universal; their ideals that of secular humanism. In this manner, NGOs fulfil a function as symbols of the ICC's *raison d'être:* the cosmopolitan, global, universal fight against impunity. One manner in which this role was demonstrated at the ASP meeting was in a confrontation with Kenya.

. . . and resistance

In the words of the ASP President, the ASP meeting in The Hague in November 2013, was 'no routine affair' (Intelmann, 2013). As one of the state delegates told me, 'There's a depth this year that we haven't seen before. Don't get me wrong, but it's not always easy reporting home about budget issues. This year, everyone is involved!' The reason for this was the intensified critique and challenge to the Court's authority from the African Union (AU) in the months leading up to the ASP meeting, which was largely orchestrated by Kenya. In the months preceding the ASP's twelfth session, Kenya's President Kenyatta and Vice President Ruto, who had been indicted by the ICC for their roles in the post-election violence in 2007/2008, deployed a number of legal and political strategies to counter the ICC, leading commentators to speculate that it is now 'unclear who is on trial: the ICC or the indictees accused of crimes against humanity' (Mueller, 2014: 36). The Kenyan authorities had challenged the admissibility, jurisdiction, and legitimacy of the Court, attempting to delay or end proceedings by exhausting all legal means available. They had allegedly also been involved in withdrawing witnesses from the cases, further delaying the trials, as the Prosecutor needed new witnesses; there are reports of the Kenyan government bribing, threatening, and killing witnesses (Mueller, 2014). On the political playing field, diplomatic channels and regional mobilization had been aimed at deferring the case through, among other things, appeals to the Security Council, threats of (mass) withdrawal of African member states from the ICC, and the issuance of an AU resolution stating that no African head of state should appear before an international court (AU, 2013).

Given these circumstances, the situation in Kenya and the looming threats from African states to withdraw from the Rome Statute came to take centre stage at the ASP meeting. At the request of the AU, a special plenary segment was included in the programme, entitled *Indictment of Sitting Heads of State and Government and its consequences on peace and stability and reconciliation*. This was *the* event at the ASP, or, as one NGO representative expressed it, 'the ASP would have been boring without it.' This is a reminder of how conflict is transformed into diplomatic drama, from the local to the global. Open confrontations between defendants and opponents of the Kenyan government's position continued throughout the ASP meeting, with, for example, the Kenyan delegation leaving a later side event in protest.[17] Throughout the ASP meeting—in the plenary debates, side events, media briefings, and via dissemination of NGO reports and position papers — Kenyan state delegates and human rights NGO representatives were at odds, contesting each other's 'truths' and legitimacy. Each side accused the other of not having the right to speak on behalf of the country. Kenyan officials questioned by whom and with what agenda these NGOs were funded, suggesting that they were puppets of western or other enemy powers. To the government-friendly Kenyan newspaper The Star, a Kenyan official confessed: 'These NGOs have really hit us below the belt

[17] 'Sitting Heads of State on Trial: A leap forward for the ICC or the beginning of the end?' organized by the Institute for War and Peace Reporting; Reporting Kenya and Wayamo Communication Foundation.

this time. We don't know how they organized themselves in such a way and I think they must have been well funded to do what they are doing. They are surely evil societies and not civil societies' (quoted in Ndanyi, 2013).

The ASP and the 'global' space provided these NGOs with access and a voice they do not have at home. As Kenyan NGOs asserted, they were having difficulty being heard at the national level, and 'the global' emerged as a political space for accessing and influencing national politics. However, this also underscores the image of human rights NGOs as 'emissaries of the West', which is partly a result of funding flows from the global North to the South and the implications thereof (De Waal, 2003). Emblematic of this resistance are the so-called 'NGOs laws' that have mushroomed across non-western states during the past decade, seriously restricting foreign funding to NGOs (e.g. Carothers, 2010; The Observatory for the Protection of Human Rights Defenders, 2013). At the ASP, the accreditation and presence of Kenyan NGOs were largely facilitated by foreign cooperation; likewise, their activities are largely funded by donors in the global North. A European state delegate explained to me that the Kenyan NGOs had an important role in contesting the official Kenyan narrative as NGOs can say things that states are prevented from saying without severely damaging diplomatic relations. I suggest this also demonstrates the sticky relations and divisions between the global North and South in the production of 'global' justice.

Conclusions

The chapter began by exploring the role of The Hague in global justice-making, and recognizing The Hague as a 'global city' for justice. It is the seat of international criminal law's major institutions, and also, giving an indication of where international criminal law is visibly and materially located, accommodates a host of academic, research and policy centres, and NGOs specializing in international criminal justice. All this makes The Hague a hub, or 'node', in the transnational networks and connections of global justice-making. Importantly, this makes The Hague the space wherein global justice is imagined. The Hague therefore stands for one way of thinking about global justice-making, and it is this way of thinking that is exported when the ICC becomes involved in a situation. Whereas The Hague remains a stable site, international criminal justice appears much more volatile in Uganda, one of its situation countries. Here, unlike in The Hague, international criminal justice is invisible, shut in behind fortified compounds in the capital, and lacking any permanent presence in Gulu, the site of mass violence. The ICC's field office in Kampala was merely maintaining presence while awaiting judicial development in the criminal case. As international criminal justice funding has pulled out, the NGOs were pursuing other forms of justice-making, yet, from the perspective of The Hague, Uganda was standing still. 'Nothing' was happening. I hold this to be an example of how globalization processes turn space into time.

The second part of the chapter identified social media as a crucial space of global justice-making. Departing from the viral success of KONY2012 in agenda-setting the LRA, the video campaign legitimized the ICC's intervention in the conflict, providing a striking example of how social media generate support and serve to build a constituency for international criminal justice. Due to the vast physical distances between different sites of international criminal justice, the use of social media for communicating global justice-making is essential. However, the digital divide continues to disconnect the periphery.

The third part of the chapter zooms in on the Assembly of States Parties meetings as a global connection. One way to understand the ASP meetings is as an annual ritual—and form of constituency building—of international criminal justice, which is pursued by invoking cosmopolitan images and sensibilities, expressed through spatial arrangements and materialities, but also through the presence and participation of 'global civil society'. In the next chapter, the notion of global civil society and the particular role of NGOs at the ASP will be analysed further.

Conceptually however, the analysis provided in this chapter demonstrates how any probing into the materiality of international criminal justice is necessarily multi-sited and multi-scalar. As such, I approached 'space' as more than geography—as more than 'absolute' locality. What has been of interest is *relative positioning* of the ICC's materiality, and how international criminal justice is arranged spatially. This is important because it is not a 'given'; spatial arrangements are expressions of social, cultural, and political relations. Confronting us with the co-existence of others (Massey, 1992), space is inherently social and political. A spatial inquiry of international criminal justice is thus an inquiry into its geography of power. Having demonstrated that NGOs are part of this geography of power, the following chapter narrows the unit of analysis: Who make up the 'global civil society' of global justice-making, and what gives them clout within the 'transnational' and 'global' spaces of politics?

3

Networks of Global Justice-Making

The Coalition for the International Criminal Court

Since globalization became part of sociology's research agenda in the early 1990s, the 'network' has become a dominant conceptualization of social organization. Facilitated by the technological paradigm, the 'network' is both a metaphor and a concept for thinking about patterns of social organization, and for making sense of how global society as an unbounded social system is formed (Castells, 1996). In international studies, transnational networks have come to be seen as central infrastructures of contemporary transnational politics and global social movements, including, as is the concern here, global justice-making through international criminal law. The previous chapter explored international criminal justice from the standpoint of space, and looked at how global justice-making is embedded in spatial relations of power. Moving on from questions of 'where', this chapter explores the 'how' of non-governmental organization for international criminal justice. It shows, quite simply, how non-governmental organizations (NGOs) organize in their mobilization for the International Criminal Court (ICC), and how structural conditions embedded in the networks and practices of NGOs shape the relationship between the so-called global civil society and global criminal justice-making.

In my conversation with western state delegates, the role of NGOs in the realization of a permanent global criminal court was referred to as an 'established fact', seen as the result of a new form of diplomacy in which non-state actors were included in deliberations on global affairs. Their presence in international law and policy making remain, however, a contested matter among

Advocates of Humanity. Kjersti Lohne, Oxford University Press (2019). © Kjersti Lohne.
DOI: 10.1093/oso/9780198818748.003.0003

academics and practitioners alike. While some point to the role of the NGO Coalition for the International Criminal Court ('CICC' or the 'Coalition') during the ICC negotiations as an 'achievement of the masses' (Cakmak, 2008), others remain critical of the concept of 'global civil society' altogether, suggesting that 'the global civil society movement might better be understood as imagining itself as the bearer of universal values, both operating in the teeth of globalisation and yet simultaneously using globalisation as its vehicle for disseminating universal values' (Anderson and Rieff, 2005: 12). Regardless of one's view, the reason for debate is, largely, a result of assumptions about who—what type of actors—are to be considered legitimate participants in international law and justice-making. The role of NGOs not only challenges 'traditional' state-centric structures and processes in international law but also causes the need to reconsider the conception of legitimate representation altogether. By questioning the historically situated framing of justice conflicts within the nation state, transnational networks 'seek to re-map the bounds of justice on a global scale' (Fraser, 2008: 1). This speaks to rescaling claims to justice as much as rescaling claims to representation: who represents what and whom within the transnational and the political spaces of global justice-making? To this end, the chapter maps out the nongovernmental *organization* for continued mobilization for global criminal justice-making, and in so doing, engages *networks* as both an empirical and conceptual feature of what makes the global.

Before digging into the contemporary networked structure of NGO advocacy vis-à-vis the Court, the first part of this chapter presents the celebratory narrative of the ICC as a global civil society achievement. Through a critical mapping and ethnographic tracing of the Coalition as a 'transnational advocacy network', the second part shows significant imbalances within these networks, as the centrality of the Coalition Secretariat and a core group of international human rights NGOs, stand in contrast to the national NGO coalition in Uganda. Against these cores and peripheries, the third part argues that the Coalition nonetheless asserts a role as reflecting *the* global civil society in global criminal justice-making by managing the 'who' and the 'what' of civil society participation in the politics around the ICC. I show how the generation of moral knowledge serves as a form of NGO currency, and that they assert a role as *mediators* between the global and the local, bridging the Court with its constituencies elsewhere. However, processes of inclusion and exclusion of global civil society affect possibilities of resistance and contestation of the way global justice materializes through institution-building and law-making at the ICC. As such, it animates broader questions of authority and legitimacy, which I begin to address in the chapter's final part. Particularly, I argue that the embeddedness of the core NGOs in the field of international criminal justice undermines the claim to moral authority, which is a critical basis of their legitimacy (see also Lohne, 2017).

The Crafting of the ICC as a Global Civil Society Achievement

In 1989, Prime Minister Robinson of Trinidad and Tobago launched a proposal at the United Nations General Assembly to create an international criminal court to deal with the international drug trade, a pervasive problem in the Caribbean region. Since then, and although the illicit drug trade has been lost along the way, Robinson is lauded as the 'grandfather' of the ICC (e.g. Song, 2014). Speaking to the Coalition's Convenor, Bill Pace, about the genesis of the Court, he explained that 'he [Robinson] knew what he was proposing. He said that the drug trafficking was not only the excuse but also the explanation for how you can get 14 Caribbean countries to endorse it,—and then took it forward.' Among NGOs, Robinson's efforts are not seen as motivated by the national and regional interests of a prime minister, but as driven by cosmopolitan sensibilities. By pointing to Robinson's affiliations to the NGOs World Federalist Movement and the Parliamentarians for Global Action, Robinson's efforts are made part of the narrative of the ICC as a 'global civil society' achievement.[1]

From Robinson's proposal in 1989 to the drafting of the Rome Statute in 1998 there was a decade of negotiations in various UN forums—from the International Law Commission, and the General Assembly to the ad hoc and preparatory committees of

[1] See for example the historic narrative of the creation of the ICC on Parliamentarians for Global Action's website: http://www.pgaction.org/ilhr/ (accessed 29 October 2014).

states' representatives and to Rome—a small network of NGOs were closely monitoring and lobbying the process. Pace explained that a lot of work in the early days of the negotiations were 'under the radar'—of both high-level state officials and the general world public: 'People would come and say [to me]: "you need your Lady Di [as] with the landmines, Bono can help you". I said, "No, the last thing we want is to alert people to what's happening. It's going very, very well".' Rather than generating public pressure on states, lobbying in corridors at the UN became the preferred tactic, as he describes his realization about the lack of lobbying at the UN compared to what there was at state level, 'short cut answer [being], there's no money, that's why the lobby isn't there':

> When I would do lobbying at the City Council, growing up in Colorado; there would be 40 or 50 lobbyists ... You went to the State house you would have 500 lobbyists; in Washington, there would be 10, 000 of us. But then, at the General Assembly at the UN, there were six of us! And I was actually representing two of the six! I immediately realized—oh my god—an individual can have an impact in the UN negotiations that you just couldn't have even at the municipal level!

Pace's experience contradicts a common assumption about how the global is imagined—expecting it to be 'bigger and better'; in this case, for lobbyism to continue the scalar hierarchy from city hall to the state house to Washington and to the UN building in New York. From six NGOs at a General Assembly meeting in 1994 discussing an early draft statute, the NGO lobby would slowly grow. When the General Assembly referred the draft statute to an ad hoc committee for further work, instead of directly to a treaty-making conference, Pace and Christopher Hall, a legal advisor from Amnesty International, set up a meeting for NGOs to increase their collective efforts. This meeting, held on 10 February 1995, led to the founding of the Coalition for an International Criminal Court (see also Glasius, 2006).

Instead of the more familiar and visible NGO strategy of generating public pressure through advocacy, the coupling of law and lobbyism as tools of justice-making is striking (see also Dezalay and Garth, 2006). In the early days of the ICC negotiations, it seems the social dynamics embedded in law and the legal profession were important. Describing the cooperation of different organizations, Pace recalls how 'the legal advisors caught fire':

The truth was the secretary generals of these groups would never have cooperated. The membership directors of these organizations would not have cooperated. Not the fundraising directors. The only ones were [the legal advisors]. 'Oh my god, look at all this work that we have to do on these different sections of this draft statute. We need help. We need to work together.' And they did work together.

Legal advisors, having law as their common language, are described as having found common ground across their individual NGO interests: law. And, moreover, the role of law as *lingua franca* further connected the NGOs with state representatives. Contrary to what would have been true of high level foreign policy elites and heads of delegations, legal experts from both NGOs and governments were able to cooperate. As put by other NGO representatives, '"NGOs and governments were the same kinds of people" ... Unlike heads of delegations, they spoke the same language, had the same education, and came from the same background' (Benedetti et al., 2014: 75). Indeed, the close relationship that developed between NGOs and the 'Like-Minded Group' of states—that is, middle and small power democracies—is recognized as one of the main reasons for the successful drafting of the Rome Statute (Glasius, 2006; Pearson, 2006; Watkins and Welch, 2011). In the next chapter I discuss how, to a considerable extent, this continues to be the case in the field of international criminal justice. As law caught on in global justice-making, so did the support of NGOs.

The Rome Conference took place from 15 June to 17 July 1998. By then, the Coalition had grown into a transnational network of over 800 organizations. Out of these, and represented by about 500 individuals, 236 NGOs were accredited to the conference. This made the Coalition the biggest 'delegation' in Rome, surpassing state delegations in numbers and expertise. They fulfilled a number of functions, such as convening seminars and conferences; disseminating the Court ideal to an outside audience; lobbying representatives from state and intergovernmental organizations; providing experts and interns to poorer and smaller government delegations; seeking and giving financial support for southern NGOs and expert participation; street action; and writing expert documents, journal articles, and reports (Glasius, 2002: 147). As concerns direct NGO influence upon specific provisions to the Rome Statute, Glasius (2002) identified significant influence upon the drafting and adoption of the independent prosecutor as well as gender-specific crimes in the Statute, while finding less success in the attempts by NGOs to include prohibitions on the use of indiscriminate weapons in the Rome Statute.

However, what has happened after Rome, after the successful campaign by 'global civil society' to create a global criminal court? Instead of reorienting to a new global cause or disintegrating after achieving its goal, the NGO Coalition has developed in tandem with the ICC's institutionalization (see also Haddad, 2013). During my research, western diplomats and ICC representatives alike characterized the relationship between the ICC and the NGOs as one of 'synergy'. Indeed, and as the remainder of this chapter demonstrates, the NGOs serve critical functions in the day-to-day operation of international criminal justice. What, then, characterizes these actors today?

The Coalition for the International Criminal Court

The Coalition for the International Criminal Court includes 2,500 civil society organizations in 150 different countries working in partnership to strengthen international cooperation with the ICC; ensure that the Court is fair, effective and independent; make justice both visible and universal; and advance stronger national laws that deliver justice to victims of war crimes, crimes against humanity and genocide.[2]

So reads the Coalition's self-presentation on their websites. From a loosely coordinated network of non-governmental activists, the CICC has formalized into an institution of international criminal justice. It has two headquarters, the 'ICC office' in The Hague and the 'UN office' in New York, and at the time of research, regional offices and representatives in Benin, the Philippines, Belgium, Peru, and Argentina, and permanent staff members.[3] It is structured as an issue-oriented coalition of organizations, with aims to (i) ensure a fair, effective, and independent ICC; (ii) campaign for a universal court jurisdiction through universal ratification

[2] 'About the Coalition', see: http://www.iccnow.org/?mod=coalition (accessed 8 February 2014). The Coalition has updated their websites since the time of research.

[3] Regional offices change depending on where they have people. At the time of writing, the Coalition website report to only have regional offices in Belgium and Peru.

and implementation of its statutes; and (iii) create awareness of the Court.[4] Through lobbyism and legal assistance, advocacy campaigns, capacity-building and outreach, to give but a few examples, the Coalition both mobilize for and monitor ongoing developments in global justice-making. In doing so, they dissolve a general distinction in the division of NGO 'labour', namely that between advocacy as the preferred modus operandi of human rights NGOs, and assistance and service-provision as predominantly carried out by development and humanitarian relief organizations (Welch, 2001; Murdie and Davis, 2012). Importantly however, activities such as capacity-building and giving assistance to local civil society organizations in ICC situation countries, or offering legal and technical assistance to governments, are still services imbued with norms and ideas of global justice. Advocacy and service provision are thus not mutually exclusive, but different strategies pursued by NGOs in their mobilization for global justice.

The Coalition's structure comprises a Secretariat, a Steering Committee, and a transnational network of supporting NGOs. The Secretariat is located in a modified apartment neighbouring Dutch ministries in Bezuidenhoutseweg 99 in The Hague. Formally, their role is to service their member organizations, which means to coordinate, implement, and facilitate civil society participation and their views. At the time of research, and excluding their interns, the Secretariat staffed approximately twenty-five individuals. The World Federalist Movement-Institute for Global Policy (WFM-IGP), with their Secretary General Bill Pace, had continued on since the Rome negotiations as the Coalition's 'convenor'. While the World Federalists were also the Coalition's initial and main source of funding, they have since received funding from a variety of donors, most of which are based in the global North, such as the Ford and MacArthur Foundations, the Sigrid Rausing Trust, Open Society Institute, the European Union, and a host of western governments.[5]

The Steering Committee consisted of a group of NGOs expected to provide policy and programme coherence for the Coalition's

[4] 'Making justice visible', see http://www.iccnow.org/?mod=makingjusticevisible (accessed 21 April, 2014).

[5] By 'western governments' I include here the Commonwealth of Australia. The other state donors are: The Grand Duchy of Luxembourg, Irish Aid, The Kingdom of Belgium, The Kingdom of Denmark, The Kingdom of the Netherlands,

activities, and included most of the founding members of the Coalition, as well as regional members following the growth in membership (CICC, 2010). Generally overlapping with the former, eight of these organizations—half of the Steering Committee members—were the most active in NGO advocacy vis-à-vis the ICC.[6] Together with the International Bar Association (IBA) and Open Society Justice Initiative (OSJI), these were known as the 'drafters' or 'usual suspects' in the field. Generally, these organizations are all international, western-based organizations with a human rights profile. Most have staff members working specifically on ICC-related issues, and have campaigns or programmes on international criminal justice specifically, which reflects both their resource capabilities and their perception of international criminal justice as a central human rights issue. Most of them have offices and permanent representation in The Hague, from where they monitor the development of international criminal law coming out of the ICC, draft proposals and recommendations to the Assembly of States Parties (ASP) and the Court, and lobby state representatives at The Hague Working Group meetings, which are diplomatic working group meetings of state members to the Court. In the everyday life of global justice-making in The Hague, the NGOs attend and participate as expert voices in conferences and seminars, drink coffee with and lobby state representatives, and attend and host receptions for international criminal justice professionals in the city.

At the same time, there are also important differences among this core group of NGOs. To maximize their combined efforts (and not step on each other's toes), the CICC organizes advocacy by thematic issues and NGO teams, which are generally headed by one of the Steering Committee members and coordinated by

The Kingdom of Norway, The Kingdom of Sweden, The New Zealand Government, The Principality of Liechtenstein, The Republic of Austria, The Republic of Finland, and The Swiss Confederation; see http://www.iccnow.org/?mod=supporters (accessed 8 February 2014).

[6] The remaining Steering Committee members are Adaleh Center for Human Rights Studies, Andean Commission of Jurists, Asian Forum for Human Rights and Development, Asociación Pro Derechos Humanos, Civil Resource Development and Documentation Centre, Georgian Young Lawyers Association, Human Rights Network—Uganda, and Justice Without Frontiers. In addition, there is an Emeritus Steering Committee Members of European Law Students Association, Human Rights First, and Rights and Democracy

one of the Secretariat's legal officers. The team structure loosely mirrors The Hague Working Group structures, and is a legacy from the Rome Conference, when the Coalition organized in thematic working groups such as gender, peace, faith, protection of children, and victims' rights. As it facilitated a strategic overview of the entire conference, this thematic organization was thought responsible for much of the Coalition's success in Rome (Pearson, 2006; Glasius, 2006). And, indeed, this strategic organization continues to be a key strength. At the annual ASP meetings as well as in the daily life of lobbying in The Hague, the Coalition is able to cover and follow, monitor and lobby ICC issues across the board, because it enables them to specialize and maximize their advocacy according to particular issues. Importantly, it also functions as a division of labour, or power-sharing element, whereby the core group of NGOs can brand and maintain areas of expertise.

Amnesty International (AI) is the most widely known international human rights organization, and has always been at the forefront of the human rights movement. It is a universal membership organization founded in London in 1961, financed by private donations, members' dues, and fund-raising campaigns. It undertakes action and research to prevent and end grave human rights abuses, and it received the Nobel Peace Prize in 1977. Its Secretariat consists of 410 people, and they have members in 167 countries and territories (see generally Hopgood, 2006; Clark, 2010).[7] Amnesty International has been involved with international criminal justice from the start, with its aforementioned legal advisor Christopher Hall described as a 'leading light in the formation of the international criminal court' (Rodley, 2013). In 2010, they began a campaign for International Justice, scheduled to run to the end of 2016. As part of this, in 2012 they set up a Centre for International Justice in The Hague (albeit consisting of only one permanent member of staff), located just underneath the CICC headquarters. Amnesty International's role in particular is explored in Chapter 5.

International Federation for Human Rights (FIDH) is a universal and federalist movement of 178 human rights organizations, founded by French and German national organizations in

[7] For a comprehensive overview of international organizations, see the comprehensive resource compiled by the Union of Internatioal Association in the online Yearbook of International Organization; https://uia.org/yearbook.

1922. It has a general human rights mandate, yet singles out core issues, such as international justice and the fight against impunity. In The Hague, the FIDH has one permanent staff member, in addition to interns. Through their Legal Action Group, which consists of a network of pro bono lawyers, FIDH provides legal support for victims of international crimes, and have inter alia represented victims in proceedings at the ICC. As legal aid is mainly provided to defendants in western domestic criminal justice systems, it is therefore interesting to note that NGOs' judicial assistance and legal aid is primarily provided towards victims of international crimes, which is discussed further in Chapter 6.

Human Rights Watch (HRW) was established in 1988, having first been set up as Helsinki Watch in 1978 (see generally Snyder, 2011). Along with AI, Human Rights Watch has set the standard for the human rights movement, and is perceived to typify 'second generation' human rights organizations, with its focus on professionalization and expertise (De Waal, 2003). They report and document abuses of internationally recognized human rights, including violations of laws of war, and 'names and shames' governments to pressure them to cease abusive practices. HRW has no direct or indirect government funding, and is financed by private individuals and foundations. It has a staff of 280, including country specialists, journalists, linguists, and lawyers. Their International Justice Program alone comprised ten 'expert staff' at the time of research, and the fight against impunity has always been at the forefront of HRW's work. The institutional apparatus alone of HRW by far surpasses that of most states, and while they do not have any permanent presence in The Hague, their headquarters in Brussels is only a few hours away by train. Along with the Coalition's Bill Pace and AI's Christopher Hall, Human Rights Watch's Richard Dicker has been active in the formation of the ICC since the early negotiations—a form of individual entrepreneurship discussed more in Chapter 4.

International Bar Association (IBA) is a federation of national bar associations, supporting human rights and the independence of lawyers and the judiciary, and fostering the science of jurisprudence and uniformity in particular fields of law. It is financed by members' dues, with a 40 per cent discount for members from 'developing countries'. It had a staff of fifty-five people, excluding part-time assistants and interns. Their International Criminal Court Programme is located on the premises of the Peace Palace, the seat of the International Court of Justice. They view themselves as a lawyers' association, not an NGO. They are, however, a member of the Coalition and cooperate with them closely. Albeit not a human rights NGO, the IBA is the only organization in this core network of advocacy organizations that focuses primarily on defence rights and due process. Chapter 5 discusses the lack of attention to these issues by human rights organizations, and the work of the IBA in more detail.

No Peace Without Justice (NPWJ) was founded in 1993 by Emma Bonino and the Transnational Radical Party, a Gandhian, non-violent organization carrying out international political campaigns, on, inter alia, human rights, the promotion of democracy, an anti-prohibitionist policy on drugs, UN reform (and the use of Esperanto as an auxiliary language in international institutions). International criminal justice is one of the three main programmes of NPWJ, the other being female genital mutilation and Middle Eastern and North African (MENA) democracy. The NPWJ does not have permanent representation in The Hague, but has offices in Brussels, Rome, and New York. Their work focuses specifically on international justice issues in the MENA region.

Open Society Justice Initiative (OPJI) is an NGO within the Open Society Foundations, founded by investor George Soros in 1984 to help countries in transition from communism, and to build 'vibrant and tolerant societies whose governments are accountable and open to the participation of all people'.[8] They have offices in over 100 countries (although membership countries are not specified), and about 2,000 members of staff. The foundation's expenditure in 2012 was approximately US$ 909 million. The OPJI promote law with a view to protect and empower people around the world. It has a permanent presence in The Hague, where one of its main activities are trial-monitoring programmes designed to 'explain what goes on in the courtrooms in The Hague to the widest possible audience around the world'.[9] Like the IBA, the Justice Initiative is not part of the Coalition, and operates somewhat on the sidelines of other human rights NGOs. Because they are not dependent on campaigns and external donors, as they are

[8] http://www.opensocietyfoundations.org/about/mission-values (accessed 25 November 2014).

[9] http://www.opensocietyfoundations.org/projects/war-crimes-trials/background (accessed 4 February 2014).

self-funded, they work closely with and fund initiatives directly at the domestic level of influence, which is described in Chapter 7.

Parliamentarians for Global Action (PGA) is a network of over 1,300 elected parliamentarians from 105 parliaments around the world, created in 1978–79 in Washington, D.C. by 'concerned parliamentarians from around the world to take joint action on global problems, which could not be solved by any one government or parliament'.[10] PGA is an institutionalized network of legislators, and is financed by members' dues, the UN, governments, individuals, foundations etc. Focused on nuclear disarmament at first, the organization has expanded to other global issues, including international criminal justice. The PGA had initiated its work with the ICC already in 1989, and advises parliamentarians on promoting and enabling ratification and implementation of the Rome Statute. It had a staff of thirteen, a third of whom were based in the Bertha von Suttner building in The Hague, an NGO office building subsidized by The Hague municipality. The objectives of the programme, or, the PGA's vision, is to 'contribute to the creation of a Rules-Based International Order for a more equitable, safe and democratic world'.[11] In The Hague, the organization participates in Coalition activities, including The Hague working group meetings, roundtable meetings with the ICC and so forth. However, its main activities are aimed at the domestic level: work with parliamentarians to advocate for universal ratification of the Rome Statute, and implementation of Rome Statute provisions in national justice systems. Their role is elaborated in Chapter 7.

REDRESS is a London-based human rights organization founded in 1992, with approximately sixteen staff. Its particular focus is torture survivors. They are funded primarily by private funds and foundations, but also sources such as the European Commission and the United Nations Voluntary Fund for Victims of Torture. They have been involved with the ICC since its treaty negotiations, advocating for victims' rights through the Victims' Rights Working Group (VRWG), a coalition within the Coalition that REDRESS facilitates. The VRWG is the biggest thematic advocacy team—a coalition within the coalition. It defines itself as an expert coalition of 300 national and international civil society

[10] http://www.pgaction.org/ (accessed 11 September 2014).
[11] http://www.pgaction.org/ (accessed 8 September 2014).

groups that, according to their webpage, 'played an historic role in ensuring that key provisions for victims were incorporated into the Rome Statute'.[12] They work to promote the rights and interests of victims before the Court, and claim to focus in particular on (i) participation and legal representation, (ii) protection and support, (iii) reparations, (iv) ensuring victims' voices are heard in considering the interest of victims, and (v) a gender sensitive approach.[13]

Women's Initiative for Gender Justice (WIGJ, or 'Women's Initiative') is a human rights organization, established in The Hague in 2004 to 'monitor the Court and advocate for gender-inclusive justice through the ICC and implementation of the Rome Statute'.[14] At the time of research, they had offices in The Hague, Cairo, Kampala, and Kitgum (Uganda), and also did work in the Central African Republic, the Democratic Republic of the Congo, Kenya, Libya, Sudan, and Kyrgyzstan where they produced reports on violations to the ICC, and did outreach about the Court to affected communities. As will be discussed in Chapter 6, the fight against impunity for sexual and gender-based crimes is a particular powerful victim narrative. Although many of the human rights NGOs are sensitive to the gendered dimensions of international crimes, The Women's Initiative is the leading NGO in this area. They act as a thematic caucus for gender issues, having replaced the Women's Caucus for Gender Justice, the coalition of NGOs credited with having ensured an explicit gender perspective in the ICC's statutes in the treaty negotiations in Rome in 1998 (Glasius, 2005). Today the WIGJ work for gender justice *through* the ICC and domestic mechanisms in the aftermath of armed conflict and international crimes, and have a role as both monitors and experts vis-à-vis the Court. The monitoring role is what is most evident in their annual *Gender Report Cards*, which offers an analysis of the ICC from a gender perspective. As experts they have also been given status as *amicus curiae*, which has given them access to file briefs before the court without actually being a legal party to the conflict. In 2012, their executive director, Brigid Inder, was hired by Chief Prosecutor Bensouda as her Special Advisor on Gender. The appointment is a testament to the close

[12] http://www.vrwg.org (accessed 4 September 2010).
[13] http://www.vrwg.org/about-vrwg/strategy (accessed 12 February 2014).
[14] http://www.iccwomen.org/aboutus/history.php (accessed 23 August 2013).

affiliations between the NGOs and the ICC, and the 'revolving door' mechanism in the field, which is discussed in Chapter 4.

The World Federalists developed from a 1947 Conference on the World Movement for World Federal Government in Switzerland, staged by fifty-one organizations fearing that 'the United Nations' efforts towards peace ... may not be successful, if the world is not willing to take this next step to World Federal Government'.[15] Since then, and now in conjunction with the Institute for Global Policy, they have worked to reform the United Nations. Bill Pace is the Executive Director of the World Federalists, and the coordinator, or 'convenor', of the CICC. In addition, the World Federalists convene another NGO coalition, namely the NGO Coalition for the Responsibility to Protect. Pace has described this as a perfect match, the one stressing *individual* responsibility, and the other *state* responsibility in dealing with international crimes.

While there are other important organizations working on international justice, these are the NGOs that are somewhat cheekily referred to as the 'usual suspects' in ICC advocacy. Notably, these organizations are all based in the global North in terms of institutional origins, funding, and metropolitan headquarters. Moreover, the role of the Coalition Secretariat stands out; in The Hague it remains the most visible, and functions more or less as an autonomous NGO, albeit speaking with the authority of its member organizations. In the global city of justice-making, it has the most staff representatives of the NGOs, and is the most active in relating to the Court and state parties, and organizing and hosting seminars and events.

However, one of the major sources of the NGOs' authority to speak in The Hague is their access and networks to the 'people', and in particular to victims and communities affected by international crimes. Local civil society organizations are fundamental to transnational networks—not only because participation and cooperation with 'local' partners is often a criterion of NGO funders, and because such cooperation may enable these organizations to leverage struggles, but also because such cooperation is perceived to guarantee a 'bottom-up' approach. The idea of the network of 2,500 organizations is thus essential to the Coalition's authority in global justice advocacy, enabling Secretariat members

[15] http://www.wfm-igp.org/site/about (accessed 4 February 2014).

to speak 'on behalf of' their member organizations, and to present themselves as 'global civil society', who, through their networks, 'bridge' the local with the global.

The third part of the Coalition's structure is thus the far reaching and extensive network of NGOs worldwide, which, according to the Convenor, make up the 'expanding circle of national and regional networks and coalitions to translate its goals into reality' (Pace and Schense, 2001: 708). The CICC claims to represent approximately eighty national coalitions in support of the ICC worldwide, coordinated by the Secretariat's regional staff serving as links between national, regional, and global levels of global justice-advocacy. But how are these networks generated?

Coalition-building is generally understood to develop out of existing networks (Yanacopulos, 2005). As concerns the CICC, the criterion for joining is plainly support for its mandate of working for a fair, effective, and independent court. Becoming a member of, or leaving the Coalition, is thus a very simple matter, indicating a loose and flexible structure. Should an organization find itself deviating from the Coalition's course, it can simply leave it. One may also opt in and out on a particular issue, pursuing one's own organization's aims if that of the Coalition is incompatible with them. However, this also means that the exact number of members varies, and, what is more, there is no list of member organizations available. Thus, although the Coalition claims to unify over 2,500 organizations across the world, this is an approximate number of listed members. In addition, many of these are 'sleeping members' who add little substance to the work of the Coalition except by increasing leverage by adding to its member constituency. The number of organizations actively working on the ICC and international criminal justice among the Coalition's extended network is thus much harder to establish.

While the network structure of the Coalition is tripartite, many of the NGO members also consist of networks in and among themselves. FIDH for instance, is a federation of almost 200 human rights organizations, and Human Rights Network-Uganda (HURINET-U) likewise comprises fifty-four member NGOs: both of these NGOs are Steering Committee members. In Uganda, I found that REDRESS, also a Steering Committee member, largely bypasses the centralized Coalition structure in its engagement, and works instead through other transnational networks, in particular the VRWG. In other words, these organizations are involved in many other networks, not the least because international criminal justice is often one amongst a portfolio of advocacy agendas and human rights issues. In this manner, the Coalition's supportive structure of NGOs and transnational networks can be understood as a web of networks, albeit one in which power and leverage are unevenly distributed.

Indeed, a question can be asked about whether the number of civil society organizations reflects actual civil society mobilization for international criminal justice, or merely mirrors the ICC's activities in the region. Almost a third of the Coalition's national coalitions are on the African continent and as put by a Coalition representative, 'management is cognizant of the fact that we don't have as many members in Asia,' a region underrepresented among States Parties to the Rome Statute. However, while there are only two States Parties to the ICC from North Africa and the Middle East, there are eleven national NGO coalitions from this region.[16]

Concerning the situation in Uganda, the Coalition's activities seem largely to have mirrored the Court's involvement, rather than setting an agenda for global justice itself.[17] When the ICC became involved in Uganda, so did the CICC, which sought to mobilize civil society participation in the process. Together with HURINET, they convened a meeting of NGOs and civil society organizations, and out of this came the Ugandan *national* Coalition for the ICC (UCICC). According to a victims' rights expert in Kampala:

> There wasn't anyone working towards the Court previously so this was the CICC's doing. There were civil society organizations in the north prior to the Court's involvement, working on different human rights issues. However, when the Court became involved, a lot of these organizations started working on these issues. The Court created a new dimension. The Court was perceived in a very negative way when it came, and

[16] The ICC and the CICC use different geographical categories in their overviews of States Parties and signatories to the Rome Statute. I use the CICC data here, primarily for the sake of internal consistency vis-à-vis national coalitions, but also because the ICC does not have 'North Africa and the Middle East' as a separate region. The lack of representation from North Africa and the Middle East should however also be seen in relation to political space for civil society organizations in the region. See http://www.iccnow.org/?mod=networks (accessed 5 February 2014).

[17] However, organizations such as Amnesty International and Human Rights Watch had produced reports on the situation in northern Uganda before the ICC became involved (AI, 1999; HRW, 1997).

the UCICC and others worked to inform and create debate, trying to get civil society organizations to appreciate what the Court was trying to do.

To this end, the UCICC conducted outreach to explain the mandate of the Court and to mobilize civil society participation in the process, for instance by facilitating relationships between the Court and local civil society. However, the close relationship between the Coalition and the Court meant that the Coalition was not only *complementing* the activities of the Court but also working *together* with the Court, holding joint meetings, seminars, and workshops: in short, doing joint outreach activities. Bearing in mind how their activity mirrors the ICC, it seemed their involvement did likewise. As mentioned in the previous chapter, when I visited their Kampala office, the UCICC had run out of funding, and were looking to redefine their mandate. Although reporting to join together more than a hundred member organizations, their representatives explains:

It becomes difficult to justify focus on the ICC when there is no progress. The member organizations are just signatures of support, not even our steering committee members are particularly active on international criminal justice in Uganda. The CICC and us (HURINET/UCICC), we have different mandates. We try to be cross-cutting. We work on transitional justice processes, but that's more on the ground—not in cooperation with the CICC. I read their emails and updates on what's going on. I also send them our press releases. I don't really interact with The Hague much.

The flows and networks of the CICC thus mirror those of the ICC. It appears relevance is decided by 'The Hague'. Without resorting to essentialism, this is a reminder not only of the imbalances between the centre and periphery of global justice-making, but also crucially of how funding-flows, to a considerable extent, determine mobilization for global justice (on power assymetries in NGO networks, see also Mutua, 2009b).

Through 'unpacking' the Coalition's institutional structure, what emerges into view is thus a 'global civil society' for global criminal justice-making with fundamental cores and peripheries. In the final two sections of this chapter, I probe deeper into the friction of these NGO networks, arguing that through 'information politics' (Keck and Sikkink, 1998) and coalition-building, the Coalition is nonetheless able to assert itself as a mediator of global justice, and as indeed, reflective of *the* global civil society. As such, the latter part of the chapter critically assesses their claims to authority and legitimacy, and suggests that their embeddedness in the field of international criminal justice fundamentally challenges their claim to either (see also Lohne, 2017).

Mediators of Global Justice

The politics of information

The production and reproduction of information and knowledge is essential to the role and participation of NGOs in international criminal justice. In the ICC treaty negotiations, state delegations and intergovernmental officials are reported to have relied on information produced and distributed by the NGOs to the extent that the 'CICC prided itself on being the "primary source of information" about the ICC' (Pearson, 2006: 272, 273). The ability to generate accurate information and use it where it will have the most impact, so-called 'information politics' (Keck and Sikkink, 1998), is considered central to the effectiveness of NGO networks. Yet in addition to the more 'traditional' role of human rights NGOs in bringing attention to human rights abuses, the politics of information also serve a role as providing the NGOs with expert authority vis-à-vis other stakeholders in the field of international criminal justice.

Through their transnational networks, such as HURINET and the UCICC, the Coalition and its core members in The Hague collect information on what is happening 'on the ground'—whether it is human rights abuses, domestic legislative processes, or public perceptions of and sentiments towards the ICC—and provide this information to state representatives and the ICC in The Hague. They provide information from The Hague—specifically on the mandate of the Court and development of the cases—to affected communities in situation countries, using the same networks. And through monitoring and lobbyism at The Hague Working Group meetings, the Coalition Secretariat and the core human rights NGOs bring information and pass it between and among the ICC and states' representatives, and vice versa from their meetings with ICC staff at the ICC-NGO roundtable meetings.

However, the Coalition does not merely transport information; information provided by the Coalition is 'filtered'—considered relevant, important, and strategic in some way to their mandate.

A lot of work therefore goes into information processing *within* the Coalition. Being essentially an information network, member organizations feed the Secretariat with information, for instance on recent activities, campaigns, and reports related to particular issues on international justice, or, more often, particular cases and situations. Along with the Secretariat's update on case proceedings in The Hague, including news and publications considered relevant, this information is digested and re-distributed to Coalition members and subscribers as email updates. Because the amount of information received by members by far exceeds the information provided to the Secretariat, and because the level of activity among its 2,500 members varies greatly, the Coalition Secretariat is predominantly a *provider of processed information* deemed relevant to its members and subscribers. In other words, information flows *to* the Secretariat from different currents and floods in the network, and then it is streamlined and re-distributed to its members *from* the Secretariat.

Thus, while the term 'intermediary' is often used in the field to describe NGOs or individuals that assist the ICC in some way (Ullrich, 2016), the role of the Coalition should rather be thought of as that of *mediators* who 'transform, translate, distort, and modify the meaning or the elements they are supposed to carry' (Latour, 2005: 39). Rather than an effortless flow of information across networks, the Coalition mediate information between and within different 'nodes' in the global chains of international criminal justice: conflict-affected communities in situation countries, State representatives, and the Court itself. Having access to major constituencies and institutions, they hold a particular central position as information becomes a valuable currency in the field, indicating how the Coalition is able to exert expert authority through a politics of information in global justice-making.

Coalition-building and gate-keeping

Building coalitions is another common strategy for NGOs. While sharing resources and costs through group specialization creates value and commitment among the Coalition members, the pooling of resources and expertise enables the NGOs to leverage their advocacy and increase their momentum by speaking with 'one voice' (see Yanacopulos, 2005). At the same time, this also means that the more organizations join the Coalition and endorse its mandate of working for a fair, effective, and independent Court, the more legitimate the Coalition's role as representing global civil society appears and the more it seems to *represent* an actual constituency. There is power in numbers. With its extensive and wide-reaching network, the Coalition manages, according to Cakmak (2008) to create an appearance of being both unified and diverse at the same time. I would add, however, that this is also a way in which the Coalition asserts itself, not only as *one* voice but as *the* voice of civil society in global criminal justice-making.

In any discussion of representation, accountably remains the other side of the coin (see Phillips, 1995). Given the fact that the Coalition speaks on behalf of others, a question must be asked about whom they are accountable to. Member-based organizations such as Amnesty International can claim to represent the views of their members. Likewise, NGO coalitions can also claim to represent the views of their member organizations—indeed, to speak with this 'one voice'. However, when the Coalition claims to represent the views of its 2,500 member organizations, this may also be seen to skew the accountability scale, removing it further from the accountability of its individual member organizations. Moreover, as member organizations can easily opt in or out, depending on the issues at hand—if, say, they disagree—it is not possible to ascertain *which* of the 2,500 organizations' views are represented on any given issues as, indeed, no official list of member organizations exists. The level of the Secretariat's agency and autonomy vis-à-vis its member 'constituency' is also important in this regard, as is the extent it prioritizes—unconsciously or not—the views of its 'parent' NGO—the World Federalists—over the views of its member organizations, and even those of its steering committee members.

A relevant aspect of inclusion and exclusion concerns formal non-state participation at the ASP meetings (Lohne, 2017; De Hoon and Lohne, 2019). While many consider the inclusion of civil society in the ASP meetings as being unique in comparison to other state negotiations, a question may be asked about who is included in these forums, and how these processes work. While the ASP Secretariat manage the accreditation process for states and organizations with United Nations Economic and Social Council (ECOSOC) Special Consultative Status, the Coalition administers the process for NGOs without such status, and others who apply to participate. According to Bill Pace, this function was delegated to him and the Coalition because of his experience with accreditation processes from previous conference work. As he explained: 'You have to have genuine NGOs—not government-controlled NGOs, NGOs that are one person, you know.'

There were several complaints about the accreditation process to the ASP meetings. For example, at a meeting between the NGOs and African governments, African delegates asked for more African civil society organizations to be accredited, and for the process to be more open and transparent. Others complained that accreditation is confirmed so close to the dates of the ASP meetings, that only well-funded NGOs can book flights and accommodation. While the Coalition also occasionally funds NGOs from ICC situation countries to be present at the ASP meetings, these processes indicate how the Coalition has come to function as a gate-keeper for civil society access, by having significant influence over who is, or who is not, to pass through the security doors and participate in the ASP meetings.

A somewhat trivial but telling detail concerning accreditation badges at the ASP meetings may also be considered. Whereas many NGO representatives, especially those with ECOSOC status, wear badges carrying the name of their organization, those accredited through the Coalition carry a generic 'Coalition for the International Criminal Court' badge. This is similarly the case for academics that manage to get accreditation to the ASP meetings too. Provided they have an individual membership in the Coalition, academics can apply for accreditation to the ASP through the Coalition. By listing my current workplace as my organization, I was thus able to get accreditation. However, instead of the 'University of Oslo', my badge read 'Coalition for the International Criminal Court'. Presumably done in good faith, as academic attention and interest in the ICC is part of the Coalition's objectives to raise awareness, the use of the Coalition's name on accreditation badges nonetheless has the strategic effect of increasing their power in numbers. Indeed, through such processes, the Coalition has become synonymous with 'global civil society' in international criminal justice, and by speaking *for* global civil society, one also implicitly defines *what* global society is—who and what are included or excluded from the category of global civil society.

The notion of speaking with one voice signifies speaking with *only* one voice. It implies creating a space for oneself, but not necessarily one for others; it implies a discursive space where there is less room for alternative voices and actors to claim equal representation to speak for 'global civil society'. To join the Coalition, one must endorse its mandate of working for a 'fair, effective and independent court'. While this may be a low-threshold principle, it is a threshold nevertheless, excluding organizations working for alternatives to the criminal justice approach to situations of mass violence. In my view, there is reason to reflect on how these accreditation processes affect ASP meetings particularly, and the field of international criminal justice generally, as a space not just for political deliberation but also for contestation. The CICC is the Coalition *for* the ICC and the ASP meetings are a pro-Court environment. Arguably, there is a lack of space for organizations or voices opposing the ICC. As a result, 'global civil society' becomes 'for' the ICC, as resistance to it is expressed through non-participation.

Through the politics of information and coalition-building, the Coalition is thus enabled considerable power of the what and the who of 'global civil society' participation in international criminal justice. It also, I would argue, demonstrates the normativity embedded in the concept of 'global civil society' altogether.

The Legitimacy of Global Civil Society

While there is no coherent definition of 'global civil society', the term is commonly used to refer to the conglomeration of civil society organizations, transnational advocacy networks, and social movements operating on the transnational and international, rather than the national, scale.[18] However, at the same time, the term is a highly contentious one, on account of two assumptions embedded in its use. First, whereas a conceptualization of global civil society as 'transnational', 'globalizing' and concerned with 'universals' would include religious missionary movements and transnational terrorist organizations alike, global civil society is imagined as a 'progressive' movement. It has a normative aspiration that an alternative term such as transnational civil society does not have. 'Just as the term "human rights" has a universalistic intent that "civil rights" lacks, global civil society can be seen as an aspiration to reach and include citizens everywhere and to

[18] For discussions, see the Global Civil Society yearbooks (e.g. Kaldor et al., 2012).

enable them to think and act as global citizens' (Glasius, 2006: 4). Second, the term rests on a dubious domestic analogy to 'civil society' in established democracies, as it is premised on the equation of the 'international society' with domestic democracies, and of the role of civil society and its 'global' counterpart fulfilling similar functions therein. Yet the 'international' and 'global' as sites of political engagement are far from democratic. In fact, and somewhat ironically, this is the oft-cited reason for the importance of including NGOs in the first place—to speak for the world's people to international institutions, to 'democratize' global governance. Yet domestically, the clout of civil society institutions is based precisely on a disclaimer to democratic or political representation. 'Citizens do not vote for this or that civil society organization as their representatives because, in the end, NGOs exist to reflect their own principles, not to represent a constituency to whose interests and desires they must respond' (Anderson and Rieff, 2005: 15).

However, global civil society scholars maintain that democracy is not the only basis for normative legitimacy. Glasius, for instance, insists that the 'most valuable contribution of global civil society to the international criminal court ... was not the dimension of increased democracy but the dimension of morality and idealism' (2002: 164). Similarly, Scholte (2018: 361) asserts that through its participation, global civil society can 'bolster public confidence in global governance by lending it moral force'. This seems especially to be the case with global justice-making, as the role of human rights NGOs can be understood to endow the field of international criminal justice with moral authority.

Generally, by producing moral outrage on behalf of victims of international crimes, human rights advocacy mobilizes attention and resources to the field from individuals, states, and international organizations (Dixon and Tenove, 2013). However, human rights NGOs claim to legitimacy is likewise premised on a notion of moral authority because 'moral capital is their most important asset' (Mutua, 2009a: 26). They assert the universality of human rights, thus representing interests that are elevated 'above' politics and multiplicity. As self-appointed speakers for *humanity*, they speak on behalf of us all. Demanding that the ICC 'does something' about global violence and humanity's suffering, human rights NGOs feed international criminal justice with moral outrage. Their embrace of and advocacy for the ICC also legitimizes the Court, as these organizations in and of themselves are powerful representatives for the 'appropriate' values embedded in notions of human rights and humanity. The ICC therefore also assumes a role as a representative of these values, the moral authority of human rights NGOs being assumed to be transferred to the Court.

However, as the moral authority of human rights NGOs is embedded in universals, their engagement takes on a spatial dimension: In contrast to, for example, expert, delegated or political sources of authority, which all assert a position of being 'inside' the field, moral sources of authority are associated with a position of externality and of being 'outside'—beyond the realm of vested interest (Hopgood, 2009). To be able to 'speak truth to power', which is arguably what has made possible their leverage within the state-centric world order, they cannot be seen to *be* power. That would undermine their moral claim to 'truth'. Their role as providers of information and the influence it yields relies upon their status as providers of objective knowledge (Price, 2003).

However, a central argument throughout this book is that human rights NGOs can hardly be seen as 'outsiders' to international criminal justice. Rather, they are significantly embedded in the 'ICC project'; beyond being stakeholders, in their eyes, they have created the Court. One way in which this deep-seated role in international criminal justice is expressed is through human rights NGOs' multiple claims to authority and representativeness. I suggest that these claims are internally incongruent and a source of tension that actually challenges the role of human rights NGOs as providers of moral authority altogether (see also Lohne, 2017). By the same token, in view of the assumption about the transfer of authority, a challenge to the moral authority of human rights NGOs is also a challenge to the moral authority of the ICC.

Human rights NGOs speak for and about victims of international crimes; it is in the name of those that have been wronged that NGOs take it upon themselves to adopt their cause. In doing so, they are part of a larger social movement calling for victim recognition in the criminal justice system—also seen in western domestic criminal justice systems. Domestically, victims' groups advocate for the needs, interests, and rights of victims, in particular as regards strengthening their participation in the criminal justice process. However, while increased attention to victims' interests and rights are advocated by victims' organizations at both the national and international level, their role is much more prominent internationally, where NGOs have a variety of functions (for a typology, see Haddad, 2012) in speaking for victims directly or indirectly (see generally Chapter 6).

NGOs in international criminal justice litigate on behalf of victims, both in *formal roles* as *amicus curiae* brief-filers and as providers of representation to victims. On the domestic level, as far as legal aid is concerned, this is generally offered to defendants lacking resources to *protect* their rights vis-à-vis the criminal justice system. By contrast, the NGO focus on legal aid, in the form of direct or indirect representation, is directed towards victims—not the defendant—and hence, is not as concerned with protection *from* as protection *by* the criminal justice system. Legal aid to victims is, thus, much more prominent at the international level than in contemporary criminal justice systems in the UK and the US, for example.[19] Furthermore, while human rights litigation and so-called 'cause lawyering' takes place at the domestic level too (see e.g. Hurwitz, 2003; Sarat and Scheingold, 2005), this takes place mainly within areas of *civil* law, not *criminal* law, which is where the ICC operates.

Moreover, NGOs fulfil *consultative roles* with ICC personnel and state representatives, both formally through ICC-NGO roundtable meetings and The Hague working group meetings, and informally. These consultative roles also develop into *advocacy* and *lobbying* for diplomatic and financial support for the Court. For example, over the years the ICC budget has become one of the major advocacy issues for the Coalition, with Amnesty International heading the Coalition's working group on budget. On the face of it, budget issues seem a long way away from what is generally considered human rights advocacy. It seems even further from Amnesty International's trademark letter writing campaigns. Budget issues are far from 'sexy' enough to attract popular support, which a member-based campaign organization such as Amnesty International relies upon. For these reasons, budget was initially a controversial issue within the Coalition, and sparked resistance from Coalition members. A Coalition representative

[19] As the rights of victims are becoming more prominent in domestic systems of criminal justice too, legal aid to victims may follow suit (see generally CEPEJ, 2014).

explained that there has been a significant change of opinion as regards budget advocacy: 'No matter what (former Chief Prosecutor) Moreno Ocampo or (former) President Kirsch said, or the Registrar, if it wasn't in the budget, then it wasn't there. So now Amnesty and Human Rights Watch are the primary monitors of the budget.'

This makes an interesting shift in human rights advocacy. Rather than monitoring states' human rights praxis directly, this is now also done through institution building. Making sure states commit enough resources to international justice therefore emerges as a critical part of the human rights portfolio. It seems nevertheless that the Coalition's preoccupation with the ICC's budget remains controversial, but not so much because it is outside the 'human rights mandate' to which most of the Steering Committee members have signed up to, but because the NGOs risk being perceived as too close to the ICC, running the Court's errands in advocating for more resources from state parties. In preparation for the annual ASP meetings, where budget negotiations have been the most important part of the agenda, the ICC and the NGOs meet in so-called roundtable meetings. A former NGO representative explained:

> With the years, it became very obvious. They (ICC officials) would come, and we would have a two-hour presentation of the budget and then half an hour presentation on intermediaries, which was what NGOs really wanted to talk about. But then the Court would draft the program, so they would have two or three hours on the budget ... the NGOs have a tendency—because they believe in the objective—to blindly take it ... but I think at some point you need to start questioning, you know. Where the hell is the money going? For me that's the big question: an institution that is spending so much money is not actually bringing in a lot of results.

What is expressed here are tensions between the multiple roles NGOs serve vis-à-vis the ICC. On the one hand, NGOs support the ICC and recognize its need for a viable budget, according to the rationale discussed above. On the other, their close involvement with the Court's 'needs' in lobbying states for resources may come into conflict with their role as monitors of the institution. To what extent can the NGOs criticize how the Court spends its money without undermining their support for the ICC project altogether?

The NGOs also serve important *information-sharing roles* in the field, passing information between the Court, states, victim communities, and the general public; finally, it has *operational support roles* such as providing assistance and helping the ICC fulfil its mandate, for example by conducting outreach on behalf of the Court in situation countries (Haddad, 2012). All of these functions are discussed in more detail throughout the book.

When compared to victims' groups and advocacy in domestic criminal justice systems, the multifaceted roles of NGOs at the international level is indeed quite striking. In fact, it is hard to imagine victims' groups fulfilling such varied functions in western domestic criminal justice systems as they do internationally. One may ask why this should be.

Within the frame of understanding international criminal justice as 'for' victims (at least rhetorically, and as opposed to other more prominent rhetorical objectives of domestic criminal justice, such as maintaining law and order), there may be more cultural acceptance for participation of human rights NGOs as spokespersons, albeit self-appointed, for victims around the world. In other words, because the role of victims is a dominant feature of the *raison d'être* of international criminal justice—not only in scale and gravity but also in participation and generation of support for the Court—so is the role of their 'representatives'.

Another explanation may be found in what can be seen as a political opportunity structure. Compared with criminal justice systems in established democracies, international criminal justice—as a *transnational* field—is much less institutionalized. So too are sources, or 'spheres', of authority (Rosenau, 2002). This enables transnational actors to draw on multiple sources of authority, which does not happen in domestic criminal justice systems, where power and authority are more institutionalized and entrenched in nation-state power (Vauchez, 2011).

In a similar vein, Haddad (2012: 126) posits that NGO participation in international courts is contingent on 'initial conditions of court creation and subsequent state financial and political support for the Court'. From this follows that the wide-ranging participation in the ICC by NGOs follows from their extensive participation in the negotiations; having a 'foot in the door' from the beginning and redefining their mandate in response to the needs of ICC institution building. Under-funded institutions, as the ICC claims to be, may also find the assistance of NGOs particularly beneficial, both in asking states for more funds, and helping them fulfil their mandate. Furthermore, a situation where the court is frequently politicized by its member states may enable a political opportunity structure for NGOs to increase their participation (Haddad, 2012). The moral authority of human rights NGOs—and particularly their role as 'disinterested' and universal bodies—become, arguably, more acutely important for the legitimacy of the Court if it is being blamed for being biased and political.

However, another problem arises, as the NGOs are so involved in international criminal justice that the CICC is sometimes mistakenly considered part of the ICC institution itself. There is a disclaimer in CICC emails and written materials: 'The Coalition for the ICC is not an organ of the court.' The difference (or lack of one) between the Court and the Coalition was also a topic in Uganda. In Kampala, a victims' rights lawyer spoke to me about the UCICC's activities in explaining the Court's mandate as both complementing ICC activities and working together with court personnel in holding joint outreach activities. He explained, 'because of this, the UCICC was perceived as part of the Court. It was difficult to distinguish the two. First of all, they have almost similar names. And second, what the UCICC was doing was talking about the Court's mandate—exactly what the Court was doing!' This illustrates the importance of how the NGOs are viewed from the outside; here, their roles as advocates of international criminal justice makes it difficult to distinguish them from the ICC, and threatens to make them appear part and parcel of the international judicial intervention itself.

Conclusions

This chapter has mapped out the organizational conditions of NGOs for the ICC. As the role of NGOs in the creation of the Court is hailed as a global civil society achievement by scholars and practitioners alike, the chapter started out from the non-state and alternative genesis of the ICC, and situated the Court as a product of NGO mobilization for law as global justice-making. There is a lot of hard work behind their advocacy; seemingly trivial legal rules, such as rules of procedure, become important, and subject to proposal drafting and lobby by NGOs as part of their larger objectives of materializing global justice. At the same time, understanding the ICC as a 'global civil society achievement' raises the question of the extent to which the ICC is an NGO project—and whether the ICC is 'NGO justice'.

The Coalition for the ICC emerges as a particularly central actor in the field of international criminal justice. Since the ICC negotiations in Rome, the Coalition has continued to play a significant part in the pursuit of global justice, fulfilling a number of functions in assisting the Court to realize its mandate. The Coalition is composed of three parts: (i) a Secretariat, which functions as an NGO within the Coalition and is the major actor in The Hague, as well as the face of the Coalition generally; (ii) a core network of primarily Steering Committee members and founders of the Coalition, most of whom are international human rights NGOs; and (iii) a web of transnational networks. Taking the example of Uganda, I discuss how non-governmental mobilization for the ICC is generated, and reflect on the imbalances there have been in these networks from the outset. Following the spatial inquiries in the previous chapter, this chapter has thus further unwrapped some of the divisions and imbalances between the global North and South in the making of 'the global'.

Through its networks, the Coalition is able to assert itself as *mediators* between these 'local' and the 'global' spaces, including the victims and affected communities in situation countries and the Court in The Hague. In this way, it seems the NGOs are able to carve out the 'transnational' as a particular space for political engagement: one that is structurally more accommodating to their participation than the traditional statist structures of domestic or international politics. In this terrain, networks and coalition-building enable NGOs to leverage their influence. As regards the field of international criminal justice, the Coalition has become *the* global civil society vis-à-vis the ICC, which is highlighted, for example, by processes of accreditation to the ASP meetings. The power to define and constitute 'global civil society' is similarly apparent in the Coalition's handling of information, where, in general, the moral knowledge provided within the field is defined by a select few, although facilitated by their web of transnational knowledge and expertise. Again, this chapter's tracing and unpacking of networks illustrate how it is that the metropole comes to speak for, and profit from, the periphery.

Another interpretation of the continued and extensive NGO participation in the ICC may be found in the contested political nature of the Court and of international criminal justice generally. Here, human rights NGOs serve an essential role as providers of moral authority, not only through their claim to universal values but also because of their claim to being outside the field: as representatives of humanity, they elevate themselves above the statist and situated realm of politics. I question this claim, however, given the fact that the role of NGOs in international criminal justice appears ever more embedded within the system of international criminal justice itself. In what follows, I will show how this embeddedness attaches not only to the organizational level of global justice-making, but also to the sorts of people involved in the field. While the focus of this chapter was on nongovernmental *organization* NGOs, the role of individuals for these organizations was also briefly commented on. It seems that a few individuals have been particularly active in advocating and realizing the ICC, that there has been a social dynamic that involves a homogenous group of people 'speaking the same language' (Benedetti et al., 2014: 75). Thus, what has also come into view throughout the chapter is the coupling of law and lobbyism as a particularly powerful mechanism for advocacy. While this shows how NGOs draw on expert and legal authority, it also bears witness to social aspects of global justice-making, including the socio-demographic backgrounds and identities of NGO representatives in The Hague. In doing so, I turn to the issue of what types of individuals are involved in global justice-making?

4

From Moral Entrepreneurs to Moral Advocates

When one explores international criminal justice as a particular site of penality, its structural conditions start to emerge, together with its embeddedness in global geographies of power. So far, I have dealt with spaces of international criminal justice, and the role of transnational NGO networks as mediators within and between these spaces. Moving from the 'where' and the 'how', this chapter takes a micro-level perspective in exploring the 'who' of global justice-making, mindful that it is not so much institutions that govern the world but the actors constituting them. To do so, I conceptualize NGO representatives in international criminal justice as global moral entrepreneurs, and draw attention to the importance of humanitarian sentiments and 'positive' emotions in feeding the development of global justice-making through criminal law. As will also be demonstrated in coming chapters, its promoters conceptualize international criminal justice as a cosmopolitan expression of social justice. At the same time, they belong to a particular segment of the globally stratified order.

More than 'mere' moral entrepreneurs, I show that human rights NGOs to a significant extent are also professionals, with considerable legal expertise. They are *advocates* of international criminal justice. As such, I draw attention to how the NGOs narrate their efforts as 'lobbying for the good', and demonstrate how the field is not only characterized by a duality of ideology and industry, but also that their role as 'advocates' is essentially a partisan position. In the chapter's second part, I situate these advocates more firmly within international criminal justice as a transnational field of practice, and specifically as part of its transnational power networks. In exploring the structural conditions of the field, particularly how internships and mobility serve as stratifying elements, I find that these advocates—as professionals

Advocates of Humanity. Kjersti Lohne, Oxford University Press (2019).
DOI: 10.1093/oso/9780198818748.003.0004

in the field generally—belong to a class of transnational western professionals. Conversely, the centre of international criminal justice in The Hague is characterized by a considerable lack of geographical representation. Lastly, I examine the social dynamics embedded in the transnational as a particular field of practice, and consider career trajectories and 'revolving door' mechanisms to indicate the close affiliations among different positions in international criminal justice, including those of human rights NGOs. These discussions not only raise the question of whether global justice-making through the ICC is an NGO project in the first place or whether the NGOs are co-opted by the ICC, but also, essentially, considers the issue of *who* drives the power to punish when punishment is disembedded from the nation state.

Global Moral Entrepreneurs

The sense of feeling good while doing good has been recognized as a familiar dynamic since Adam Smith's (2006) writings on *Moral Sentiments*: to measure one's own humanity by feeling compassion towards others. Yet, while early theorists on sensibilities such as Smith and David Hume stressed the embeddedness of moral bonds in tender-heartedness, in empathy and sympathy, the return of emotions to criminological scholarship has generally emphasized negative emotions—disgust, shame, vengeance—and their impacts on penal policy and criminal procedure (Karstedt, 2002; Karstedt et al., 2011). In contrast to this, the moral sensibilities invoked by human rights NGOs are positive ones: indeed, compassion, sympathy, and solidarity with distant others appear as constitutive of global justice advocacy as the 'call for revenge' and punitive sentiments associated with 'penal populism' do in late modern societies (Pratt, 2000; 2007).

In The Hague, NGO representatives spoke of their work as being part of a larger global social movement towards a more 'just' world order. 'Making a difference' was a recurring refrain in talk about what motivates them, as indicated here:

> On the substance, (the work) is extremely interesting. There is so much developing that I really have the feeling that I am making a difference through my work, and I am making a difference and making the world better. And that is very much an underlying motivation that I will always have, and those are discussions that we have with our colleagues here as well: we are making a difference!

Writing on the evolution of global prohibition regimes, Nadelmann (1990: 480) notes how they, 'like criminal laws, tend to involve moral and emotional considerations more so than most other laws and regimes', connecting transnational norm scholarship with Becker's concept of *moral entrepreneurs*, familiar to scholars of crime control and deviance. Becker emphasizes the moral impetus of norm entrepreneurs, or 'rule creators', operating with 'an absolute ethic' in making rules to fight 'what he sees is truly and totally evil with no qualification' (Becker, 1991 [1963]: 148). The moral crusader is not interested in forcing their own morals upon others; rather, 'many moral crusades have strong humanitarian overtones. The crusader is not only interested in seeing to it that other people do what he thinks is right. He believes that if they do what is right it will be good for them' (Becker, 1991 [1963]: 158). It is therefore interesting to draw parallels with how humanitarian principles are invoked by NGO representatives when they describe motivations for their work, and how, to a significant extent, they can be understood as a type of global moral entrepreneur.[1]

Most of those I met working in international criminal justice were so-called 'progressive' people, using human rights as an emancipatory language to frame claims to justice, development, and social change on a global scale. Their motivations for working in international criminal justice were not necessarily based on international *criminal* justice but rather in international, or global, *social* justice. Consider the following explanation from one of my informants:

> Why am I doing this? Generally, I have an interest in social justice issues and development. To my mind, this (international criminal justice) is closely linked to development issues. I also took an interest in participatory democracy during my studies … that led me to the work of the Coalition. It was serendipity that I ended up working here. I harboured no real desire to come to The Hague to work in international justice.

Instead of a preoccupation with international crimes and criminal law, what is emphasized is the struggle for global social justice, in which international criminal law functions as a tool.

[1] While Nadelmann uses the term 'transnational moral entrepreneurs', I prefer the prefix 'global' to emphasise the cosmopolitan as opposed to the nation-state perspective of the human rights NGOs. As such, the actors dealt with here are not dependent on the 'transnational hook' to generate moral concern.

The significant role of NGOs within international criminal justice is likewise identified as inspiring. Within this conceptualization, international criminal justice becomes a cosmopolitan expression of social justice. As part of this, the work *feels* good and becomes a motivation in and of itself, proving that, indeed, it is possible to do well while doing good. 'We are not selling pants or whatever,' explains another informant,

> And that motivation is something that you need to restate for yourself. Because it is hard work, we do long hours. We are getting paid much less than we could if we were to be lawyers in law firms. But we are getting so much more out of in terms of motivation, being able to do something better, to have a feeling that you make an impact.

Compared to what they *could* be doing—making more money and having better job security—what emerges is a sense of activism, a collective determination to make the world a better place for others. As part of this, there is sense of *relative* sacrifice, as expressed by yet another NGO representative:

> Job security is very limited, and that definitely affects your morale and what you are doing. But I think everyone in this field is so dedicated to the issues that—yes, you're doing it! You want to do it! You will find something else if you can't. It is not as much about the job. It's just being part of this.

These narratives point to the notion of being part of a social movement towards global justice—of being part of history-making and global justice-making. Advocates of international criminal justice conceptualize, or *frame,* international criminal justice as part of the 'global justice movement', and accordingly leverage *retributive* justice onto the agenda of a movement that is generally associated with economic, environmental, political, and social notions of justice (Della Porta, 2007). Notions of 'development' and 'progress' emerge as moral and righteous—or self-righteous—claims to legitimacy for their (pre)occupation.

Paraphrasing Kenneth Burke, Becker (1991 [1963]: 153) writes that a 'man's occupation may become his preoccupation. The equation is also good the other way around. A man's preoccupation may become his occupation.' In doing so, he conceives a dimension that, I suggest, accurately describes the field of international criminal justice, namely one that comes between ideology and industry. Work in international criminal justice, and particularly work in the NGO sector, is as a *moral job,* and as such, an aspiring professional one. Yet while Becker (1991 [1963]: 153) describes how a successful rule creator moves on to find other issues, becoming 'a professional discoverer of wrongs to be righted, or situations requiring new rules', and leaves rule implementation and enforcement to 'other' professionals—in particular lawyers—NGOs in international criminal justice largely carry out roles as (legal) professionals themselves. It is precisely the *coupling* of moral and expert authority that distinguishes them. While Becker's moral crusaders are concerned with ends rather than means, human rights NGOs apply and specialize in law as a means to global justice, and in the process become legal professionals themselves (see also Dezalay and Garth, 2006).

Thus, rather than being 'mere' entrepreneurs, human rights NGOs are *advocates* for international criminal justice. In addition to publicly supporting the idea of international criminal justice, they are also, in most cases, lawyers, and frame global grievances through law and rights-claims. After all, the human rights movement is driven by a lawyer's worldview (De Waal, 2003). The way human rights advocates use the law, however, is closer to the 'position of a solicitor, or a partisan legal advisor, than to the position of a judge or neutral academic writer. The law is applied in ways that helps the case; counter arguments are not necessarily engaged with full candour in a way we would expect an academic to do' (Dudai, 2006: 789). In considering the role of international justice advocates as *lobbyists*, then, the manner in which law is *applied* should not be lost sight of because of the fact that law per se has become their information (see also Chapter 7). While Becker distinguishes between 'rule creators' and 'rule enforcers', it appears this distinction is much more uneven as regards NGOs in international criminal justice.

'Lobbying for the good': balancing claims to moral and expert authority

To be able to claim expert authority, human rights NGOs cannot be perceived as too engaged or too vocal in their advocacy vis-à-vis state parties. As professionals they must contrive a role closer to the disinterested other, whose advice is based on facts rather than politics (see also Jakobi, 2013). As lobbyists, they must therefore necessarily mute their moral cries and put on more 'objective' expressions. A Coalition Secretariat representative explained that he tries to 'avoid taking the kind of moralistic advocacy approach. If you appeal to people's reason, it is a lot more effective. People can get turned off by crusades, moralizing crusades.' In conversations with state delegates, the Coalition's 'professional' character was pointed to as a justification for their participation in the field altogether, to the extent that 'professionalization' became an indicator of influence. Yet, crucially, it is *diplomats* that can get turned off by moralizing crusades. As Pearson (2006: 279–80) notes from the Rome negotiations:

> Some NGOs were also identified as using heavily emotive arguments and not presenting an objective, informed point of view. Such behavior was felt to be intrusive, obstructive, and counterproductive to the negotiations and to the relationship between NGOs and states on the whole ... [H]ostility encountered by some NGOs shows states' preference for NGOs in roles of 'neutral' knowledge experts as opposed to advocates, though the reality is that the two roles are often interlinked.

The Coalition seems to have perfected this role, juggling moral claims and expert knowledge, to the extent that this is indeed what has facilitated their access to the diplomatic corridors in The Hague. Accordingly, human rights NGOs draw on multiple sources of authority depending on where and with whom they are engaged: while the creation of moral outcry over distant suffering to get other more powerful actors to 'do something' is their *raison d'être*, it seems that, to engage these more powerful actors, 'reason' is back in the game.

In discussing their role as lobbyists, one of the Secretariat representatives said:

> Some may think that this is not what we want to be doing, this state level thing. 'We are human rights activists! We want to be making a lot of noise!' which is not necessarily diplomatic ... It is a matter of influence. If you walked in with jeans and a t-shirt, looking like a tramp and just said 'You should do this!' they are not going to do it. But if you put on a suit and conduct yourself, you get things done.

The Coalition representatives thus perceive behaving more like diplomats than the 'traditional' image of activists engaged in contentious politics as a more politically effective strategy. In formal attire, armed with law as the *lingua franca*, attending receptions and networking with other experts and professionals—aspiring to *behave* like diplomats—has become part and parcel to the everyday lives of global justice advocates in The Hague.

However, who is able to 'put on a suit' and 'get things done'? And how do they talk about their work and what they do? Are they activists or professionals, or does the distinction between the two blur in the way they narrate their professional identities? A Coalition Secretariat representative described work in the following manner:

> I normally say that I give legal advice to human rights organizations, that I work in human rights, and that I work with victims of mass crime. It's all true—and specifically international criminal law. Maybe it is the people I hang out with, but the general response is not one of 'God, you are one of those, are you?' It is 'good for you!' So that is how I describe it, and that is why I say that no one knows what I do. No one really knows or understands what we do. It is completely a bit of a mix and a bit of a mess. I am not a lawyer—I am not strictly a lawyer as such; I am not strictly doing diplomacy but I am doing a lot of that; I am not a lobbyist, but I do lobbying. You lobby for good as opposed to other reasons, you know.

Again, I would like to draw attention to the duality of idealism on the one hand and industry on the other. Lobbyism is indeed an activity and a term associated with industry, with money and in particular with the competition for financial capital based on self-interest; what my informant refers to as 'other reasons'. The Coalition, by contrast, 'lobby for good', and thus, allegedly, for something beyond self-interest. Nonetheless, it appears that it is also important not to be seen as too idealistic, as if an appeal to emotion would undermine the appeal to reason. Although the juxtaposition of emotion and reason is deeply embedded in social and political thought in late-modern societies, it is interesting to observe how NGO representatives, whose participation is largely legitimated by reference to moral sensibilities, also navigate this landscape, 'so that emotions do not intrude into the true preserve of law: reason' (Karstedt, 2011: 2). As one of my informants put it when discussing the aspiration to universal ratification and enforcement of the ICC statute: 'I don't know if the world would be a better place. It is a little bit *fleur bleue*—a little girl's dream.'

However, if one considers the domestic terrain of crime policy in late-modern societies, it is hard to imagine that the drivers of crime policy would ever be referred to as *fleur bleue;* quite the contrary, crime policy today seems to shun what it now considered naïve: the idealistic aspirations for reform that characterized post-war penal-welfarism (Garland, 2001). In later chapters, I probe deeper into some of these differences and similarities between cosmopolitan and domestic penality as a way of dissecting the imaginaries embedded in the field of international criminal justice; or, to stay with the metaphor, the contents of the little girl's dream. Nevertheless, I would like to stress the need to *renounce* idealism, once more reflecting the aforementioned duality of idealism and industry:

> I would not like to picture myself as the saviour of anybody or anything because I do not believe I am doing anything of that sort. I don't want to be either the caricature of the humanitarian worker—because I have seen too many of them, thinking you have saved an African child. It is not how I conceive what we do or anything ... I think the real humanitarian workers do not even picture themselves like that. They know what they are doing and they do not have pretentions. I was working for a few months with the Director of Operations for Doctors without Borders. This guy did not have the impression that he was saving anybody or anything. He was just doing his job and he was doing it well.

In her perceptions of what underlies 'real' humanitarianism, she emphasizes work, not charity: doing 'good' is associated with being a good professional. This notion is also discernible in relation to the renunciation of *sacrifice,* traditionally coupled with contentious politics, activism, and humanitarian work (Douzinas, 2007a; Hopgood, 2013). Apart from the low wages relative to their fellow law graduates, most of my NGO informants in The Hague do not mention sacrifice or inconvenience. Rather, they draw attention to how enjoyable their work is, often describing it as diverse and social, in terms of both meeting interesting people and liking their colleagues. There is also a sense of 'being' or 'living' 'the international', as demonstrated here:

> I find the work really interesting. No two days are the same in terms of what you deal with. I like that we are at the forefront of a lot of things that are going on—within the Court as well. And we work with people from all over the world, daily having conversations with people from all over the world, which I just find fascinating. World events and what is going in the world effect your next day at work. I just find that really exciting. If you watch something on the news—remember when Libya was happening—and thinking I will be dealing with that tomorrow. And you are!

Dealing with international events is associated with global importance—of being *part* of the global, of something great that is developing and progressing for the good of humanity. Moreover, notions of 'contributing', of 'sacrifice', and of 'the global' are brought together in notions of space and geography by an informant in The Hague, explaining that: 'We all are living in the West, and it does take a bigger effort of will to say, "well, I can be doing something outside of this comfort zone", if you know what I mean.' I ask him to elaborate:

> I would like to go and work in the 'field', whatever that means, but more for my own sake, to explore and continue seeing the world. I am very realistic in the amount of what I could contribute to any sort of these problems on the ground, and actually, for quite a while I have always had a preference for trying to effect the suprastructure of issues rather than going down [at the micro level], which is of course invaluable work to do, but I think my skills are better suited to, at the moment anyway, this type of work, trying to influence the structures of power.

It is interesting to note how he depicts a disconnection between sacrifice and influence in work for the greater good, and further, how this type of influence plays out at the global level. Significantly, 'the global'—the structures of power—is located inside the comfort zone.

Epistemic Communities and Transnational Power Networks

The professionalization of human rights NGOs in relation to international criminal justice can be understood as reflective of the general professionalization of western societies, and the human rights movement in particular (De Waal, 2003). Their ability to draw on multiple sources of authority and exert themselves as moral entrepreneurs and professionals at the same time must also be understood, however, in the light of the particularity of the transnational as a site of political engagement (Dezalay and Garth, 2006; Vauchez, 2011). One of the major features of the decline of penal welfarism in domestic crime discourse was a parallel decline in western societies in public deference to expert knowledge and public authority (Pratt, 2007). This development is in itself one of the main explanations for the upsurge of civil society organizations claiming to speak on behalf of 'the people' domestically, but can also, arguably, be associated with the rise of transnational advocacy networks, social movements, and international human rights NGOs. It is therefore interesting to note that, somewhat paradoxically, some of those claiming to be more interested than representatives of the state in what is really of concern to people now sometimes claim greater expertise than do state representatives.

This is not only explained by the fact that the major international human rights NGOs have a significantly larger legal apparatus than most state delegates, and often more representatives too at the ASP meetings in The Hague (or New York). It also has to do with the fact that individual moral entrepreneurs have been involved since the early days of the ICC negotiations: people such as the Coalition's Convenor William (Bill) Pace, Amnesty International's Christopher Hall[2], and Richard Dicker of Human Rights Watch. This gives them individualized power—an institutional form of power—in an otherwise transient field. As a state delegate at an ASP meeting put it, Pace is 'one of the more familiar faces in these circles'. While this does not apply to NGO representatives generally in the field, it neither applies to NGO representatives exclusively. There were also academics and state representatives with significant individualized power in the field, such as Mahmoud Cherif Bassiouni and Prince Zeid bin Ra'ad. However, to understand the role of NGOs in international criminal justice it is essential to recognize that individuals with considerable power represent them. These are actors who belong to the field's 'epistemic community', that is, the field's 'network of professionals with recognized expertise and competence in a particular domain and an authoritative claim to policy-relevant knowledge within that domain or issue-area' (Haas, 1992: 3). Derived from Foucault's more abstract sense of 'episteme' as defining 'the conditions of possibility of all knowledge' (2005: 183), members of an epistemic community—although coming from a variety of backgrounds and disciplines—share the same normative and causal beliefs, notions of validity, and policy enterprise. Crucially, what the epistemic community approach draws attention to is the role of actors, and in particular expert actors, in transnational governance and global norm formation.

[2] Christopher Hall passed away in 2013.

In keeping with findings on the imbalances of global civil society (Chapter 3), there are however, considerable nuances here also. Just as not all organizations are equally powerful, neither are individual NGO representatives. Individuals such as Bill Pace or Richard Dicker are better examples of international criminal justice's epistemic community than an intern on a short-term contract at the Coalition's Secretariat. However, the role of NGOs in international criminal justice cannot be understood properly without recognizing their considerable expert authority and their role as epistemic-like communities (Glasius, 2010). It also opens up the possibility of seeing their contribution as part of 'the political infiltration of an epistemic community into governing institutions which lays the groundwork for a broader acceptance of the community's beliefs and ideas about the proper construction of social reality' (Haas, 1992: 27). For these reasons too, it becomes increasingly interesting to enquire into *whose* beliefs and ideas, as in approaching transnational legal governance,

> it is not the institutions as such, the ICs [international courts], that govern the world but the transnational power elites constituting and instituting them. To make intelligible the power and interest of global legal governance, it is important to invert the common logic of inquiry by asking not only which organizations and rules govern but also, more importantly, who governs those organizations and rules. (Madsen, 2014a: 334)

Attention is thus directed towards what is often downplayed in studies of international law, namely demographics, social interest, and, ultimately, class—features of international criminal justice that are already conspicuous as the level of entering the field.

Entering the field: trials and tribulations of internships

Many of those advocating for international criminal justice in The Hague have started their professional career as interns at one of the international criminal courts or core human rights NGOs, to the extent that internships make up a substantial part of the 'work force' in the field. For example, in April 2013, the ICC's work force of 1024 included 118 interns and visiting professionals (ICC-Registry, 2013).[3] While this is already a substantial proportion (11.5 per cent), the figure increases further if one adjusts for

[3] Because of the high turnover—contracts last for a minimum of 3 to a maximum of 6 months—the number of interns at the Court at any given time varies,

staff categories applied by the Court, as interns are recruited for 'work [that] will generally be comparable to the work of the upper general service category or junior professional level'.[4] Including the interns and visiting professionals, the total number of staff includes sixty-five consultants or contractors, 151 individuals on what is called General Temporary Assistance, a further 334 general assistance staff in established posts, and 356 professional staff members. When comparing the number of interns and visiting professionals to the professional staff employed at the Court, unpaid positions increase to just over 33 per cent.

Likewise, the Coalition Secretariat in The Hague recruits a substantial number of interns. Especially in preparation for and during the ASP meetings, they recruit about a dozen short-term interns to assist during the two intense weeks of the meetings: they mostly write up summaries from the various General Assembly meetings and side events, take pictures, and provide lunch. Most of them will return to their universities after short dipping into the everyday life of international criminal justice. At any given time however, the Secretariat also has a few more 'stable' interns who usually, as is generally the case with internships in the field, work on contracts lasting from three to six months.

For the aspiring professional in international criminal justice, these are the prevailing conditions. In The Hague, one of the advocates explained that, despite having extensive legal experience on human rights issues in her country of origin, she saw internships as the only way to 'enter' international criminal justice:

> I came here three years ago. You know, I was 33, and had to apply for an internship. I was told by many people: 'Look, I've got some good advice: It is so competitive to get into the court or any of these institutions. It is beyond your credentials. You have to know somebody or have a little bit of experience'. Fair enough. So I did that.

Internships are the gateway to white-collar work well beyond The Hague. However, there are particular aspects of this form of (un)employment in international criminal justice that I suggest warrant further attention. Reflecting a 'curious blend of privilege and exploitation' (Perlin, 2012: xv), internships are perceived

but averages around 80, which amounts to roughly 25 per cent of the Court's professional staff.

[4] Correspondence on file with author, ICC intern coordinator, 2013.

as unfair among young professionals in the field. Yet they also serve as a type of gatekeeper to the field, enabling certain individuals and disenabling others. Hence, internships are influential in affecting *who* is eligible to become an advocate for and professional in international criminal justice—a crafter of global justice. Because these processes of inclusion and exclusion are intrinsically linked with international criminal justice's centrality in The Hague, it also illustrates previous arguments about the spatial arrangements of international criminal justice, and how its materialities are bound up with global geographies of power.

An internship is not considered work, but is rather conceptualized as an extension of one's education—a necessary *rite of passage* into becoming a professional in international criminal justice. However, despite not being legally recognized as work, interns do indeed work (although not all they do may be as relevant to their education as foreseen). For example, interns provide ground work for much of the material products of international justice, whether legal analysis and research to support arguments and judgments at the ICC, summaries of witness statements that become their evidence, or reviews of cases, written in their capacity as trial monitors for the Coalition. Rumours abound among interns and young professionals about the nature of what many refer to as unpaid work and labour exploitation (see also Perlin, 2012), as the following quote from an NGO representative demonstrates:

> I have been told that ten years ago the jobs interns do were [professional] entry-level jobs in institutions. I don't know about the Coalition as such, but certainly at the ICC. That is what I have been told: that what the interns are now doing is what you'd be doing when you first started at the lowest [professional] level.

Because what they do is not formally recognized as labour, they are not considered staff, which especially at the tribunals has brought frustrations: although working for free, they have to pay full price in the canteen and pay for their language classes—perks that paid staff benefit from. As the working conditions in international criminal justice, these practices convey messages of the inequality and injustice embedded in its structures, and its lack of attention to social inequalities. As non-employees, interns have no standing in court and enjoy no workplace protection such as health insurance. Besides other regulatory issues such as overtime and working conditions, this also bypasses intern protection in case of sexual harassment; this in a highly competitive and hierarchical field which may leave some young people particularly vulnerable vis-à-vis fellow interns, intern coordinators or other professionals (Schonfeld, 2014).

In response to this, The Hague Intern Association was created in 2012 to '*improve intern* welfare *and promote intern* rights', including increasing participation from 'developing' nations.[5] The intern organization arranges social and academic events such as Thursday Night Drinks and panel debates on current topics, surveys property owners, and provides useful tips to interns in a welcome booklet. Organizationally, the intern association resembles many other non-profit organizations in The Hague, structuring their activities and volunteers in working groups of social, welfare, and advocacy and communications teams. At the time of my visit to their General Assembly meeting, held at the premises of the former ICTY, their president had just returned from travels to other European capitals to strategize with similar intern associations. The 'fight for intern rights' was gaining traction internationally, with organizations such as Intern Labour Rights (US), Geneva Intern Associations, and even street protests in Brussels (Nielsen, 2013).

Organization requires agency and resources, both of which the privileged yet exploited interns in The Hague possess. The form this organization takes, however, resembles the institutions and organizations of international criminal justice, and as such may offer an indication of how institutional culture is adopted. While most interns will return to their countries of origin, and may well end up in high-level positions in government or the private sector, a few will go on to become advocates and professionals in international criminal justice. Either way, probing into the conditions of internships reveals more than just how the field recruits professionals, since it begins to unwrap how attitudes and skills are transferred within the field. It also shows what type of people become part of international criminal justice, and how they come to embody their working conditions.

Although some get by on scholarships from their universities, most interns are self-funded. This raises the question of who can

[5] http://hagueinternsassociation.org/about/ (accessed 20 March 2014). Their homepage has since shut down. Although they do keep a presence on Twitter and Facebook, their online activities are much less than at the time of my research.

afford to work for free for three months, six months, or even a year. And further, and most crucially, who can live and work for free for an extended period of time in The Hague, a city in the midst of Europe. Processes of inclusion and exclusion are not only based on socio-economic backgrounds but also on citizenship, as the prospects for acquiring an internship and entering the community of international criminal justice seem to a large extent to depend on one's citizenship.

Several of my informants spoke of the unfairness of intern recruitment and its relation to global inequalities. One of them explained:

> I can speak because I am probably one of the examples, but you can only really do internships if you are middle class or affluent enough to do your internships—certainly in The Hague—and be supported from home. That really narrows down who can work in the sector and who can move forward into working in the sector ... And the EU is cutting down subsidies at the ICC for internships. There used to be certain developing nations internships—there was internships for people specifically from Africa. I think they have stopped that subsidy program.

While the financial crisis was blamed for the cuts, the Coalition Secretariat said that they try to mitigate some of the geographical inequalities embedded in the field. Besides their focus on geographical representation in their network of membership, they also say that they, at least to a certain extent, have the same aims as regards their recruitment of interns to the Secretariat. However, there are practical challenges because of their location in The Hague. Their intern coordinator explained:

> I try to do [screenings] months ahead to give other people from different regions a chance because it takes time for them to get a visa. A lot of people apply early on, and then you just try to see what you can do for them. That helps—we have had quite a few interns from all over the world as of late. But there's definitely an advantage to EU citizens. Logistical considerations, you know.

The location of international criminal justice in the EU is thus of considerable significance for who is recruited to the field, and favours those with an EU-friendly passport. Although non-EU citizens may be able to get a visa to do an internship, they might not be able to prolong their stay and continue with 'intern rounds' and apply—hang around and wait—for paid positions. In addition to the economic barrier, non-EU citizens without the 'right' background are also confronted with the restrictive visa and residence policies of the Netherlands and the European Union. Thus, even at the level of internships there is a considerable lack of geographic representation in international criminal justice. Because of their effect on recruitment to professional positions, these asymmetries persist in the field, influencing who is able to advocate and work for global justice through international criminal law. Crucially, this also illustrates how space matters and how international criminal justice is materially brought into a particular kind of being through its location in The Hague specifically, and the EU generally.

The 'politics of presence': representation and international justice professionals

In The Hague I talked to two non-European NGO representatives about geographical representation in the field:

Informant 1: Ideally, it (international criminal justice) is supposed to be very international but it is much harder for non-Europeans. For example in The Hague-based courts, if I had an internship offer or a job offer, I would have to first get a visa, and then if it is not approved, then that's it. If it is approved, then you come here, and still your status is pending on whatever you are doing. It is much harder. I don't know if you have heard this, but to work in this field, you have to stay around and see what comes out.

Me: Because it's a lot about networking?

Informant 1: Exactly. Networking and doing internships and getting to know people. The applications take a long time so you have to stay longer to get into the field.

Informant 2: Up to a year the applications take.

Informant 1: So for example if you are from South America, you can't do that. You have to go back. You lose your chance because it is most likely that someone who has been here the whole time will get it. And you probably know that they do internships in different courts. They go from the ICTY to the ICTR and then ICC, just to get the time and try to come up with something. So again, it is easier if you are an EU citizen but much harder if you're not—and especially not if you have visa requirements.

Me: Have you seen this reflected in the people that work at the courts?

Informant 2: Well, look at the barristers, the defence—they're all Queen's Counsel Brits! I mean, what is that about? I don't want

> to blame it all on this because there are other issues, but for sure, that has to be looked at: the staff at the court. It is a constant struggle to have—and this is public information—representation from all the state parties. It's not there. Not at all! There are qualified people all over the world—it's a big gap—and I think it is a problem for the Court when you're trying to build credibility, and be—and look like—they're international …

The five countries with the topmost professionals working at the ICC in 2012 were France (45), United Kingdom (27), The Netherlands (17), Canada (15), and Germany (13). By comparison, the situation countries Côte d'Ivoire, the DRC, Mali, and Uganda had two professionals each working at the Court (ICC-ASP, 2013; but also WIGJ, 2012).

In liberal democracies, difference is primarily conceptualized as a matter of ideas, and hence, representation becomes a 'politics of ideas', reflecting more or less the beliefs, ideas, and opinions of one's constituency. Besides the democratic deficiency inherent in the international system generally, many of the challenges facing global governance institutions centre on demands for political *presence*, as the lack of even-handed geographical representation can be read as an indicator of global inequalities. As Phillips (1995: 5) notes, in this 'major reframing of the problems of democratic equality, the separation between "who" and "what" is to be represented, and the subordination of the first to the second, is very much up for question. The politics of ideas is being challenged by an alternative politics of presence.' In pointing out the lack of geographical representation at the ICC, my informants shed light on some of the dilemmas involved in 'trying poor countries' crimes in a rich city' (Verfuss, 2004). As explained above, some of the problems have to do with obtaining visa and residence permits to live and work in The Hague, a non-issue for EU citizens, but a significant barrier to others. This demonstrates how political and spatial relations affect the structures of international criminal justice. It demonstrates a significant discrepancy between the Court's claim to the 'global' and the images it projects of itself.

However, there is also a considerable lack of geographical representation in *advocacy* on international criminal justice in The Hague: the vast majority of the people there are EU citizens too (Lohne, 2017). At the time of research, of the Coalition Secretariat's eight staff members in The Hague, all but one were European citizens. The exception was North American. Among the core group of NGO representatives in The Hague, there is only one with an African background. Talking about his work lobbying state representatives, he asserted that 'it was challenging for me being the only African representing an NGO in The Hague. All other NGOs are represented by westerners.' I asked him to elaborate:

> It is in The Hague so I can't complain, right? If we were in Africa, then I'd say, you know. It has its own challenges. When I first got here it was easier for my other NGO colleagues to access the state officials than me. And this has nothing to do with racism. It just has something to do with maybe it is somebody that you identify yourself with more, somebody you think you have more things in common with.

Besides indicating which regional states are subject to the most lobbying in The Hague, geographical place is invoked as a rationale for this unevenness, despite *global* justice being the professed concern. As the making of global justice mainly takes place in the heartland of the European continent, it becomes somehow accepted, or normalized, that the *makers* of global justice also mainly originate from the European continent.

Things were different in Uganda: European and North American citizens were not in the majority. However, while most staff were Ugandan nationals, international human rights NGOs had 'expats' in charge ('expats' is generally shorthand for westerners). The presence of international staff was explained by reference to administrative and technical *expertise*. Locals, on the other hand, were seen as crucial for *communicating* with recipient communities. The ICC outreach officer confirmed. 'The presence of local staff is extremely important. There is a big need for local staff to explain what is going on. International staff is here too. They are also needed—as figureheads, and to administer internationally and so on.' Local staff are thus important for building credibility and local legitimacy whereas international staff are important for their expertise in the subject at hand. In The Hague, the dominance of EU citizens is explained and in part made 'natural' by virtue of its geographical location; in Uganda and presumably in other situation countries, local and national staff are considered necessary for the implementation of international criminal justice. This begs the question whether the politics of presence is recognized in situation countries in part to affirm the politics of ideas constituted in The Hague, the centre of international justice-making. Generally, in both contexts, the global justice expert seems to hold a western passport.

Transnational mobility as capital

The majority of the NGO representatives in The Hague are what is popularly described as 'third culture kids', that is, individuals who have grown up outside their parents' cultures and lived and studied in multiple countries (Pollock and Van Reken, 2001). High mobility has been part of their lives for shorter or longer periods, and for some, for their entire childhoods: they have moved countries every two years or so because of their parents' belonging to a class of mobile western professionals. People's attachment to nation and locality are ways in which cosmopolitan orientations can be operationalized (Roudometof, 2005). It is therefore interesting to observe how some of my informants talked about 'home', often employing the functionalistic term 'base', or the more unflattering metaphor of getting 'anchored' as expressions of the notion of staying in one place. On the subject of how transnational and mobile backgrounds have played into contemporary lifestyle choices, one of my informants said:

> I always think that I have a lot broader outlook than most of my friends—and I'm not saying it is a bad thing but obviously I've moved houses about 18 times in my life; I've lived all over Europe, I've spent summers working in America, I've spent other years working in New Zealand, I've worked all over, and I don't know, I think that's partly what it was. The idea of sitting in an office in a little town in England just filled me with dread.

Almost all of the international justice advocates are graduates in international law or international relations, or a combination of the two. High-end schools such as Sciences Po in France or Yale in the US are not uncommon. Their transnational experience while growing up and getting a university degree (or two or three) thus serves as an example of how modern mobility functions as a stratifying concept in the global order (Aas, 2007): for advocates of international criminal justice, their 'third culture' backgrounds confirm their membership to a class of hyper-mobile global professionals. However, as much as mobility becomes an important signifier of 'being' cosmopolitan, in the field of international criminal justice, it is also coupled with legitimacy to speak for the global. Consider the following NGO representative:

> Out of me and my NGO colleagues, I'm the person who travels more than all of them. They can do their engagements about the Court's budget, about this and that, but when I go to Africa, I bring views from the continent. And when we sit in meetings and the Court says one thing, I'm able to sit there and say 'Hey, I was in Côte D'Ivoire last week'. I bring in news from the ground, and I say, 'Hey, I was in Kenya, this is what is happening'.

Even among colleagues, mobility serves a stratifying purpose. Travelling is associated with local knowledge, and therefore the right to speak. Another NGO representative elaborated:

> I've been to Uganda twice this year, Ivory Coast twice, probably going to Congo or the Central African Republic by the end of the year. It's not just based on books or what you read, you actually meet the people, you work directly with victims so you really get both sides—it's kind of a bridge, we're basically trying to bring the voice of the ground to the Court and from the Court to the ground.

Travel and personal encounters are not only identified with a heightened expertise and increased entitlement to speak for the global, but is ultimately imagined as constitutive of a global *connection*: through her travels, she connects the global with the local, the Court with the victim and vice versa. Importantly however, it is not Ugandans connecting the victims with the Court, but predominantly western advocates of international criminal justice who have *been* there.

Career Trajectories: Global Justice-Making as Industry

As mentioned previously, the advocates of international criminal justice in The Hague are very diverse. While individuals such as Bill Pace and Richard Dicker belong to the top end of NGO professionals, the discussion above shows how the field is also full of interns and others in junior positions, many of whom hope to advance in the field of international criminal justice. While the average age of the Coalition Secretariat staff is approximately just under thirty, and working there is often considered the first *relevant* job for those working there, the international justice liaisons and senior counsel staff in the core human rights NGOs are generally older (in their late thirties and forties), hold more important positions and have more legal expertise. Nonetheless, despite belonging to a group of predominantly transnational western professionals, if the advocates of international criminal justice are compared to lawyers in other global cities—New York, London, Tokyo—advocates of global justice are by no means *global elites,* although they certainly do contribute to transnational network governance. Particularly for Coalition Secretariat staff and the younger professionals in the field, international justice advocacy seems fuelled by pragmatism as much as ideology. Perhaps due to the high competition for jobs in international criminal justice, and the lack of job security in a financial crisis-stricken EU and The Netherlands in particular, some of the younger advocates did not aspire to work on the NGO side of international criminal justice specifically, but rather 'fell into it', often due to practicalities. As one representative said:

> I just saw an advertisement for this internship position on one of the websites of the university ... I had no idea about how NGOs work and even that they had such a big influence, and I thought it could be an interesting angle—and also because internship applications at the ICC, they take six months to get back to you, and I thought I don't want to do that.

As work in the NGO sector is still considered 'relevant' and 'work experience', the motivational factor may not be found in advocacy for international justice at all, or in an ethos or a calling to end impunity, but rather in a much more mundane and sober interest in the field, whether legal, political, or social. Working as advocates for international criminal justice is first and foremost working *on* international criminal justice. This is a reminder of how, while moral sensibilities are basic to the project of global justice-making, international criminal justice has also become an industry. Many of my informants expressed gratitude and considered themselves lucky to have a job at all.

At the time of research, job opportunities in international criminal justice were becoming scarce: The ad hoc tribunals were winding down, which meant that many international justice professionals would be out of a job (Christensen, 2015b). This raised the question of where the international criminal justice professionals would go, and if they would be able to create a demand for their skills in other fields. In Chapter 7, I return to this topic, as I relate the notion of 'positive complementarity' as part of opening up a market for international justice expertise in rule of law development at the domestic level. However, it is interesting to consider how these dynamics affects the NGO sector, and more generally, the mobilization of international criminal justice advocates. One of my informants who had worked in the field for over a decade explained that 'One of the things that attracted me to the field was that there was so much to do! It was so new!' Graduating with a topical master thesis on victims' rights in international criminal law or the equivalent, the field's newness added to this informant's sense of purpose: a sense of *making* international justice. The strengthening of human rights through international justice mechanisms and the establishment of the ICC created a market for young and ambitious mobile western professionals seeking not just to get a job but also to specialize. A question thus remains whether the lack of job opportunities in international criminal justice will influence this sense of purpose and ambition, or the attractiveness of the field. In Chapter 2, I described how the ICC field office's downscaling in Uganda resulted in a spill over into the NGO sector. Will there be a similar dynamic in The Hague whereby professionals from the tribunals move into lower paid jobs in the NGO sector?

Revolving doors and identity-switching

For many NGO representatives, human rights advocacy on international justice is considered highly relevant work for graduates in international law and relations, a view confirmed by the ICC, who often recruit from the NGO sector. A number of former employees from the Coalition Secretariat had 'moved on' to the ICC, and several Coalition staff members admitted that the Court was a viable 'way forward' for them. The expertise of the international justice advocate is, after all, international criminal justice.

There is thus a considerable 'revolving door' dynamic within international criminal justice, which means that the same people may occupy different positions in the field at different times. This phenomenon is already apparent at the entry level, with so-called 'intern rounds', that is, people interning with different courts and organizations in The Hague, or with the international criminal tribunals in Arusha and Phnom Penh. Many of the advocates of international criminal justice have therefore previously held internships at the ICC or in one of the other tribunals. Some have also had short-term contracts at the international criminal courts before joining an NGO. As a result, advocates of international criminal justice are significantly socialized into the field from early on, gaining not only an overview of who's who, but also a network with which to cooperate and draw on later in their careers.

The revolving door phenomenon in international criminal justice extends well beyond what Baylis (2009) has referred to as 'tribunal hopping' as it is not uncommon for professionals in international criminal justice to engage in 'identity-switching' between practitioner (court officials), academic (writing scientific articles, holding academic positions), policy work (for international organizations, NGOs or states) and activist (through NGOs). For example, during the ICC negotiations, the aforementioned Professor M. Cherif Bassiouni held positions as president of the *Association Internationale de Droit Pénale* (NGO), vice chair of the Preparatory Committee and Chair of the Drafting Committee in Rome (government), leader of the Egyptian Delegation to the Preparatory Committee and to Rome (government), chair of the UN commission of inquiry on crimes in the former Yugoslavia (international organization), and president of the International Institute of Higher Studies in Criminal Science in Sicily, Italy (academic) (Glasius, 2002).

Besides building networks, through identity-switching, professionals may be able to draw on knowledge derived from one 'identity' as a means to increase their position in another 'identity', thereby asserting themselves as people who 'know well' across the field:

> For example, if this professional is involved in the determination of policy for an international organization, she may be able to use her relations within the different network domains to make claims to knowing well that favour her particular view of policy. Better still, she may persuade professionals across the network domains that she knows well and that her views should be adopted by all concerned. (Seabrooke, 2014b: 336)

The use of NGO representatives as Special Advisors to the ICC, such as the Women's Initiative for Gender Justice's executive director Birgid Inder, is an illustration of how international justice advocates may be able to perform this role in international criminal justice, with Inder positioned as a 'gender expert' in global justice-making.

The revolving door phenomenon is not uncommon among transnational professionals. Unlike domestic fields where power and epistemic authority is more institutionalized (and more embedded in processes of state-building), professionals in transnational fields are able to draw on and exploit opportunities *between* different domains of knowledge. They may occupy what is referred to as *interstitial* positions (Vauchez, 2011), or structural holes, 'missing relationships between nodes in a network, unmade possible ties, which inhibit flows of information' (Seabrooke, 2014a: 51). In this manner, 'the transnational' becomes a particular space of political engagement, and transnational authority a form of symbolic capital structuring the field. That advocates of international criminal justice are able to switch positions within the field can thus be seen as their engaging in a form of transnational issue professionalization.

Nevertheless, and as with previous discussions on budget (Chapter 3), one can ask whether these close affiliations between the Court and the NGOs risk undermining the NGOs' ability to critically monitor the Court from the position of outsiders. It is unclear how far it is a deliberate court strategy to co-opt the NGOs in order to silence critical voices. However, speculations abound in the field, for instance concerning ICC's hiring of Brigid Inder as Chief Prosecutor Bensouda's Special Advisor on Gender. In some respects, what follows from this discussion on the entrenchment of NGOs in the professional field of international criminal justice is the question of how not only advocacy, but their roles as critical monitors of global justice-making are affected by the fact that the ICC is a former or potential future employer.

The ICC vs. the NGOs

My NGO informants identify a number of interesting differences between working in the NGO sector and working in the ICC. For example, 'real lawyers' with a higher level of legal expertise fill legal officer positions at the ICC. At the ICC, staff also make significantly more money. However, work there is not considered as 'stimulating'. In the NGO sector, there is a sense of 'no two days being the same' and work being much more variable—much more fun. As an NGO representative, one is able to access high-level people, arguably achieving a level of influence much quicker than if one worked at the ICC. An NGO representative explained:

A large part of why I also love my job is because I am 27, and doing things I almost shouldn't be doing at my age … I am meeting people who work in the Court who are really influential in drafting things, and I am working with human rights activists and we're actually working on those things. I know a lot of people my age and if I compare it, even if they are doing international (work), at the ICC, they just sit in an office doing a little project. I'm addressing The Hague Working Group.

What is expressed is a sense of recognition gained from working in the NGO sector, a feeling that individual influence and importance is greater if you work in the NGO sector rather than at the ICC. I ask whether work in the ICC is still attractive.

I couldn't go into a job at the (same) level of influence. I don't think I can be a legal officer at the ICC anyway; I haven't reached that level of legal scholarship to be able to do that. I'd go in at the very lowest level, and I don't think what I would be doing would be as interesting. I don't think it would be as stimulating, the job wouldn't be as changeable—I wouldn't meet the people, the people that you meet here are great. One thing you get if you work there is great money, and it is still interesting work, but if you work in civil society, if you work here, you don't make great money but the job you do … I genuinely enjoy it, I really landed on my feet with the job because I am very much a people person. I just naturally form rapport with most people—diplomats, ambassadors, down to anybody.

On the one hand, the NGO track enables quicker access to high-level influence and recognition; on the other, there might be lower standards of legal expertise than there would be if they were not representing civil society. Instead, the NGO lobbyists have a more generalized expertise, where their function, *namely that of NGO representatives* cannot be undermined: as representatives of global civil society, the 'people', affected communities, and even victims of international crimes, they can claim both moral *and* legal expert authority.

For others, prior experiences working at the ICC have made them more inclined to work on international criminal justice from what they consider 'outside' the system. One of my informants who had worked with victim representation at the Court, expressed profound disappointments over experiences that had made her question her engagements with international criminal justice altogether. She explained that at the ICC

> There is this sense of being in a bubble: very distant from the field, very distant from the realities of the field. And for me, having worked with NGOs and being in that relationship with local organizations, I was so puzzled. You know, having to explain (to the Court) why we needed to have people in Kenya! … I would rather become a cashier at Albert Hein (Dutch convenience store) than to work with the Registry again.

Others too were reluctant to return to the ICC, with expressions such as 'now that I've seen what it's like'. A related perception of work in the NGO sector is that it gives them a freer role from which they can monitor and comment on the direction of international criminal justice. Working in the NGO sector is perceived as a way to stay involved with ICC issues, yet from 'outside' the system. An NGO representative explained: 'When you're inside an institution, whether it is psychological or whatever, you're going to be less critical. You're *in* it … It's always good to have an outside view. I've worked in the Court, by the way. I worked there for a year and a half.' Here, the NGO position is considered a strength precisely because it is seen as having outsider status. From this perspective, criticism of the Court is considered important because NGOs are imagined as being an external partner in the development of international justice. This is an example of how the moral authority of NGOs is closely connected with a claim to outsider status—they see themselves as external and expert commentators—as this type of authority and influence is dependent on their role as providers of objective knowledge (Price, 2003). At the same time, her statement vividly illustrates the revolving door dynamic of the field; she can hardly be seen as an outsider to the ICC, having worked there for more than a year, and having access to former colleagues in her contemporary position as an NGO representative.

Conclusions

This chapter has explored international criminal justice as a transnational field of practice, and examined the kinds of people inhabiting it; in short, inquiring into *who* has access to global justice-making. It conceptualizes agents working in international criminal justice NGOs as global moral entrepreneurs and shows how they use humanist discourses to promote criminal global justice-making through law, turning them into advocates of international criminal justice. In the second part of the chapter, I make two central claims, namely that advocates of international criminal justice are deeply entrenched within the field of international criminal justice itself, and that these advocates—as professionals in the field generally—originate from a class of transnational western professionals.

These findings have implications for a number of assumptions about the making of global justice. First, there is a discrepancy between international criminal justice's global claims, and its lack of geographical representation, which appears, at least to some extent, justified by the ICC's geographical location in The Hague. Second, human rights NGOs' claim to moral authority through their 'outsider' position seems more and more open to question. The advocates for international criminal justice must therefore continuously navigate the line between being 'inside' and 'outside'; on the one hand, to be close enough to be taken seriously as experts, and on the other, distant enough to be able to offer an 'external' perspective based on their moral authority. This animates a question whether global justice-making through the ICC is an NGO project in the first place or whether the NGOs are co-opted by the ICC.

Having situated the presence of where, how, and who of the purported global civil society in global criminal justice-making, my concern in the coming chapters are now with the assumptions, discourses, and imaginations that give force to this cosmopolitan penality. How do human rights NGOs as penal actors contribute to the imaginary and global travel of criminal justice and penal values?

5

Penal Imaginations of Global Justice-Making

Rwanda, March 2013:

I am at Mpanga prison in the Southern District, the largest prison complex in Rwanda. I am here with a group of people, about 20 of us, mostly Europeans, on a study tour of transitional justice. We are graduate students, professors, civil servants and teachers, women and men, travelling around the country to talk to and learn from people in high and low places. How is Rwanda as a nation—and as a people—moving on after the atrocious events in 1994?

Mpanga's Deputy Director has welcomed us into a meeting room. Sitting on long wooden benches in front of him, we listen as he gives us the administrative facts in Kinyarwanda. Our group leader translates: We are told Mpanga houses approximately 7500 inmates, who are mostly *genocidaires*: those convicted for participation in the genocide. These are housed in the Golf Wing; ordinary criminals in Romeo; females—ordinary and *genocidaires*—in Juliet. The Delta Wing is for foreigners, we are told: Eight Sierra Leoneans convicted of war crimes and crimes against humanity by the Special Court.

We visit the Golf Wing first. We learn that there are currently 5916 male *genocidaires* detained here, some of who are out working in the neighbouring fields or on the roads. Preceded by the Deputy, and one or two armed guards, we enter a massive compound. We are guided up some stairs and onto a gallery overlooking an open space that must be as big as a football field. Groups of men in red and pink robes are crowded everywhere—standing, sitting, in the open yard, on the stairs, throughout the gallery. Some look at us. Most mind their own business, playing cards, talking, going about with their everyday lives. I don't know how many groups like us visit, but since this is Rwanda's finest prison

Advocates of Humanity. Kjersti Lohne, Oxford University Press (2019). © Kjersti Lohne.
DOI: 10.1093/oso/9780198818748.003.0005

complex, I'm sure it's quite a few. Our intrusion into what remains of their privacy is deepened as we are seated down at the short end of the gallery, visible to all, and all visible to us, the foreign prison visitors. We are then welcomed by singing, drumming and dancing robes in the yard. One of us, a Dutch professor, is asked to say a few words. As he expresses our thanks through the microphone, one of the prisoners makes sure its cable is long enough, removing it gently from the feet of the Deputy. When the Deputy isn't speaking, he moves around, talking to prisoners, smiling, joking. There are barely any guards; if there are, they're invisible to me, hidden amid the thousands of robes covering the bodies of convicted *genocidaires*.

We walk out the same way we came in, across the gallery and down the stairs. We leave the compound and continue our visit to the Delta Wing, on the other side of the Mpanga complex. The Delta Wing is the UN-financed compound housing eight Sierra Leoneans, including Issa Sesay, the former leader of the rebel army Revolutionary United Front, infamous for their 'short sleeve/long sleeve' amputations. The UN finances the Wing because these individuals have been convicted by an international tribunal—the Special Court for Sierra Leone. They are serving their sentences here, on the other side of the African continent, because their own country does not have prisons meeting the international standards required for international convicts.

We have only walked a hundred meters or so, but entering the Delta Wing, we enter the international realm. Here, each prisoner has not only an individual cell, but two rooms at his disposal. Pictures of families are on the wall, and paper with scribbles and writing lies on their desks. They have their own chef—with separate kitchen and food storage. Everything is UN approved.

In the common room one of the prisoners is watching a football game. He's in his towel, apparently just out of the shower. Focusing on the game, eating an apple, he barely turns his head to watch us stroll past, in contrast with three other prisoners who are actively interacting with their visitors. As soon as we enter, two of them approach us, loudly lamenting their unlawful conviction and horrible treatment. They yell at the guards, and particularly at the Deputy, who brush them off. Can we notify Human Rights Watch? Can we pass on a letter to Amnesty? they ask us. A third prisoner is taking us around, showing us their cells and common

> rooms, talking about the absurdity of his conviction for acts that, after all, are what happen in war. He was unfortunate enough to be on the losing side. As we leave his prison and walk out onto their recreational football field, he shakes our hands.

Within the same prison complex, Mpanga prison presents us with two different penal materialities—one the 'national section' and the other the 'international section'. As such, it reveals some of the asymmetries and unevenness characterizing international criminal justice: how the master minds of mass violence are punished according to state-of-the-art international human rights standards, in contrast to the punishment imposed for 'ordinary men' and those further down the chain of command. This chapter delves further into such 'frictions' in international criminal justice by explicating the cosmopolitan penal imaginary animating it, and the consequences for 'justice' it generates.

After the Rwandan genocide in 1994, where an estimated 1 million people were massacred, and an equal number allegedly participated in the violence, the government pursued extensive prosecution and punishment of those involved. Five years after the genocide, approximately 125,000 people, roughly 10 per cent of Rwanda's adult male Hutu population, were detained in prisons designed to hold a maximum of 15,000 prisoners, leaving them 'hopelessly overcrowded' (Drumbl, 2000: 291). That same year, 3,000 prisoners died behind bars (Christie, 2004).[1] In addition, the number of cases not only created a huge backlog of cases in Rwanda's already strained criminal justice system, but led to compromises in criminal procedures and legal safeguards for those accused (Drumbl, 1997). While Rwanda pursued aggressive implementation of retributive justice, through the UN International Criminal Tribunal for Rwanda (ICTR), national prosecutions, and later through local *Gacaca* courts, Sierra Leone opted for a less comprehensive, but more familiar (and perhaps more viable), official response after the conflict occurring between 1991 and 2002: prosecution and punishment of *selected* individuals. A so-called 'hybrid' or 'internationalized' Special Court was set up, consisting of both international and national staff. In contrast

[1] As observed by Morrison (2005), had Rwanda's state-sponsored crimes been included in prison population rates, it would skew all criminological and penological analysis.

to the ICTR, which is located in Arusha, Tanzania, the Special Court for Sierra Leone is situated *in* Sierra Leone. For security reasons, however, eight of the nine men convicted by the court were transferred to the UN detention unit attached to Mpanga prison in 2010.[2] The Delta Wing at Mpanga is therefore one of three international detention units: apart from the ICTR detention unit in Tanzania, which ironically detains Rwandans, the third 'international prison' is located in Scheveningen on the outskirts of The Hague. Here, defendants from the International Criminal Tribunal for the former Yugoslavia (ICTY) and the International Criminal Court (ICC) are held, in addition to those already convicted who are waiting to be transferred to other countries.

While Rwanda exemplifies an exhaustive retributive approach to mass violence, and arguably at the expense of what many would consider basic human rights, retributive justice is core to the 'fight against impunity' movement, in which human rights non-governmental organizations (NGOs) are at the forefront. At the same time, human rights norms have also been key in setting standards for international imprisonment and sentencing (van Zyl Smit, 2005; Schabas, 1996). As these 'international standards' are often considered too luxurious—in the meaning of not being 'harsh' or 'punitive' enough in comparison with the relative standards of penal and non-penal materialities in the global South—these developments nonetheless illustrate that the human rights movement carry both punitive and non-punitive elements.[3]

As has been clear from previous chapters, the engagement of human rights NGOs with the ICC is no novelty, but rather a contemporary manifestation of a continued effort to hold individuals criminally and individually accountable for large-scale physical violence. Because of their embrace of the criminal justice system, they have become significant carriers of penal discourse. Yet why do the human rights NGOs embrace the criminal justice system as the proper way to 'deal' with conflict and mass violence? After all, as an enforcement tool, the system is not very successful. The vast majority of individuals involved in international crimes have not been held legally accountable, and most likely never will be. Even when, as is the case with the ICC, indictments and arrest warrants are sent out, enforcement is low, as the ICC is dependent on

[2] See http://www.rscsl.org/detention.html (accessed 13 November 2018).

[3] For a conceptual discussion on 'punitiveness', see Matthews (2005).

cooperation by states to carry out arrest warrants. International relations scholar Sikkink (2011: 20) has suggested that one 'key explanation for both the initial adoption and the spread of the criminal accountability model was that it was familiar and obvious to people from their experience with it domestically'. Yet, within criminology, it has become widely known general knowledge that punishment at the domestic level is '"irrational", "dysfunctional", and downright counter-productive' (Garland, 1990b: 4). How are we then to understand the extension of criminal accountability from the national to the international? What makes it 'the obvious' thing to do?

In putting sociology of punishment to work on international criminal justice, this chapter explicates the cosmopolitan penal imaginary, an imaginary crafted at the intersection of human rights sensibilities and criminal justice. In previous chapters, I focused on the situatedness of its advocates, whereas now I turn to the logics, values, and penal sensibilities embedded in the fight against impunity, increasingly framed as the 'fight for global justice'.[4] Moving from a position of scepticism towards the criminal justice system, the chapter's first part brings attention to how human rights NGOs have embraced criminal law as an instrument of human rights enforcement. This shift indicates a deep-seated conviction of the deterrent effects of the criminal justice system, which has manifested itself in a complete rejection of amnesties as a mechanism of transitional justice. As regards the situation in Uganda, international human rights NGOs have strongly opposed amnesties for crimes committed by the Lord's Resistance Army (LRA), despite the fact that local civil society groups initiated this. I then move on to discuss non-punitive elements of international criminal justice, and especially the lack of calls for punitive sanctions and higher sentences. It becomes clear that in the fight against impunity, the human rights movement brings with it particular ideas about punishment. For example, as foot soldiers of legalism, human rights NGOs express an extraordinary faith in the ability of criminal justice to achieve *social* justice. This is particularly noteworthy in light of the domestic penal imagination in the West that by and large has ceased to regard criminal justice as a tool of social engineering. As international criminal justice

[4] E.g. http://www.coalitionfortheicc.org/fight-global-justice (accessed 10 July 2018).

develops from the two philosophical currents of legalism and liberalism, both firmly situated within the legal structures of western societies (Drumbl, 2007), the domestic analogy is a useful one, albeit far from uncontested (e.g. Tallgren 2002). As regards their similarities and differences, the final part of the chapter applies and develops a sociology of punishment for international criminal justice further by a general yet analytical comparison of its patterns and tendencies compared with crime control and criminal justice in the West.

The Turn to Criminal Law

Philosophically, notions of human rights find their origins in natural law and the Age of Enlightenment, inspired by such figures as John Locke, Jean-Jacques Rousseau, and Immanuel Kant, and the idea that individuals simply by existing possess some absolute and inherent rights. The modern human rights movement, however, is commonly seen as dating from the 1970s and specifically the 1973 coup in Chile, which catalysed the growth of a transnational movement. In the bipolar and politically tense landscape of the Cold War, human rights offered a 'third way' of framing interests, rights, and politics that retained the language of universality. Following the Cold War, however, the field of international human rights expanded while becoming increasingly embedded in the liberal world order. It also professionalized. Amnesty International (AI), who in its early days primarily organized letter writing and public protests, now became part of a plethora of human rights organizations subject to increasing accountability, including employment law, management, and public relations.

Intrinsic to rights-claiming, law came to form the backbone of the development of the international field of human rights. As part of this, legalism, 'the ethical attitude that holds moral conduct to be a matter of rule following, and moral relationships to consist of duties and rights determined by rules' (Shklar, 1986: 1), became the dominant frame for making sense of injustice and human suffering, as well as human conduct in general. In addition to the allure of neutrality and universality, the force of law confers authority. As discussed in previous chapters, human rights NGOs claim, make use of, and exert considerable *legal* authority in their assistance, advocacy, and lobbyism. This not only indicates the professionalization and dominance of lawyers, but also suggests that the human rights movement is essentially 'driven by a lawyer's world view' (De Waal, 2003: 478). The normative diffusion of human rights in the form of proliferation of international human rights instruments—conventions, principles, and recommendations on the rights of victims and prisoners alike—is therefore not only the result of concerted transnational advocacy networks, but also reflects the emergence of a professional field of practice, replete with legal expertise, experts, and elites (Dezalay and Garth, 2006).

However, despite the development of an international human rights framework, a corresponding decline in human rights violations did not follow suit, and the lack of compliance was pinned on the lack of enforcement mechanisms. 'There were lots of rules, but they didn't have teeth' (Sikkink, 2011: 15). The criminal turn in human rights can thus partly be understood as a strategy of 'hardening' soft law (see generally Engle et al., 2016), offering a means to *enforce* human rights, as expressed here by one of my informants:

> We're trying to establish a system of international justice that makes it more likely that those that are responsible for human rights abuses will be held to account, and to give the human rights movement this enforcement tool that until 15 or 20 years ago it didn't have. We could name and shame human rights perpetrators, or governments that are (committing) human rights violations, but we didn't have available the ability to hold individuals criminally responsible... This is what we're trying to build up, this tool that is available to enforce human rights ... The enforcement is key to stopping new abuses, the enforcement is key to justice.

Besides rendering 'criminal justice' synonymous with 'justice', she highlights the forward-looking and utilitarian rationales ascribed to international criminal justice. Before elaborating on this consequentialist logic, it is worth pausing to consider that the turn to criminal law has required a significant adjustment of thinking for human rights organizations. In the early days of the movement, the criminal justice system was associated with repression—a system *inherently repressive* by nature due to its violent potential (Engle, 2012). Vis-à-vis states, the human rights focus has generally been on defendants' rights. Indeed, *amnesty* and the release of political prisoners were at the very core of Amnesty International's foundation in 1961. Now, however, amnesties are seen as *antithetical* to justice, because of a belief that they 'ingrain cultures of impunity', as put by several of my informants (see also Houge and Lohne, 2017). Thus, from a former position of scepticism, human rights NGOs have come to embrace the criminal justice system as a tool for the work of liberation and emancipation *from* repression. The case of Uganda is particularly illustrative in this respect, as the ICC's intervention in the country sparked the crucial and recurring debate on 'peace versus justice' in transitional justice settings, and the role of amnesties therein.

Punitive Forces of Human Rights: The Rejection of Amnesties

Amnesties exempt individuals from prosecutions and punishment, and have commonly been applied in state transition processes, whether so-called 'blanket' or unconditional, such as the self-made amnesties by military dictators in Latin America in the 1970s and 1980s, or as in South Africa, whose use of amnesty is best known, and where it was made conditional upon disclosure of the 'truth', and admission of individual guilt (Hayner, 2002; Gibson, 2005). Proponents of amnesties will generally point to the *realpolitik* of armed conflicts and political transitions, and the ways in which amnesties can 'bargain' atrocious actors out of powerful positions, and thereby effectively bring about peace in violent contexts. Others will claim that amnesties are a denial of justice, constituting legal amnesia and an obstruction to 'real' peace (see McEvoy and Mallinder, 2012).

In northern Uganda's protracted conflict, amnesties for rebels, most of whom are kidnapped child soldiers, have been framed as both an incentive for peace and an impediment to justice. These two opposite frames, however, have generally been voiced by what can be conceptualized as 'local' and 'global' voices. In 2000, the Ugandan government passed an Amnesty Act exempting LRA rebels from prosecution. The passing of the act was the result of a lengthy campaign by local civil society organizations, and in particular, the Acholi Religious Leaders Peace Initiative (ARLPI). ARLPI was formed in 1998, bringing together leaders in the north from the four major religious groups: Catholic, Anglican, Orthodox, and Muslim. In their report *Quest for Reconciliation*, they write: 'Not seeing an end to the war in sight and having witnessed that military action only exacerbated the suffering of the people, ARLPI began to advocate for the implementation of an amnesty act to work as an incentive for LRA combatants to defect' (ARLPI/Snowdon, 2008). As the Amnesty Act did indeed increase the numbers of defecting rebels, contributing to a substantial reduction of LRA forces (Agger, 2012), the ICC indictments were perceived as a 'big blow to the pursuit of peace for northern Uganda' (ARLPI/Snowdon, 2008). In an interview with a Gulu-based human rights NGO, the perception was still dominant that the ICC's involvement was an obstacle to peace in the region, rather than something that facilitated this.

The Amnesty Act—it got thousands of our people back every month! Once the ICC got involved, no one came. I said that the ICC only goes after the big five, but they (the LRA) don't know that! They told their own people that everybody would be slaughtered like chickens—that was the term they used—slaughtered like chickens. No, then they rather chose to fight and die.

In addition to pointing to the complexities of 'truths' in conflict situations, he still talked of the rebels as 'our people'. This conception was likewise reflected by Bishop Ochola from ARLPI, who stated that 'Justice is achieved when an offender is not [*sic*] viewed as the enemy' (ARLPI/Snowdon, 2008). In addition to offering incentives for the rebels to lay down their arms and return to their communities, ARLPI argued that to punish the rebels, who did not fight voluntarily but as a means to survival, would result in their double victimization.

International human rights NGOs, by contrast, adopted a prosecutorial approach. They dismissed amnesties on principle and supported the 'ICC track'. There were, of course, tensions. As explained by an international NGO representative, 'In Uganda it's tricky because many of the victims in the north are actually in favour of the amnesty. And because of the way we work, we would not want to go against what the victims say but we can't go against international law either.' Her reasoning illustrates the tension between their roles as representatives of victims' voices and their role as legal advocates, between their claims to both moral and legal authority. What do they do when international criminal law—the tool of human rights enforcement and the apex of global justice—is rejected by those in whose name justice is done? In managing this palpable tension between international law, which is their moral compass, and the political agency of those they aspire to help, it may seem as if the former takes precedence, as they 'would not want to' go against victims, but 'can't go against' international law. She further explained how they worked on this particular issue, bringing together a civil society group for a seminar on amnesty:

> We try to make them come up with a statement on what they think of the issue... It is a network, they're all based in the North, and working with victims. And it was very interesting because you can actually see after a while that while they don't agree whether there should be an amnesty, they kind of all agree that you shouldn't have amnesty for the most serious crimes... So you can help them frame that in a way that actually reflects what they want and what they say, but also explain to them what international (law) says, so that they can fit that in what they decide to come out with.

Human rights activists typically oppose amnesties for international crimes on the grounds that they are impermissible according to international law. However, there is no direct prohibition of amnesty in international law (McEvoy and Mallinder, 2012). Notwithstanding the object and purpose outlined in the Rome Statute's Preamble, 'there are several articles of the Rome Statute that might be read as permitting the Court under certain circumstances to recognize an amnesty exception to its jurisdiction,' leaving Scharf (1999: 522, 526) to conclude that the 'Rome Statute is purposely ambiguous on the question of whether the International Criminal Court should defer to such an amnesty-for-peace arrangement in deciding whether to exercise its jurisdiction'. Hence, the legal argumentation and reasoning of international human rights NGOs is worth particular attention; importantly, it is *their* interpretation of international law that is put forward in their advocacy.

AI's position is of particular interest, both for being a strong representative of the human rights movement generally, but also due to their aforementioned shift in perspective and approach towards criminal justice. Following the opening of ICC investigations in Uganda, they issued a press release stating that '[u]nder no circumstances should amnesty laws include crimes under international law,' and that 'Amnesty International opposes amnesties, pardons and similar measures of impunity for crimes under international law in all circumstances where they would prevent a judicial determination of guilt or innocence, the discovery of the truth or full reparations' (AI, 2004a: 2). In a report commenting on an agreement between the LRA and the Ugandan government on Accountability and Reconciliation resulting from peace negotiations, they reiterated their position four years later by stating that the

> Amnesty Act of 2000 is a serious barrier to accountability and justice to tens of thousands of victims of Uganda's conflict... Amnesty International has repeatedly called on Uganda to repeal the Act and revoke all amnesties granted to ensure justice, truth and reparations for all crimes under international law committed during the conflict. (AI, 2008: 21–2)

Not only does the organization oppose the use of amnesties, but they also advocate that Uganda should revoke those amnesties already granted to defected LRA rebels, as the agreement between the LRA and the Ugandan government 'severely undermines the commitment to accountability by exempting the more than 20,000 persons who have been granted amnesty' (AI, 2008: 21).[5] Human Rights Watch has taken a similarly punitive position towards post-conflict justice, both on specific cases such as the situation in Uganda, and generally, saying 'No Amnesty for Atrocities' (Human Rights Watch, 2010). It becomes clear that, in the fight against impunity, amnesties must be opposed. For Coalition representatives in The Hague, amnesties are presented as *intuitively* wrong, because they ingrain 'cultures of impunity': 'The idea is just unbearable; that you can do whatever you want, and just retire free... It is necessary for people to know that they can't commit crimes with total impunity.' It is a view presuming that: 'If the world can see that if you kill a thousand people—a million people—but you're let off, peace might come to the region, but in the future, someone else will do it... (Amnesties) ingrain a culture that you can get away with those crimes.'

These accounts underline the deterrent rationality embedded in the cosmopolitan penality: in order for war not to return, in order for people to be *deterred* from committing mass violence—to prevent 'someone else'—criminal punishment is considered not only justified but also imperative. Amnesties, by contrast, are seen as a cause of impunity, and therefore to be done away with so

[5] AI refers to the entire number of rebels granted amnesty under the Amnesty Act of 2000, not only LRA rebels, which make up a smaller portion than the number given here.

that justice may be done. In a public statement commenting on the peace talks between the LRA and the Ugandan government in 2006, AI writes that 'implications of amnesties are of course broader than legal issues. Without justice, the rights and needs of victims are often forgotten' (AI, 2006: 2). By justice, the organization means prosecutorial justice handed down by the criminal justice system, in effect excluding amnesties from the discourse on justice altogether by presenting them as diametrically opposed to 'justice'.

In Gulu however, NGOs painted a radically different picture of what 'justice' entails in ongoing armed conflicts:

> People were still being killed! One cannot talk about justice here as one can with courts in the West. This was different. Was this the right moment for justice? We worked for peace, and the ICC came in when peace talks were happening—the ICC spoiled the peace talks! This was an active conflict, and we believed that first and foremost we had to end that conflict. And the ICC's actions, the way they acted told us: nah, the killing can go on—it is justice we're after!

In view of the positioning on amnesties, and illustrated by the 'debate' on peace vs. justice in northern Uganda, international human rights NGOs embrace prosecutorial justice and the ICC. Through the fight against impunity, justice as expressed by prosecutions and punishment has become *the* expression of global justice, to the extent of crowding out other conceptions of justice, such as restorative justice, and, as most critically as expressed by informants in Uganda, ending ongoing violations (see also Nouwen and Werner, 2015b). It illustrates how the international field of human rights have come to embody punitive forces worthy of more critical attention by the sociology of punishment.

Non-punitive Forces of Human Rights

There are, however, other elements of the cosmopolitan penality that resonate much better with a view of human rights as a *non-punitive* force. Moving from the premise that prosecution and punishment are considered central to justice and social repair after mass violence, the *amount* of punishment, the length of sentences—remains noticeably 'limited' compared to that imposed by domestic justice systems, not least if the gravity of the crimes in question is taken into consideration. The ICC's maximum sentence is thirty years[6]—'a joke' according to my fellow (American) participants at a summer course on international criminal law in The Hague. The NGO community, however, has been remarkably silent on the issue, to the extent that my questions on punishment during interviews often appeared to startle my informants. One Coalition representative said that she had 'never thought of the ICC as a penal institution' and another confessed: 'I don't really have strong views on it.'

At the time of interviews, the ICC had achieved only one guilty conviction, which was often pointed to as an explanation for the lack of 'thinking' about the ICC's punishment. Many were unable to recall Lubanga's sentence of fourteen years, six of which had already been served (see Chapter 1). In discussing his sentence, one of my informants said that 'locking him up forever is not going to solve the problem,' and another admitted, 'you couldn't find any proportionate harm anyway—the death penalty not being an issue.' These two statements indicate some of the hybridity characterizing the ICC project: On the one hand, it is important to fight impunity and hold perpetrators accountable; on the other, they should be punished 'appropriately', that is, according to international standards and human rights.

Rather than his sentence, the *charges* brought against Lubanga attracted considerably more attention from the NGOs, concerned as they were with widening the scope of the charges, in order to have the Court recognize more people as judicial victims of the case. It was not the fact that Lubanga 'only' got fourteen years for conscripting and enlisting child soldiers that primarily affected the NGOs' engagement with the verdict; rather, it was concern about the fact that the Court had not paid attention to sexual violence, since this was not reflected in the charges against him. In the advocacy for justice for victims, it is the *legal recognition* of them in the charges brought against the defendant that becomes important, and not the demand for longer and more severe sentences. Prosecution is more important than punishment; judicial recognition of victimhood takes precedence over moral calls for revenge.

This view resonates with seeing international criminal trials as fulfilling objectives of transitional justice. In the transitional

[6] According to Article 77.1(b) of the Rome Statute, the Court may impose a life sentence in exceptional circumstances.

justice literature, criminal trials in response to mass violence is commonly justified by a need to establish the truth of events, rather than passing judgment on individuals per se (Akhavan, 1998; Fletcher and Weinstein, 2002; generally, see Minow, 1998; Teitel, 2000). This reasoning is also prevalent among NGO advocates in international criminal justice. A Coalition representative, for example, said the following:

> [The ICC] is a rule of law institution. At the end of the day, it is about punishing, but if you put it like that, you can say that the ICC is an institution to punish. And it's not. It's an institution to establish what happened. And who did it. If they can't, then someone is acquitted, and if they can, then that person is convicted. But it's not there to punish. Its consequences will be that the person will be punished, but it's a consequence.

Rather than a call for retribution, she ascribes the ICC in a broader societal and communicative role.

The 'human rights sensibility' is particularly discernible as regards the death penalty, which has been abandoned by the contemporary international penal regime. For example, the ICTR's exclusion of the death penalty was one of the reasons why the Rwandan government voted against the UN resolution establishing the tribunal. As lower-ranking perpetrators faced the possibility of capital punishment in Rwandan courts, the government thought that this would create penal disparity, since those in leadership positions facing trial at the ICTR would not (Akhavan, 1996). In contrast to human rights as a punitive force in the fight against impunity, this shows how human rights also function as a normative bulwark against penalties considered 'inhumane'. Although prosecution remains central to the ICC project, severe punishments do not.

If the ICC is not viewed as a penal institution among its NGO advocates, how, then, is it conceptualized? During fieldwork, I was intrigued by talk about international criminal justice being a 'social concept'. I asked a Coalition representative to elaborate on what he meant:

> It's hard to describe, I don't really know, but why is it that international criminal justice has developed into being this more of a role for NGOs than for perhaps any other body? Is it because NGOs put their foot in the door to start with? Maybe, as it's not the same in any other field. But, I think it's because justice is ultimately about and for victims, and ultimately for people. That is why people—and civil society as that embodiment—have such a vested interest in it, because ultimately international criminal justice is for them, and not so much for states and governments.

Another Coalition representative similarly expresses the view that 'international criminal justice is certainly more of a social concept. It is not a concept of armed force, which is a state concept. State security is more of state issue as opposed to a social and human [concept].' But what, I ask, does he mean by international criminal justice 'being' social? 'It is a social concept as it is more about people. It is more about protection of regular people. It is more about people ... compared with issues of international security, military interventionism, that sort of thing.' It appears that the referent unit in 'social justice' is conceptualized as individuals, or 'the people', rather than states, as it is the rights of individuals that are emphasized in social justice. International criminal justice, as social justice, is imagined as protection of these rights. In accounts of their motivations for working in the field of international criminal justice (see Chapter 4), NGO representatives also highlighted 'social justice'. They were interested in 'social justice issues' and this line of work emerged out of that motivation.

In light of the conceptual linkages between human rights and criminal justice outlined above, it becomes clear that human rights NGOs conceptualize international criminal justice as part of social justice-making, albeit on a universal scale, and hence, dressed in cosmopolitan clothing. In subsequent chapters this claim is further elaborated, particularly in Chapter 7, where I discuss how the Rome Statute system of justice is put to work by human rights NGOs as a tool in the development of domestic criminal justice systems. Before doing so, however, it is important to further dissect the cosmopolitan penal imaginary constitutive of global justice-making.

The Cosmopolitan Penal Imaginary

Several scholars have noted the lack of attention to penological thinking at the international level (e.g. Tallgren, 2002; Holá and van Wijk, 2014). International criminal justice, 'when deconstructed, truly does not have its own theoretical foundations' (Drumbl, 2003: 268) but is rather premised on the theoretical bedrock of ordinary crimes and domestic criminal law deeply embedded in western social and legal thought. As such, the criminal accountability model was not only 'familiar' and 'obvious' to the activist mentality (Sikkink, 2011), but relied upon a set of measures and morality already taken for granted with the workings of the nation state. However, while the domestic analogy is much debated in international criminal law (Tallgren, 2002), I will now consider some of the tensions inherent in the domestic analogy from a sociology of punishment perspective, examining international criminal justice as a particular site of crime control and penality. As such, it also connects with the debate prompted by Posner and Vermeule (2004) in their critique of transitional justice for overstating the exceptionality of the field, thereby denying the relevance of comparisons between regime transitions on the one hand, and the variety of transitions that occur in established democracies on the other. Social phenomena—whether the cause or response to violence—are seldom best approached as self-contained objects of study. However, in spite of their claim that 'legal and political transitions lie on a continuum, of which regime transitions are merely an endpoint' (2004: 763), their concern with justice—ordinary or otherwise—remain state-centric. International criminal justice, however, transcends the nation state framework, and as such disrupts the truism in political theory and criminology alike that the power to punish is the prerogative of the state (Zedner, 2016), compelling the need for a sociology of punishment for international criminal justice.

Offering an extensive diagnosis of late-modern penality, Garland's *The Culture of Control* (2001) is arguably the foremost contribution to a theoretical criminology of changing patterns of crime control in late-modern western societies since the 1970s (see also Feeley and Simon, 1992; O'Malley, 1999; Christie, 2000; Pratt, 2000; Simon, 2000). He describes and analyses changing and developing—albeit unstable and uneven—patterns and directions in crime policy. Against the background of *penal welfarism*, the penological project of 'civilization' and 'rationalization', the new terrain of crime policy is marked by a rise of punitiveness and a return to retributive rationalities, with an emphasis on the control, management, and incapacitation of 'risky' populations. There are, however, several caveats to Garland's analysis, among others the fact that his broad-brush interpretations are based on the US and the UK, both of which are relatively more punitive in their approach than many European countries (Cavadino and Dignan, 2006). How far his analysis of these two societies apply to crime policy outside the global North is, of course, yet another question. However, in order to identify patterns and trends, nuances and subtleties must necessarily give way to simplification; his analysis is intentionally general.

As such, it offers a useful point of analytic departure for a sociology of punishment for international criminal justice.

The rehabilitative ideal

Garland (2001) identifies several indices of a move away from penal welfarism. A strong yet uneven force is the decline of the rehabilitative ideal of punishment. While rehabilitation programmes still exist, and the ideal still has traction, particularly in Scandinavia (Pratt, 2008; Ugelvik and Dullum, 2011), it no longer claims to express the overall ideology of the penal system.

Rehabilitation of 'international criminals' has never been a dominant objective in international criminal justice. Deterrent justification of punishment is *general*, directed outwards towards an imagined global community, rather than being *specific*, that is, inward-looking and directed towards the perpetrator's prospects of rehabilitation. In fact, 'drafters of the tribunals' Statutes almost entirely neglected questions regarding the enforcement of sentences' (Holá and van Wijk, 2014: 8). One may of course interpret this historically because of the fact that the international regime emerged as a system of justice in the 1990s, when the rehabilitative ethos of criminal justice had already declined. Another explanation may be sought in the extraordinary nature of the crimes committed, and of the individuals held responsible, as the collective nature of international crimes brings into question any possible relevance of rehabilitation programmes. In research carried out by Holá and van Wijk (2014: 15) on the enforcement of 'international' sentences, they find that due to the 'character of international crimes, international convicts are often classified as "the worst criminals" by domestic authorities. In practice however, many of them are former politicians or military/state officials who according to our respondent [a former employee of the ICTY] pose no danger to society.'

Without commenting on the working practices found in this research, there is an absence, rather than a decline, of a rehabilitative ideal in international criminal justice. In any event, the lack of attention to the *content* of international punishment is noteworthy, together with trends outlined in the 'new penology' in late-modern societies (Feeley and Simon, 1992). Apart from the International Bar Association (IBA), no major human rights NGO is much concerned with the treatment of ICC detainees and convicts; rather, the International Committee of the Red Cross (ICRC) has signed an agreement with the Court giving the organization unrestricted access to ICC detainees on humanitarian grounds (ICC-PRES/02-01-06, 2006).

Punitive sanctions and expressive justice

Another current of late-modern penality is the re-emergence of punitive sanctions and expressive justice which is viewed as having 're-established the legitimacy of an explicitly retributive justice' (Garland, 2001: 9). Instead of being shaped by professional and expert knowledge, crime policy becomes an expression of presumed public sensibilities, where the language of condemnation and 'just deserts' has become legitimate. This is also reflected in normative theory, which increasingly emphasizes the communicative, expressive, and symbolic aspects of sanctions and punishment.

International criminal justice can be understood as part of the retributive and expressive turn; both rationalities surface as dominant factors in the field (Drumbl, 2007). However, as discussed above, calls for 'punitive' sanctions and more severe sentences are absent from The Hague and from human rights sensibilities in the field—absent are connotations of 'excess' punishment. The language of condemnation, however, is remarkably strong, with constant reference to the need to 'combat', 'fight', and 'end impunity' (Houge and Lohne, 2017). NGOs and the ICC alike invoke these objectives, indicating not only how the ICC project is conceived in absolute terms, but also how the Court and the NGOs are unitedly 'determined to put an end to impunity for the perpetrators of these crimes' (the Rome Statute's Preamble).

However, quite unlike the way 'penal populism' operates in the UK and the US, where punitive sanctions are seen as expressions of public sentiment (Pratt, 2007), it is the experts and professionals—here the ICC and the NGOs—that are the drivers of international punishment. One might object that it is precisely the NGOs that make up the 'global public' through their positioning as 'global civil society'; yet, as argued in this book, I position their role in international criminal justice much closer to that of the professional than to that of the lay person. In subsequent chapters, I demonstrate how an important part of this role is thus, in fact, to *generate* moral outrage, so that international criminal justice may impose punishment for breaches of our purported common moral order. In this way, international criminal justice both echoes the national, and departs from it. While it relies upon retributive and expressive undertones, it makes no appeal to punitive sensibilities: a fact that should be understood in the light of the close relation between international criminal justice and human rights NGOs.

Public emotions and representations of crime and criminals

As part of the re-emergence of punitive sensibilities, there are changes in the emotional tone of crime policies.

> Crime has been re-dramatized. The stock welfarist image of the delinquent as a disadvantaged, deserving, subject of need has now all but disappeared. Instead, the images conjured up to accompany new legislation tend to be stereotypical depictions of unruly youth, dangerous predators, and incorrigible career criminals. Accompanying these projected images, and in rhetorical response to them, the new discourse of crime policy consistently invokes an angry public, tired of living in fear, demanding strong measures of punishment and protection. The background affect of policy is now more frequently a collective anger and a righteous demand for retribution rather than a commitment to a just, socially engineered solution. (Garland, 2001: 10–11)

In late-modern societies, changing images of the 'criminal' is associated with shifting notions of the crime landscape: images of 'dangerous predators' feed a 'culture of fear' (Furedi, 2002), which again give rise to punitive sensibilities. This is in contrast to previous times when penal reforms were justified in a 'progressive sense of justice, an evocation of what "decency" and "humanity" required' (Garland, 2001: 10).

As regards international criminal justice, this plays out rather differently. First, there is indeed an image of ICC indictees as 'dangerous predators': being wanted or prosecuted by the ICC attaches a 'special stigma' (Mégret, 2015): such people are *hostes humani generis*—enemies of the human race, and hence, the quintessential Other. One of the major features of the 'new penology' is the image of crime as 'everywhere', random, pervasive, and ready to strike anyone at any time. However, rather than being in our midst, ready to strike anyone at any time, the crime landscape of international criminal justice is *differentiated*—it is the violence of African conflicts that is dealt with by the ICC. Rather than 'unruly youth' and risky populations *within* late-modern societies, the ICC criminal emerges from the 'global borderlands' (Duffield, 2001), the imagined geographical space where breakdown, brutality, and excess dominate. In this way, the representation of the African villain indicted by the ICC is one of someone totally outside society, reminiscent of Christie's portrayal of 'suitable enemies'—black against the (metaphorically) white victim: 'He is a dangerous man coming from far away. He is a human being close to not being one' (1986: 26). The LRA's Joseph Kony epitomizes this image of the African villain/warlord—of meaningless and barbaric brutality—of evil incarnate. A similar image is that of the despotic other, for instance embodied by Sudan's President al-Bashir, and most topically during my fieldwork, President Kenyatta of Kenya.

Yet rather than a 'collective anger', the background sensibility of international justice policy is collective moral outcry, a humanitarian impetus to 'do something' about distant suffering caused by distant others (Boltanski, 1999). There is a distinct dichotomy between the victim in need of international criminal justice and the criminal whose impunity make international criminal justice necessary, representations that function to 'corroborate cosmopolitan social narratives of legitimacy and illegitimacy, justice and progress' (Sagan, 2010: 9). Thus, while retributivism is central, there is a stronger commitment to 'socially engineered solutions'. As discussed in Chapter 7, the fight against impunity and the Rome Statute system of justice is associated with development of criminal justice systems and 'penal aid' (Brisson-Boivin and O'Connor, 2013) in the global South, a view of (international) criminal justice as incorporating a potential for social reform.

The centrality of the victim

As part of the resurfacing of public punitive sensibilities, Garland (2001: 11) also points to the 'remarkable return of the victim to centre stage in criminal justice policy'. In crime news reporting, stories have become victim-focused, and victims' interests and sensibilities are regularly invoked in support of punitive responses.

On the one hand, international criminal justice chimes very well with the domestic terrain of criminal policy wherein the victim now has a much more prominent role. The victim is indeed the figure in whose name international criminal justice is done, and a dominant representational figure in the fight against impunity (see Chapter 6). However, the cultural representation of victims in international criminal justice differs radically from that in late-modern western societies. While victims of crime in the global North have taken on a representational character, whose experience is put forward as everyday and collective rather than atypical and individual, victims of international crimes are distant and powerless, and their highly publicized images are part and parcel of the humanitarian communication that feeds the fight against impunity. Although the notion of victimhood is critical and routinely invoked in support of 'justice' at both the domestic and the international level, who and what are recognized within this category differs. As a result, the role of the victim at the domestic and international levels is necessarily different too. While the victim in the first case is a reminder of the unpredictability of ordinary crime, and thus serves the purposes of punitive force, the victim of extraordinary crimes represents the incredible and remote, a spectacle of humanity's suffering.

Importantly, the centrality of the victim to international criminal justice has some important implications for the defendant (Lohne, 2018a). The representational dichotomy between victim and criminal, distinct in domestic penality but absolute in its cosmopolitan manifestation, is one of the reasons why attention to victims and criminals in criminal justice systems often become caught in a 'zero-sum' game.

During conversations with a Norwegian state representative in The Hague, he emphasized the primacy of victims over defendants in international criminal justice, in contrast to how he perceived criminal justice systems in the Nordic countries: 'The criminal justice systems in the Nordic countries give more attention to perpetrators than victims. This is therefore a debate that we are familiar with—the call to make sure the criminal justice system is not overshadowed by concern for the defendant.' At the international level, however, and in the human rights imaginary, the victim occupies centre stage, with the effect that less attention is given to the perpetrator. There is a conspicuous lack of NGO attention to the rights of the defendant in international criminal law: in The Hague, *none* of the main human rights NGOs working on ICC issues focus specifically on defence issues. As an NGO informant explained, 'victims are much more interesting for NGOs,' since they are directly related to funding flows. In the moral economy of international justice, victims are the driving engine, just as they are the expressed *raison d'être* of human rights NGOs. Defence rights are simply 'not as sexy', explaining, plainly: 'This isn't for the perpetrator. It's for the victims' (Lohne, 2018a).

The focus on victims rather than perpetrators is not just a question of NGO resources and interests: defence rights are also considered a difficult topic to focus on vis-à-vis general public opinion. 'It's more difficult to come home and say "I'm going to represent Gbagbo" than to say "Hi, I found a job at ICC in Chambers",' she says. 'That's just how it is.' Apart from some slight attention by HRW, the organization that focuses primarily on defence rights in The Hague is the International Bar Association (IBA), a legal professionals association. Their representative explains:

There was an enormous gap in this area … (Defence rights) are not what many states and many people in this field want to focus on. Atrocity crimes bring a lot of emotion, and obviously, the first thing on people's minds are the victims, which is very understandable. Most NGOs in the field are looking at human rights and victims, making sure states are signing up, that arrests are happening. The train is always moving in that direction, and yes, fair trial rights do get lost in the shuttle.

The IBA's ICC programme is twofold. The first part of their mandate is to monitor the ICC as a legal institution and workplace, representing the 'global voice of the legal profession'. The second part of their mandate is geared towards advocacy and monitoring the ICC, as is the case for the other NGOs. However, in contrast to the 'fight against impunity' focus of human rights organizations, the IBA promotes a 'rule of law' focus, indicating an emerging distinction between human rights activism on the one hand, and rule of law on the other.

This separation can be seen to reflect an ambiguity concerning the type of 'justice' international criminal justice is imagined to provide (see also Sander, 2018). While legal professional associations emphasize the comparison with domestic systems of justice in terms of due process and the objectives of criminal law procedures, human rights NGOs appear to put a greater emphasis on international criminal justice *as part of transitional justice*, out of a desire that the criminal justice process should establish 'truth' and 'memory' and public recognition of suffering. However, where does one draw the line 'between impunity and show trials' (Koskenniemi, 2002a), or, rather, when does victims' justice become victors' justice?

The IBA's ICC programme comments critically on what they identify as 'legal lacunas' in the system (see also van Wijk, 2013;

Reijven and van Wijk, 2014). For instance, after Ngudjolo Chui was acquitted of all charges in the Court's second verdict, he applied for asylum, claiming he was unable to return to DRC for security reasons. At the time of research, he was awaiting the decision of a Dutch district court on his appeal. Spending the first months following his acquittal at Schiphol's immigration detention centre, he was then under the ICC's 'protection ... in a hotel in The Hague' (Lingsma, 2014). A representative from the IBA's ICC programme voiced her frustration regarding these developments:

> The Court hadn't imagined what would happen after someone was acquitted. They had only imagined what would happen if someone was found guilty, convicted. They hadn't imagined what would happen if witnesses claimed asylum, and what their legal status would be after finishing testifying if they were actually in detention.

What is referred to above as legal lacunas is in my view testament to a general lack of penal imagination in the international arena. In fact, acquittals have been a recurring headache—a 'forgotten party' (Henry, 2005)—particularly for those concerned with the principle of legality, and with the right to effective remedies at the international level. Of the ten people acquitted at the ICTR, nine still remain in the UN safe house in Arusha, unable to return to Rwanda because of security concerns, and unable to relocate to third countries because of, inter alia, the Refugee Convention which excludes individuals from protection if there are 'serious reasons for considering' they have committed war crimes (Heller, 2008; van Wijk, 2013). As is also the case with ICTY acquittals, compensation claims for time spent in detention (bearing in mind that it is not uncommon for trials to last a decade) have been rejected on the grounds that they 'might open the floodgates to an unmanageable host of compensation claims'.[7] As well as indicating serious legitimacy deficits in the legality and much vaunted rule of law of international criminal law, this also very much raises the question of what kind of justice is conceived of and administered by international criminal justice and its advocates. A question must be asked to what extent, if at all, has the prospect of acquittals been part of the penal imagination of international criminal justice.

[7] *Protais Zigiranyirazo v The Prosecutor*, Trial Chamber III, 'Decision on Protais Zigiranyirazo's Motion for Damages', Case no ICTR-200 1-01-073, 18 June 2012.

Punishment and politics

In his diagnosis of late-modern societies, Garland (2001: 13) sees a 'distinctly populist current in penal politics that denigrates expert and professional elites and claims the authority of "the people", of common sense, of "getting back to basics"'. This echoes what Pratt (2007) refers to as penal populism when describing penal policy driven by the pursuit of electoral votes rather than the reduction of crime and motives associated with penal welfarism, thereby further entrenching the relationship between punishment and politics through a politicization of crime control.

When evaluating how international criminal justice resembles or departs from how populist currents drive crime policy in late-modern societies, it is imperative to consider the radically different political dynamics of domestic and international criminal justice. Crucially, international criminal justice is a criminal law without a state (Mégret, 2015): There are no electoral votes to pursue. International criminal justice has no self-evident sovereign or public constituency comparable to the citizens of a state that are the subjects of domestic criminal law. One interpretation of the legitimacy of international punishment rests on the presumed consent of ratifying states. However, this concerns the relationship of states in an international community of, namely, states: the relationship between individuals in an international 'community' are ignored—despite it being individual accountability that is at stake, and the international community constituting the punishing authority (Tallgren, 2002). Therefore, the 'sovereign' of international criminal justice—interchangeably embodied in notions of 'international community' or 'humanity'—as well as its 'constituency' has to be actively constructed in legitimation processes that far exceed its domestic counterparts (see Chapter 7). As Hoyle and Ullrich (2014: 700) observe,

> domestic criminal courts are rarely challenged on substantive grounds. It is not questioned whether these institutions should exist in the first place and what type of justice, if any, they bring to victims or society at large ... However, as a new and *sui generis* institution in the international arena, the ICC lack the habitual legitimacy and the established procedures concerning justice of domestic criminal courts.

What emerges into view is therefore international criminal justice's lack of political constituency, of 'supporting votes'.

Fundamentally, it is here that human rights NGOs play a fundamental role in constituting the Court's constituency. Yet, while human rights NGOs claim authority as representatives of 'the people' and 'global civil society', I have shown how, as far as the ICC is concerned, they should be regarded more as professionals, practitioners, and part of its epistemic community rather than as outsiders. Rather than a 'highly charged political discourse' of crime control (Garland, 2001: 13), theirs is a highly charged *moral* discourse on the humanitarian imperative to 'do something', this 'something' being to 'end', 'combat', and 'fight' impunity. Instead of a politicization of crime control within the national, it therefore appears to be a moralization of politics within the global, in which the language of crime and law comes to takes the place of the language of war and politics.

In the Netherlands I talked to an NGO representative who had been working and interning in The Hague for some time. We were at her place, talking about the ICC's standing in world politics:

> Every time a government is overthrown, the first thing that you say now is 'I want the former leaders to be tried before the ICC.' In a way it's recognition of a certain legitimacy. Like in CAR (Central African Republic) when the Bozizé government was overthrown last January, the first requirement for the peace talks was that Bozizé would be tried before the ICC.

In its early years, the ICC and the NGOs had to bring the existence of the Court to the attention of various audiences, but now the ICC is being invoked by a variety of actors in response to violence, injustice, and suffering. From police brutality on the streets of Kampala to protests in Oslo on behalf of the Tamils or the Palestinians, the ICC is being called upon to 'do justice'. One should be wary of giving this the same favourable interpretation as that of my informant, who saw it as a sign of the Court's legitimacy, but it certainly points to a recognition of the Court, and its perceived ability to apply leverage to and adjudicate political struggles (independent of its jurisdiction), transforming political claims into legal rulings. I would suggest that, without calling into question the claims of Palestinians, Tamils, or those subject to Ugandan police brutality, these calls for prosecutions in the immediate aftermath of political changes is also a way of criminalizing and depoliticizing political opponents.

Again, the case of Uganda may provide an illustration. When the ICC issued arrest warrants only for the LRA, and none for the crimes committed by government soldiers, an initial enthusiasm for international and external intervention rapidly cooled. In Gulu, I was told:

> When it became clear that it was de facto impunity for the government—that the Court would only go after the rebels—the (local) NGOs started this campaign called 'Justice for all'. The government reply was 'Nah, we're not against this. If there is documentation of crimes committed by the UDPF (government soldiers), send them to us. We'll handle the cases ourselves.' People realized that the government didn't want justice in northern Uganda, but help from the international community—the Court—to win the war.

What is presented here is a different narrative about the conflict than the one given in western media, by the Court, and not least by NGO advocacy campaigns such as Invisible Children's KONY2012 video (see Finnström, 2008). The narrative includes recurrent criticism of international criminal law for asserting, basically, winners' justice, a criticism also made by the convicted Sierra Leoneans at Mpanga. The narrative clearly illustrates the deeply political situations in which the ICC intervenes, and how the Court runs the risk of being instrumentalized.

Mindful of such dynamics, HRW has been critical of the Prosecutor's prosecutorial strategy, complaining that it has not given sufficient consideration to the *perception* of its work. Rather than pursuing prosecutions of the two or more sides to a conflict simultaneously, the Office of the Prosecutor (OTP) has adopted a sequential prosecutorial strategy, which means the Court becomes vulnerable to this type of criticism. A representative explains that 'In Uganda, what we've called on them to do is to explain what they've done, and I really think it's been far too long, and it doesn't get you very far to continue saying: "well, investigations are still open".' HRW has also been noticeably critical of the ICTR and the tribunal's failure to prosecute crimes allegedly committed by the Tutsi-dominated Rwandan Patriotic Front.[8] Because of the ICTR's one-sided prosecutions, her view is that 'the institution will probably not contribute what it could have to either justice

[8] For a sharp critique of HRW's 'discourse' in Rwanda, see former US diplomat Johnson (2013).

or reconciliation as a result. I don't think there's any question there, in my mind or in this organization's mind that those were crimes that should also have been tried by the ICTR.' I ask her to elaborate on seeking a balance that reflects the underlying pattern of the crimes committed in the conflict, which she identifies as critical: the gravity threshold that international courts and tribunals necessarily must pursue because of resource restraints, and the need to counter myths of collective innocence and guilt which make international justice vulnerable to the 'winners' justice' critique (Fletcher and Weinstein, 2002):

> I can imagine some situations at the ICC where the crimes on both sides are not of such magnitude that they don't have to go the ICC, but yeah, in most situations they do. Libya is a good example right now. We haven't called on the Prosecutor to take up rebel crimes, but we have called on her to watch and look closely.

As much as the ICC might have legitimized President Museveni's brutal military politics in the eyes of outsiders, who then also see the Court as dispensing winner's justice, such 'use' and subsequent criticism of the Court is arguably inevitable as long as it relies on cooperation with the state in question. Indeed, the Court essentially *needed* protection from the government to do its work in northern Uganda. The conflict was ongoing at the time of intervention, as has been the case in most situations in which the ICC has intervened. Thus, in most of the situations before the ICC, the Court has followed rather than opposed State power, meaning it has conducted prosecutions of political adversaries of sitting governments.

This was also how it seemed to members of the Ivorian diaspora following the proceedings against former Ivorian President Gbagbo at the ICC. Exchanging views on the proceedings at the end of the day, they asked me rhetorically why the sitting President Alassane Ouattara was not also in the dock, along with the former colonial power, France—*their* violence in the country was not on trial. For them, Gbagbo was the victim of a political show trial, winners' justice, and western justice. A different critique of the Court, though one which also charges it with neo-colonialism, maintains that the ICC is not necessarily criminalizing Africa, but rather censoring African governments by criminalizing 'non-western endorsed' political figures. Or, as has been argued as regards the situation in Uganda, that by referring the 'situation of the LRA' to the Court, the ICC is being used by State power to delegitimize political adversaries, and to legitimize military interventions (Branch, 2007; 2011). According to Nouwen and Werner (2010: 949):

> The Ugandan government thus redefined the conflict in northern Uganda in terms of international criminal law in order to use international criminal justice as another instrument to defeat its enemy. Following the Ugandan government's previous attempts to brand the LRA as 'irrational', 'religious fundamentalists', or 'terrorists', the ICC could brand the LRA as internationally wanted 'criminals'. The ICC could turn the LRA from enemies of the Ugandan government into enemies of the international community as a whole.

There is thus significantly different political dynamics at play, if one compares international and national criminal justice. Within this political landscape, human rights NGOs have a critical role in generating a constituency for international criminal justice, as its lack of 'statehood' means it has no political constituency of legal subjects. While the 'crime complex' is profoundly politicized at both levels, it appears that the populist current permeating the domestic crime discourses takes on the language of humanitarianism at the international level.

Conclusions

From a review of how international criminal justice compares to that on the national level, this chapter has begun to make sense of the cosmopolitan penal imaginary, which draws on but also, critically, departs from western domestic penality. In contrast to criminal justice in late-modern society, international criminal justice is imagined, above all, as a type of social justice, yet on a universal scale informed by cosmopolitan sensibilities.

The chapter began with a description of penal materialities at the Mpanga prison complex in Rwanda, which holds national prisoners convicted by national courts, and international prisoners convicted by an international court. Within the same prison complex, the Mpanga visit offered important glimpses into some of the asymmetries, seen here in the form of prison conditions, arising from the penal imagination of international criminal justice. International criminal justice cuts across a geography of inequalities, which becomes conspicuously apparent when comparing prison conditions and standards of living. It also becomes clear that those imagining what 'doing justice' entails—to the extent this *is* imagined at all—do not do so from the perspective of where the crimes took place, but from that of experts on how justice *ought* to be done, who are situated elsewhere. These are not criminological or 'penological' experts, but human rights experts: punishment is imagined from the human rights point of view. Furthermore, international criminal justice does not seem to have its own penal theory, relying instead on justifications and rationales from national systems and western liberal legalism in particular. International criminal justice has been spearheaded by human rights NGOs, not criminological and penological expertise.

In the embrace of criminal law, human rights NGOs have moved from a position of scepticism regarding criminal justice to essentially viewing criminal law as a tool of human rights enforcement. Discussing how human rights NGOs approach amnesties in transition processes, and using Uganda as an example of such categorical opposition, it is shown how human rights carry punitive forces, which stood in opposition to the views and voices of civil society groups in northern Uganda where the violent conflict took place. Compared to a 'pure' retributive rationale however, international criminal justice is characterized by human rights sensibilities that also function as punitive restraints. Retributive and prosecutorial justice can therefore be seen as an explicit and deeply moralistic element in how global justice-making is imagined. Animating the cosmopolitan penality, human rights, simultaneously, engage both punitive and non-punitive forces. In contrast to 'just deserts' and cries for harsher sentences—expressions of punitive populism in western domestic penality—international sentences are neither punitive nor severe; in fact, it seems sentences are barely on the agenda at all. Moreover, none of the major human rights NGOs focuses on defence issues, indicating a lack of penal imagination in the field generally. Rather than being 'hard' justice, international criminal justice is imagined as social justice—as a social project of civilization and development.

This brings us to a critical juncture in this fleshing out of cosmopolitan penality: Compared to the national terrain of crime control and policy in late-modern societies, the penal imagination demonstrates a remarkable faith in the utilitarian and transformative effects of criminal law and punishment. In contrast to the return of retributive sentiments nationally, internationally, there is a significant unsettling of the traditional retributive paradigm (Hoyle and Ullrich, 2014). The next chapter therefore turns to how international criminal justice is conceptualized as 'victims' justice', before moving on in Chapter 7 to show how the Rome Statute system of justice is implemented as a deliberate and engaged process of social engineering in contexts of failed justice in the global South. However, this chapter has shown how the penal imaginary driving the project of global justice-making through international criminal justice is characterized by hybridity and tension, between punitivism and non-punitivism, human rights and the rule of law, and, not least, between the national and international, local and global.

6

Victimological Imaginations

From Criminal to Victims' Justice

As is clear from the previous chapter on the cosmopolitan penal imaginary, the figure of the victim holds a particular role in international criminal justice. While the rise of victims' rights and a more prominent role of victims' advocates is familiar from western domestic criminal justice systems, this chapter demonstrates how 'victims' have come to animate the project of international criminal justice altogether, legitimating both the need for global justice intervention as well as those that advocate on their behalf.

Putting a victimological imagination to work on international criminal justice (see McGarry and Walklate, 2015), the chapter probes two lines of inquiry. The first part delves into how justice for victims is imagined in international criminal justice, focusing on a conspicuous discrepancy between the ideals of the International Criminal Court's (ICC) 'ground-breaking provisions' regarding victim participation and reparations, and their implementation in practice. For example, at the time of research only thirteen individuals had actually appeared in court, five of whose statements were later dismissed as unreliable (Kendall and Nouwen 2014). Albeit semi-independent from the ICC, the Trust Fund for Victims (TFV) also raises questions about the connections between criminal justice, development, and humanitarianism, and to what extent its activities contribute to 'juridify' humanitarian suffering and consolidate global victim hierarchies.

The second part focuses on the notion of victimhood in international criminal justice—of victims for justice—and situates victim imageries as a source of moral authority claimed in representational practices by both human rights NGOs and global justice-making generally. I argue that the figure of the victim is culturally represented through imaginations from the global North

Advocates of Humanity. Kjersti Lohne, Oxford University Press (2019). © Kjersti Lohne.
DOI: 10.1093/oso/9780198818748.003.0006

and becomes universalized as a symbol of 'humanity,' of which the gendered and racialized victim of sexual and gender-based violence (SGBV) provides a particularly powerful victim imagery. The image of the victim of international crimes is characterized by her essential 'otherness'; it is humanity that suffers. Yet, the kind of victim needed by international criminal justice disregards political subjectivity as the conflict is not only 'appropriated' by the state (Christie, 1977) but removed by the 'international community' altogether. A sociology of punishment for international criminal justice thus reveals how when disembedded from the nation state and its legitimacy, criminal justice and penal power seem especially justified by humanitarian reason (Lohne, 2018b).

Justice for Victims

In his inaugural lecture to the Centre of Criminological Studies at Sheffield University, Christie (1977: 7) made the following observations:

> The victim is a particularly heavy loser in this (criminal justice) situation. Not only has he suffered, lost materially or become hurt, physically or otherwise. And not only does the state take the compensation. *But above all he has lost participation in his own case.* It is the Crown that comes into the spotlight, not the victim. It is the Crown that describes the losses, not the victim. It is the Crown that appears in the newspaper, very seldom the victim. It is the Crown that gets a chance to talk to the offender, and neither the Crown nor the offender are particularly interested in carrying on that conversation.

In later decades, the figure of the victim has become a dominant reference point in discourses on crime and punishment (McGarry and Walklate, 2015), and there has been increasing recognition of 'victimhood' through material structures of law and justice-making, as victims' rights are now invoked, recognized, and codified in national, regional, and international legal instruments. Of particular importance has been the UN 1985 Declaration of Basic Principles of Justice for Victims of Crime and Abuse of Power, which deals with the rights of victims to access, participation, and reparation vis-à-vis the *domestic* criminal justice system. Focusing on victims of *international* crimes, the UN Basic Principles and Guidelines on the Right to a Remedy and Reparation for Victims of Gross Violations of International Human Rights Law and Serious

Violations of International Humanitarian Law was adopted in 2005. Restorative Justice initiatives have been developing in parallel, and codified, for example, in the UN Basic Principles on the Use of Restorative Justice Programmes in Criminal Matters, adopted in 2002. Alongside the development of 'soft law' instruments, criminal justice systems have also increasingly seen the emergence of policies such as 'victim impact statements' and adoption of legislation referring explicitly to the suffering of victims, such as Megan's Law in the US and Sarah's Law in the UK (Griffin and Blacker, 2010).

Underpinning this recognition is the development of a victims' movement operating at both domestic and international levels, organizing to provide services, and to advocate and lobby for legal and institutional change. Emanating from social movements developing in the late 1960s in the US and UK, victims' organizations have become increasingly prominent since the 1990s, with examples such as Victim Support in England & Wales and the European Forum for Victim Services (Williams and Goodman, 2007).

As regards the ICC, the strengthened status of victims before the Court is widely accredited to the work of NGOs (Wemmers, 2009). At the Rome Conference, victims' rights were at the top of many of the NGOs' agendas, uniting under the Victims' Rights Working Group (VRWG). Today, the VRWG remains the largest 'coalition within the coalition' of NGOs advocating for international criminal justice.

According to legal professionals, the ICC provides the most important recognition of the victim as a subject of international criminal law, with provisions regarding rights for victims of international crimes *as victims* celebrated as one of the main innovations of the Court (Bassiouni, 2006). The Rome Statute and Rules of Procedure and Evidence recognize and outline principles of (i) victim participation in court proceedings, (ii) protection of victims and witnesses during proceedings, (iii) rights to compensation or reparations, and of (iv) the creation of the TFV from which reparations may be made. In practice, however, things have been different. The implementation of victims' rights at the ICC has remained unclear and ad hoc, with procedures varying from situation to situation. The participation regime has been subject to continued advocacy and critique (Pena and Carayon, 2013), for example for its complicated application process (Pena, 2009), the limited capacity of victims to influence the charges and scope of cases (Ferstman, 2012), and for the failure of ICC personnel to properly consult victims in the process (Wemmers, 2010). Most critically, the implementation of victims' rights at the ICC has been criticized for proceeding by 'trial and error', and of being constitutive of 'experimenting laboratories' (McGonigle Leyh, 2012: 407).

Nonetheless, the unsettling of the retributive paradigm in (international) criminal justice has led to a 'proliferation of different concepts of justice in a contested justice making process at the Court' (Hoyle and Ullrich, 2014: 684), with different 'justice deliverables' claimed by different stakeholders in international criminal justice. The Court itself, for instance, posits that it is 'this balance between retributive and restorative justice that will enable the ICC to not only bring criminals to justice but also to help the victims themselves rebuild their lives'.[1] In what follows, I probe deeper into what 'kind' of justice the ICC is imagined to provide for victims of mass violence, along with the efforts of bringing them into effect.

Victim participation: promises and pitfalls

For the first time in international criminal law, the Rome Statute introduced the rights of victims to participate in judicial proceedings before the Court. To participate, persons fill out an application to the ICC's Registrar, and the application is transferred to the appropriate Chamber, which rules on who, when, and how participation will take place. Because of the large number of affected individuals, a common legal representative represents them, and can, subject to Chamber's approval, make opening and closing statements, participate in hearings, and question witnesses, experts, and defendants.

Victim participation is an important advocacy issue for most of the human rights NGOs, with the International Federation for Human Rights (FIDH) and REDRESS being particularly active. During fieldwork, a major concern among the NGOs was ensuring adequate funding to the legal aid programme. 'One of the main worries at the moment is that they are not trying to make

[1] See http://www.icc-cpi.int/en_menus/icc/structure%20of%20the%20court/victims/Pages/victims%20and%20witnesses.aspx (accessed 5 March 2015).

the system better; they are trying to make it cheaper!' explained an NGO representative. Another shared the concern:

> How to represent victims is being viewed from a purely budgetary perspective, like 'what's the way we can represent a thousand victims?' Our point of view is that it should be the other way around: What do victims need? And then look at how much it will cost and the most efficient way of doing that.

Unlike domestic systems of justice, the ICC has to negotiate its budget annually at the Assembly of States Parties (ASP) meetings. Hence, the legal aid programme has to demonstrate to the ASP how it contributes to the ICC's objectives. As discussed in Chapter 3, NGOs have a particular role in these budget negotiations, advocating for more funds for the ICC by citing the Court's growing number of investigations and prosecutions. Because the legal aid programme funds both victims and defendants' legal counsels and representatives, the budgetary discussion adds another dimension to a more familiar argument concerning the inclusion of victims in criminal justice proceedings—namely the extent to which victims' rights come at the expense of defendants' (Zappalà, 2010). Most human rights NGOs focus on the cost implications for the role of victims (e.g. FIDH and Carboni, 2012). Whereas human rights NGOs stand up for victims, defence rights—by all standards also *human* rights—are monitored by *rule of law* organizations, such as the International Bar Association (IBA) (see also Chapter 5). This separation among NGOs indicates a tension concerning what type of 'justice' international criminal justice is imagined to provide (Lohne, 2018a). While legal professionals' associations emphasize parallels with domestic systems of justice, focusing on the adjudicative roles and importance of due process, human rights NGOs ascribe the (international) criminal justice process with goals of establishing 'truth', 'memory', and public recognition of suffering, in short, to the socio-political goals of transitional justice (see also Sander, 2018). This latter view of justice is particularly discernible when probing why victim participation matters to human rights NGOs.

Imagining victim participation

Human rights NGOs see victim participation in the criminal justice process linked to process, rather than merely judgment. An informant explained that 'part of the reason we are pushing for participation so much is (because) we are strongly convinced that this in itself is a form of reparations to victims. The process is as important as the result,' she said, pointing out that 'if you involve them, if you consult them, if you give them a voice, then that process is reparative.' Through participation, the victim is not only 'accounted for' and 'recognized' by being able to have a say in the deliberations on justice, but the process is also considered *therapeutic* for victims. In recognition that prosecutorial and retributive justice is insufficient (Schabas, 2011; Pena and Carayon, 2013), the ICC is credited with integrating *restorative justice* in its proceedings, and what is more, of having a *transformative* potential, as suggested here by another NGO representative:

> You already have women willing to participate to the proceedings and facing their abusers when I am sure even a decade ago it was so taboo and so shameful to come forward as victims of rape and as victims of abuse. So now to see that they are coming forward and saying: 'I want to participate in the proceedings because these people caused me a great deal of harm that has impacted all my life.' I think that is the way the system goes down to the roots and to the field [ICC situation countries]. And not only that: it has empowered women, given them their dignity back to say 'well, you have taken my will away from me by raping me, but now I am here and I am going to stand in front of you and take my will back. And I will stand in front of you'. I think that is a great way to do it.

I asked whether all women should be allowed to participate.

> I definitely think that everybody, every victim should be allowed to speak and say what they have to. I think that is what they want also—that is why so many people turn to international justice. Like in the case of ICTY, the proceedings took so much time because there were so many victims who wanted to talk and say something. And I think yes, there should be. You can't say that international justice and especially the ICC is focusing on victims and that its primary goal is victims if you do not give victims a voice. There's no point.

However, contrary to the aspirations expressed here, victim participation at the ICC means *indirect* participation through legal representation, that is, a lawyer acting on their behalf. For most victims given status as 'participants', it is the voice of their legal representative that is heard—not theirs; their only contact with the Court will be through their legal representative. As Judge Van den Wyngaert (2011: 480) asserts, although 'it is theoretically possible for victims to appear individually, this would be totally impractical in view of the high number of victims'. For example, the common legal representative appointed to the Kenyatta case in the Kenya situation was estimated to 'speak for' approximately 20,000 victims (The Hague Trials Kenya, 2014). As Kendall and Nouwen (2014) observe, direct participation is very rare: only thirteen victims had appeared in Court at the time, five of whose statements were later dismissed as unreliable.

The distinction between direct and indirect participation, however, is a meaningful one: especially if one recalls previous arguments on the recognition of victims' experiences and political agency *as* restorative, as having a legal representative 'speak for' victims essentially reduces their 'views and concerns' into a legal argument. Through indirect participation, another principle of restorative justice is neglected, namely the meeting of 'victim' and 'perpetrator'. This space for dialogue, which is at the core of restorative justice, is absent from proceedings at the ICC (but see Hoyle, 2011).

Besides the anticipated benefits participation may have on victims, NGOs also point to the advantages victim participation has for the criminal process itself, contributing to 'facts', 'truth', and 'memory'. For example, my informants pointed to how victims participating in the Lubanga case helped illustrate how the use of names is used in the Democratic Republic of Congo (DRC). Another such example was the way in which SGBV was brought to 'public' attention through victims participating in the ad hoc tribunals as witnesses (see also Pena and Carayon, 2013). As part of this, a central issue has been to advocate for ICC charges being reflective of the conflict. An NGO representative explained that, 'as a victims' advocate, I think one of the main reasons why you want to have victim participation is to have some sort of control on the type of charges that are brought being representative of what actually happened.' This is viewed as an important element in considering trials as establishing the 'truth' of events, as part of writing history. As such, the rationale is closely associated with a preference for the ICC's prosecutorial strategy to be reflective of the underlying patterns of the conflict in question, as discussed in Chapter 5 with reference to prosecuting 'all' sides of the conflict in order to avoid narratives of collective guilt and innocence (see Fletcher and Weinstein, 2002). This approach to prosecution is sometimes at odds with the 'mandate' of international criminal justice to pursue the most serious crimes, and to ignore the difficulties with obtaining sufficient evidence for prosecutions in these situations (see generally Bergsmo, 2012). However, in terms of victim participation, it is also considered important to obtain a broad set of charges in order to legally recognize victims *as* victims. This is because only victims of the specific charges brought before the Court are able to participate in the case, and to acquire the status of legally recognized 'victims'. In Uganda, this has meant that victims' applications have been left 'in storage' pending judicial development of the cases. Victims are 'put on hold', as the judicial process narrows the category of those legally recognized as victims (Kendall and Nouwen, 2014).

Implementing victim participation

When the Court began its investigation into the situation in DRC, it was unclear how victim participation was going to be realized, as this was at the very beginning of the ICC's endeavours, with no prior case law on participation. The FIDH became involved to facilitate victim participation in the situation, and filed applications on behalf of victims. As explained by one of those involved at the time, FIDH undertook a mission to the DRC in 2004 and collected testimonies about the conflict. These testimonies were collected through local grassroots organizations, today referenced as 'intermediaries' (Ullrich, 2016). From about a hundred different testimonies, approximately twenty were selected for consideration, on the basis of consent from the victims involved, their safety, and their level of victimization, that is, whether they had been harmed themselves, or 'merely' witnessed crimes (so-called 'direct' or 'indirect' victims). For an initial application for participation, FIDH selected six testimonies, which comprised a variety of crimes and types of victimization, in different regions. This was a strategic choice by the organization to show the ICC the range of crimes being committed, challenging the Office of the Prosecutor (OTP) on cases and charges by using victim participation as a means to make advocacy (see also FIDH, 2006).

However, significant problems emerged from both the Court's administrative approach, and from it being an international NGO that was trying to implement it. For example, in addition to a long, complex, and risky process of applying for victim participation, the early standard victim application form attracted substantial criticism. From The Hague, it is difficult to reach (out to) victims. Yet, while the ICC arguably wanted as much information as possible from victims who wanted to participate, it created, according to my informant, 'a seven-page form which was very difficult to fill out, and very difficult to understand for expats like me, let alone the NGOs on the ground and victims'. Moreover, the form linked participation with *reparations:* 'The fact that they were asked what type of reparations they wanted gave them expectations that they would get reparations!'

Another set of challenges emerged not from the ICC's system per se, but from the role that international NGOs had in implementing it. As a French organization, FIDH facilitated representation of victims by their French pro bono lawyers: lawyers who were accustomed to the French legal system and the representation of cases under universal jurisdiction. Victims' rights under international criminal law however, were not only unfamiliar legal territory but also *new* legal territory. It has therefore been asserted that, as pro bono lawyers and non-specialists in international criminal law, these legal representatives had neither the time nor the expertise needed for the job. While this does not apply to all international NGOs, it illustrates some of the challenges involved in global justice-making and international law development, worthy motives notwithstanding.

Yet most critically, the charges against Lubanga ended up being significantly narrower than anticipated. Lubanga was charged with and convicted of enlisting, conscripting, and using child soldiers in the Union of Congolese Patriots (UPC). Human rights NGOs vehemently opposed the narrow charges in the case, claiming that 'the failure to include additional charges in the case against Mr. Lubanga could undercut the credibility of the ICC in the DRC,' and, moreover, that 'the narrow scope of current charges may result in severely limiting victims' participation in the first proceedings before the ICC' (Avocats sans Frontières et al., 2006). One of the victims' rights advocates involved remained clear in sharing her evaluation with me: 'The system was a failure, and that was not anticipated.'

Because of the commitment the organization had made to the victims, they submitted all twenty applications to the Court. However, due to the narrow charges in the case, none of the victims were eligible for participation, as participation was decided by the chambers to be dependent on victims' connections with the charges in the case, and not to the Court's jurisdiction, as had previously been ruled (see also Wemmers and de Brouwer, 2011).

While the six applications were initially recognized by the Court as 'participants in the situation'—an event publicly celebrated by FIDH (2006)—my informant said that, due to subsequent changes in the ICC's rulings: 'Participation in the situation ended up meaning nothing.' She expresses not only disappointment but also guilt for having created expectations—and having contributed to 'mobilize' victims—only for these persons to be excluded from the process as well as from being legally recognized by the Court *as* victims:

> 'What about *our* crimes?' It was difficult to explain it to them, and I thought it was as difficult to explain it to the so-called intermediaries; not that they wouldn't understand it, but it was a hard thing to swallow. I remember I was there, and we were trying to look at the positive side. We would tell them that there may be possibilities in the future, because you never know—the ICC is a permanent institution—and also look at the more abstract notions and impacts, like 'You were the first victims, and that opened a door!' But you know, telling that to people who are in need, hoping for reparations, wanting something concrete for their lives.

This is the moral landscape in which NGO advocates turn to the ICC as a panacea for global justice-making. They view the ICC as much more than 'merely' being about prosecutions and perpetrators; it represents the potential for a more victim-oriented justice. An informant noted that while he is 'all for prosecutions', 'there are times when justice could mean several other things.' Traditional objectives of criminal courts—adjudication of guilt and innocence and administering punishment—are recognized as insufficient; the ICC must do more; it must incorporate additional notions of justice, of justice for victims.

Victim reparations: promises and pitfalls

Following a conviction at the Court, the ICC may award reparations to victims of crimes. This is familiar from domestic systems of criminal justice where reparations are conceptualized as a form of compensation for the harm committed against them (Ashworth, 1986; Zedner, 1994). Reparations may be awarded as (i) (monetary) compensation for 'moral, material and physical harm'; (ii) restitution, for instance by restoring property in an attempt to re-establish the situation prior to the atrocities; and (iii) rehabilitation in the form of medical, psychological or psychiatric care, 'as well as social, legal and other services needed to restore victims' well-being and dignity' (ICC, 2009). At the time of research, there was a lot of anticipation but also considerable confusion about the implementation of reparations, for instance whether or not there would be individual or collective reparations, and on the 'appropriate' application procedures. There had only been *court ordered* reparations once, namely in the Lubanga case.

In recognition of the fact that those prosecuted by the Court will rarely possess the means to give 'adequate' reparations to their victims, the ASP had established the TFV. The fund is a body semi-related to the ICC, and is responsible for reparations. In addition to court ordered reparations, the TFV also has an *assistance* mandate, which enables the body to award reparations to victims *of crimes under the jurisdiction* of the Court. The role ascribed to the TFV demands some further analysis, as it illustrates the force of humanitarian reason for the justification of international criminal justice (Lohne, 2018b).

Among advocates of international criminal justice, there was a concern about the ICC being too perpetrator-focused. An NGO informant asserted that 'If we do not do something to raise the profile of the Trust Fund, people are going to think that this Court is all about grabbing perpetrators. Let us get the world to know that the Trust Fund is also doing something to better the lives of victims.' The work of the TFV is described as having the potential to bring the discussion back to what it should 'really be about': what the ICC is doing for victims. In Chapter 5, I referred to a Norwegian state representative who had a similar worry about the criminal justice system being overshadowed by a concern for the defendant, as opposed to that of victims. He explained further that 'the care for perpetrators is usually more prominent than the care for victims in domestic criminal justice systems. The Trust Fund for Victims prevents that from happening in international criminal justice.' In this manner, the TFV is regarded as 'balancing' the administration of justice vis-à-vis victims and perpetrators; as ensuring a more 'holistic' form of justice.

In Uganda, the TFV had been involved in implementing its assistance mandate despite the criminal cases being at a standstill. Some of my informants saw the role of the TFV as a way of building momentum for the ICC amongst victim communities. 'If you want to get people in affected communities to really accept the Court, we need to pay more attention to the work of the Trust

Fund for Victims. Victims want perpetrators held accountable, but they are also concerned about the greater and broader issues.' By 'greater and broader issues', this NGO representative brings up what is often at stake in complex and protracted humanitarian emergencies, namely access to basic needs such as food and healthcare. While the cases have been at a standstill, the TFV had been the only 'presence' in northern Uganda. At the ICC field office in Kampala, I was told that 'the Victims Trust Fund is more active—they have more funding, programs are being implemented, they have helped over 40 000 victims'. The TFV had funded programmes through NGOs as 'implementing partners' providing psychological and physiological rehabilitation (provision of prosthetics, for instance), as the conflict left many of its victims lacking body parts such as lips, noses, ears, and breasts (see also TFV, 2014). A Ugandan victims' rights advocate explained that 'at first, victims were scared to get this help because they thought it meant them having to witness at the Court. That has changed now. Now, individuals cry to be on the list, but there's no funding.'

These developments raise several questions about the extent to which the TFV's activities are part of the ICC's overall contribution, or legacy, in northern Uganda. Institutionally, it is. The ICC and its advocates can claim to 'have done something' in the region, to have contributed to justice, albeit not necessarily to the retributive and prosecutorial kind. This is, after all, in agreement with those that claim that the ICC is not 'all about' prosecutorial justice anyway, but that its purpose is to bring justice to victims. A more critical reading would challenge the Court by asking to what extent the TFV serves, at least partly, as a fallback option for the ICC. Where arrests cannot be made, because of lack of state cooperation or some other reason, the ICC still delivers.

Yet, the TFV's very existence raises the question of what type of justice 'ICC justice' is—is it criminal justice, development, or humanitarianism (Lohne, 2018b; Kendall and Nouwen, 2018)? When do assistance and reparations merge into aid and humanitarianism, or when does a social justice-oriented criminal justice develop into, well, development. After all, what separates the work of TFV from other development funds? These types of questions hold great significance in a world fraught with suffering from poverty, curable diseases, and global inequalities, and 'where it is unclear why victims of international crimes should "jump queue"' (not to mention victims of certain international crimes rather than others)' (Mégret, 2010: 127).

Criminal justice, development, or humanitarianism?

The TFV consists of voluntary contributions from states as well as private entities, becoming an opportunity for states (and non-state actors) to express humanitarian concern through dedication and support to 'ICC justice'. This was the case at an ASP meeting, where Sweden held a reception together with Women's Initiative for Gender Justice to mark their donation, as the funds were earmarked victims of SGBV. Indeed, earmarked contributions make a significant part of TFV funding: out of a total of approximately nineteen million Euros, over five million were earmarked donations to SGBV crimes. The TFV's winter report of 2014 says:

> Already in 2008, the TFV Board of Directors launched a call for earmarked contributions to address the harm suffered by SGBV victim survivors, in recognition of the pattern of harm resulting from SGBV being prevalent in most situations before the ICC ... Next to this being a remarkable fundraising success for the TVF, it also reflects a strong policy-based engagement by States Parties. Already since 2010, Finland and Norway have notably and consistently supported the TFV with SGBV earmarked donations ... The significance of the United Kingdom's initiative to associate the TFV with its Preventing Sexual Violence Initiative (PSVI) has also been that other donors have been inspired to earmark their voluntary contributions to the TFV for SGBV victim survivors. (TFV, 2014)

The UK were the TFV's biggest donor, with Norway in second place. For Norway's part, a representative explained that earmarked funding to the TFV is a consequence of the government having money in the aid sector 'needing to be channelled in this direction', along with the fact that SGBV are a stated priority for the ICC. Earmarking funds for SGBV is unproblematic. By comparison, he explained, 'earmarking funds to child soldiers is harder because they are both victims *and* perpetrators.' In recognition of the contribution that the TFV makes, this illustrates how it has become part of humanitarian funding flows, including their hierarchies of victimhood and suffering.

The way international criminal justice can be seen to merge into the field of development is not a popular subject for discussion in the field. The Norwegian representative explained the importance of separating objectives and consequences: the ICC has a *legal* mandate, but *development* may result. A victims' advocate confirmed 'This is not development, it is reparation.' 'You need to make that link between responsibility and harm ... You can't just run and say "I'm building a school". You need to say, "I'm building a school out of a recognition that the kids in this specific village have suffered this or the other".' Building a school, to continue her example, necessitates linkage between the beneficiaries of the school and a categorization of suffering as a result from a specific type of harm identified by the Rome Statute. Whereas suffering denotes an internal state, reparation is generally material in recognition that what people lack is often access to basic needs. Yet, it distinguishes what types of suffering, understood to have been caused by particular acts, are worthy of 'repairing'. In the case of two villages without schools, where the inhabitants of one are classified as victims of international crimes, the reparations scheme may legitimately provide assistance to one village but not the other. On the one hand, one might say that one school is better than none. On the other, however, it demonstrates how global inequalities come to be juridified and depoliticized. 'By not building two schools, the reparation scheme fosters the illusion that one type of harm—international crimes—is remediable, and worse than general poverty and structural inequality, which are just facts of life' (Lohne, 2018b: 12).

Victims for Justice

In Chapter 5 I discussed how a feature of late-modern penality is the image of crime as 'everywhere'—random, pervasive, and ready to strike anyone at any time. There, the figure of the victim has taken on a representational character, where '[p]ublicized images of actual victims serve as the personalized, real-life, it-could-be-you metonym for a problem of security that has become a defining feature of contemporary culture' (Garland, 2001: 11). That 'we' are all potential crime victims is foregrounded by media interest, yet one that varies according to the victim's background. If the victim is male, and/or working class, of African or Asian descent, has drug problems or is a prostitute, the case receives less publicity as reporters assume their audience will neither empathize nor relate with the victim's case. Being the representative character whose experience is seen as common and collective, the white middle-class victim generates the most media attention (Jewkes,

2011). In this way, the notion of 'universal victimhood' arising from conceptions of crime as 'everywhere' in a 'risk society' (Beck, 1992) presumes an undifferentiated public, and, moreover, an undifferentiated *global* public (Aas, 2012). While the threat of terrorism is blamed for being the emblematic universal risk, 'the terrorist victim we are invited to imagine is an affluent White urban Christian Anglo-Saxon, not an impoverished Baghdadi Muslim' (Mythen, 2007: 470).

By contrast, the victim imagery invoked in international criminal justice is that of the distant, powerless, helpless other. She is characterized by her essential 'otherness' from the intended recipient audience, symbolizing the part of humanity that suffers, and whose highly publicized image is part and parcel of the humanitarian communication that feeds the fight against impunity. In contrast to the victim in western domestic discourses on crime, the victim of international crimes *couldn't be you.* Rather than resembling the figure of the *crime* victim in western penality, the victim of international crimes echoes those calling for humanitarian interventions, an imagery criticized for depicting victims as 'hordes of nameless, despairing, and dispirited masses' (Mutua, 2001: 229):

> To the extent they have a face, it is desolate and pitiful. Many are uneducated, destitute, old and infirm, young, poorly clad, and/or hungry. Many are peasants, the rural and urban poor, marginalized ethnic groups and nationalities, and lower castes, whose very being is a state of divorce from civilization and a large distance from modernity. Many are women and children twice victimized because of their gender and age, and sometimes the victim of the savage culture is the female gender itself.

Although the figure of the victim is routinely invoked in support of 'justice' at both the national and international level, who and what are recognized within this category differs. While the victim in the first case is a reminder of the unpredictability of ordinary crime, the victim of extraordinary crimes represents the incredible and remote—a spectacle of humanity's suffering.

Scales of victimhood

'These are crimes that no one owns. These crimes are of concern to the whole world.' I was talking to a Norwegian state representative about international crimes and amnesties. In his view, because 'no one owns' them, no one is in position to give amnesty for international crimes. Without questioning how someone is then in a position to *adjudicate* international crimes, his views illustrate interesting notions of ownership, responsibility, and victimhood in international criminal justice.

As crimes against humanity, international crimes are of 'concern to the international community as a whole' (the Rome Statute's Preamble). As such, they are injected with a higher victim profile as it is not only the *direct* victim that is wronged, or, by extension, the State as a result of breaches to the domestic criminal code, but comprises an elevated form of universal victimhood embodied in the notion of humanity (Findlay, 2011). These are crimes against 'us all', scaling up victimhood from that of domestic and 'ordinary' crimes. Here, the work of the universal is at play, as it is the invocation of universal victimhood that justifies 'doing something' about humanity's suffering—intervening not only for the sake of individual victims but for the sake of us all; for the 'delicate mosaic of humanity' (the Rome Statute's Preamble).

In the early days of international attention to the conflict in northern Uganda, Amnesty International (AI) stated that 'These are crimes against the entire international community and the fabric of international law. Amnesty International calls on the international community to fulfil its responsibilities by assisting the ICC and by helping Uganda to develop and implement an effective action plan to end impunity for these crimes' (AI, 2004b: 2). In addition to making the international community the victim of the crimes, it was postulated, as a consequence of this universal victimization, that the international community had a responsibility to resolve it because of its ownership of the conflict, through being its victim. What responsibility, then, remains for direct victims of international crimes?

An implication of this scaling of victimhood is the way it makes it difficult to decide 'who' is included in the constituency of victims. Is it the direct victim, all our fellow humans, or the value system embedded in the notion of the 'humanity'? Moreover, to what extent are the interest of these categorizations shared? In advocacy on international criminal justice, the conceptual ambiguity of victimhood is applied to leverage advocacy issues. However, when 'humanity' becomes the victimized, it may be asked whether individual experiences of violence, suffering, and of the quest for justice is devalued. In the move to the global, the production of a universal category of victims risk denying the political agency of individual victims as it transcends nation state sovereignty: it is the international and not the national that is recognized to act out of humanitarian concern (Clarke, 2007).

According to the Rome Statute's Article 53, the 'interest of victims' shall be taken into account by the Prosecutor in deciding whether or not to investigate and prosecute international crimes. AI has been particularly active in the legal wrangle concerning the meaning of the 'interests of victims', arguing as follows:

> The interest of victims must be taken into account, but guidelines emphasise that the prosecutor acts in the interests of the public generally (which necessarily include the interests of victims), and not on behalf of individual victims. Indeed, one of the major advances in criminal law was the shift from seeing crimes of violence as crimes against the public, to be prosecuted by the state, rather than private matters to be resolved by the families of the criminal and the victim, who could easily be intimidated into settlement. (AI, 2005: 13)

According to Amnesty International, 'individual victims' should not be the concern of the Prosecutor; rather, the 'general public', which must be interpreted as the 'international community', or 'humanity', is the primary interest group which the Court must act on behalf of. Reminding the Court that it has 'a duty to prosecute such violations and to respect the rights of victims to justice', the organization clarifies its stance further:

> In carrying out these duties, prosecutors must take into account the personal interests of victims, which would necessarily include such considerations as the need to provide information about the conduct of the proceedings, to assist in participation in proceedings, to secure effective protection and obtain necessary support when participating in the proceedings, but there is not the slightest suggestions that prosecutors should decline to investigate grave crimes or to prosecute them because some victims personally opposed investigation or prosecution. (AI, 2005: 5)

The interests of victims are, in effect, taken into account when they correspond to the interests of prosecution and criminal proceedings. In AI's view, victims' interests are relevant insofar as they strengthen the arguments for prosecuting, on the grounds that the 'basic presumption should be that it is always in the interest of justice to prosecute' (AI, 2005: 8).

In the move to 'the global', Christie's (1977) thoughts on the appropriation of conflict by the criminal justice system takes on an additional dimension, as conflict is not 'appropriated' by the state, but by the 'international community' embodied in the ICC. In this 'elevation' of conflict appropriation, victims may be further disassociated from their conflicts as the 'international community' reflects the relationship between states. These are states that have ratified the Statute. Albeit dealing with individual responsibility, it disregards the relationship between individuals (Tallgren, 2002). Thus, while this scaling of criminal justice is intended to extend access to justice in situations where domestic criminal justice is perceived to fail, Clarke (2007: 139) pertinently asks 'what kind of victims does the ICC require northern Uganda's citizens to be?' While national processes, including offering amnesties to alleged perpetrators, (at least theoretically) recognize victims as political agents, the 'articulation of justice that advocates international law over national law reduces citizens in Uganda (and elsewhere) to victims whose very exclusion from political life is the necessary condition for political intervention by international legal regimes such as the ICC' (Clarke, 2007: 135–7; Mamdani, 2010). It may thus be asked whether the scaling of victimhood from the national to the international involves a way of 'extending' conflict appropriation, not just 'stealing' the conflict but ignoring victims as owners of the conflict altogether.

Global identities of suffering: victims of sexual and gender-based violence

Imageries of humanitarian suffering are at the core of global justice-making. As part of the visual nature of contemporary social life, and of humanitarianism as powerful social imaginary, representations of a suffering humanity animate ideas of universal justice as expressed through international criminal justice, human rights, and humanitarianism. Global identities of suffering, that is, 'generic categories [which] include a range of experiences pertaining to acute social vulnerability, infliction of physical pain and conditions of emotional and psychological trauma', have become key to 'the regulatory project of global legal liberalism' (Sandvik, 2012: 248). Without questioning the harm to and suffering of people affected by these types of crimes, victims of sexual and gender-based violence (SGBV) have a particularly powerful victim-status. With the 'fight against impunity' overwhelmingly adopted as a panacea for these types of crimes (Houge and Lohne, 2017), this victim-status must be recognized as a significant force in global justice-making through international criminal law. In so doing, I echo previous criminological debates on the criminal prosecution of violence against women as a punitive force in domestic systems of justice, and that challenge the idea of criminal punishment as the scale by which victims' dignity should be measured (Ericsson, 2007; Houge et al., 2015).

When violence against women during relative peace and conflict finally became part of international norm and policy agendas, it did so rapidly. Indeed, in the international area, no other issue has undergone a more accelerated process of criminalization than that of sexual and gender-based violence (Sandvik, 2012). Reminiscing about the NGO mobilization in the ICC treaty negotiations, a senior NGO representative explained: 'We tried two or three times to create a gender caucus. Finally, we succeeded in creating it, because I had seen what a powerful tool that was in the global governance movement that was going on in the world conferences. This was all happening parallel to those world conferences.' What he referred to is a wave of UN meetings on women's issues: in Mexico City (1975), Copenhagen (1980), Nairobi (1985); they spanned the UN Decade for Women (1976–85) and created advocacy networks and momentum for further conferences in Vienna (1993), Cairo (1994), and Beijing (1995). As observed by Keck and Sikkink (1998: 169), in 'each of these cities, increasingly large parallel conferences of NGOs took place at the same time as the official conferences; more than 14,000 women from 150 countries attended the NGO forum in Nairobi, and 20,000 attended the one in Beijing in 1995.' Through these global spaces of interaction, the formation of transnational agendas, coalitions and organization became possible. At the 1993 Summit for Human Rights in Vienna, 'women's rights became human rights', with women's interests first framed within a rights terminology and then incorporated into the conference's human rights declaration (Bunch, 1990). In the continuum from relative peace to armed conflict, legal strategies have since been central to fighting gender-based violence and discrimination, with a particular emphasis on 'rights' discourse and the human rights frame.

In parallel, recognition of *gendered* forms of suffering in conflict were gaining increasing traction in the ad hoc tribunals, which established significant case law on sexualized violence as an international crime. For example, the Akayesu case at the International Criminal Tribunal for Rwanda (ICTR) and the Foca judgment at the International Criminal Tribunal for the Former Yugoslavia (ICTY) were among the first international criminal cases to establish rape as a constitutive element of genocide and crimes against humanity. In the Akeyesu case, sexual violence charges were not included in the initial indictment but were included after evidence of such crimes appeared in the witness testimonies. According to Carla Ferstman (2012), the Executive Director of REDRESS, the NGO Coalition for Women's Human Rights in Conflict Situations submitted an *amicus* brief that led the ICTR's prosecutor to amend the charges. This supports Haddad's (2011: 109) conclusions that 'transnational advocacy helped generate the necessary political will to adopt and implement legal norms regarding crimes of sexual violence at the ICTY and the ICTR.'

Hence, the build-up to a 'strong' gender-sensitive ICC was marked both by the women's movement as a particularly strong force of transnational advocacy, and by a substantial legal recognition of how violence in conflict is gendered. Activists from the women's movement became part of the Coalition by 1997, developing into the Women's Caucus (for Gender Justice) during the Rome negotiations. According to Spees (2003: 1238),

> the Women's Caucus worked to reveal and correct the deficiencies in existing humanitarian law with respect to crimes of sexual and gender violence. Furthermore, the Women's Caucus was among the strongest voices calling for a more active role for victims and witnesses in the justice process, a broad reparations scheme, strong mandates for protection of victims and witnesses, and gender experts and women on the court and among staff at all levels.

Although at times criticized both by other NGOs and government delegations for being 'too aggressive' in their lobbying, the Women's Caucus worked intensely to incorporate rape and gender crimes in the Rome Statute. And indeed, the Rome Statute became the first international treaty to codify acts of sexual and gender-based violence as among the most serious crimes in international criminal law, explicitly criminalizing rape, sexual slavery, forced prostitution and sterilization, as well as other acts of sexual violence of 'comparable gravity' (Steains, 1999; Glasius, 2006).

The Women's Caucus for Gender Justice concluded its work in 2003 and has now been replaced by the Women's Initiative for Gender Justice (WIGJ), which continues to monitor and support the ICC (their website being www.iccwomen.org, as against the Coalition's www.iccnow.org). The WIGJ has established a role as both a watchdog and an expert body on gender issues at the Court. Their work not only encompasses the judicial development of the fight against impunity for SGBV crimes, but also focuses on gender balance in staff and expertise in the Court, including in the selection of judges. Besides their *amicus curia* status at the Court, they have increasingly taken on a role as 'gender experts' at the ICC, formalized in the appointment of Birgid Inder as the prosecutor's Special Advisor on Gender in 2012.

When Bensouda took office as Chief Prosecutor in 2012, she promised to 'guarantee that the primacy given to the gender related crimes will stand and will even be furthered' and made the investigation and prosecution of sexual and gender-based crimes one of the OTP's strategic goals (CICC, 2012: 13; see also the OTP's strategy plan ICC-OTP, 2013). In June 2014, the OTP launched a 'Policy Paper on Sexual and Gender-Based Crimes', confirming their prioritization of the issue as 'among the gravest under the Statute' (ICC-OTP, 2014: 5). The launch of the report coincided with the Global Summit to End Sexual Violence in Conflict, a summit co-chaired by the UK Foreign Secretary and Angelina Jolie, Special Envoy for the UN High Commissioner for Refugees, and was attended by 1,700 delegates from 123 national delegations including seventy-nine ministers. Setting out to take 'practical steps to tackle impunity for the use of rape as a weapon of war, and to begin to change global attitudes to these crimes', it was the 'largest gathering ever brought together on the subject'.[2]

Despite the considerable 'global' attention paid to SGBV crimes, NGOs have criticized the Prosecutor for failing to allow the systematic and widespread use of SGBV to be reflected in the charges brought before the Court. As mentioned, in the Lubanga case, NGOs and legal representatives requested that the charges should include SGBV crimes, in order for these crimes to be properly reflected in the Court's proceedings (see also Ferstman, 2012). As discussed above, the legal recognition of victims is considered

[2] See https://www.gov.uk/government/topical-events/sexual-violence-in-conflict (accessed 8 March 2015).

important not only in its own right but also, at the ICC, for triggering right to participation. Victimhood is therefore essentially a 'juridified' concept, despite its abstract use as the justification for humanitarian interventions. For those who speak on behalf of victims it becomes important to ensure that those whom they speak on behalf of—whether authorized or not to do so—are reflected in the charges against the alleged perpetrator. A recurring dilemma in international criminal justice is whether to pursue leadership cases, that is, to go after high-level alleged perpetrators, or *thematic* cases, such as those involving sexual and gender-based crimes. While these crimes may not necessarily be the 'gravest', the symbolic value of prosecuting these crimes is considered particularly important by its proponents (Hagan, 2010; Bergsmo, 2012).

Moreover, the embrace of international criminal justice by the women's movement generally, and by core human rights NGOs in particular, cannot be seen in isolation from how international law, here the Rome Statute, is seen as a way of influencing *national* criminal justice systems by using the Rome Statute as a model standard, as also suggested in legal scholarship:

> In countries that ratify the Rome Statute, the gender provisions could help strengthen the capacity to address violence against women at the national level via the inclusion of additional crimes of sexual and gender violence, progressive definitions of existing crimes, and more gender-sensitive procedures for the trial of these crimes. (Spees, 2003: 1234, 1246)

This form of rights-based development, or 'gender justice-making', through criminal justice has implications that merit further scrutiny.

The DRC has become infamous for widespread sexual and gender-based crimes, to the extent that it has been labelled the 'rape capital of the world' and the 'world's worst place to be a woman' (e.g. BBC News, 2010; The Guardian, 2011). However, critical scholars are increasingly drawing attention to the way dominant narratives underpinning international efforts in eastern DRC, including dominant narratives about gender relations and sexual violence (Autesserre, 2012) are having unintended consequences. Eriksson Baaz and Stern (2013) point to how global flows of images and funding flows have created what resembles a 'rape industry' in the DRC with false rape claims and so-called 'would-be victims'; the international funding flows being blamed for having created an incentive structure around this type of crime, contributing to increase its 'occurrence' and skewing the statistics to ensure that DRC is indeed the world's rape capital. Albeit conscious of how such a critique may affect much needed attention to the plights of women in DRC, 'rape is much too serious to be rendered banal through its commercialization' (Eriksson Baaz and Stern, 2013: 104).

Domestic courts in eastern DRC were the first in the world to invoke the Rome Statute in their conviction of seven soldiers in 2006 for crimes against humanity and war crimes, and it has since frequently been applied to sentence soldiers for sexual and gender-based crimes. If the following figures on judicial attention to sexual and gender-based violence in eastern DRC are accurate, they do, however, 'stand in stark contrast to statistics from other countries' (Lake, 2014: 3):

> [F]or the months of June and July 2012 (for which the author monitored and observed judicial proceedings), the Juvenile Court in Goma heard 97 cases in total, of which 78 were SGBV cases. In this period, more than 70% of those detained in Goma's central prison in 2012 were alleged SGBV perpetrators ... The decisions themselves are also striking when contrasted with the treatment of rape in other domestic settings, which boast considerably greater resources, more progressive human rights records, and stronger legal infrastructures.

While acknowledging that the fight against impunity is contributing to a significant increase in the frequency of criminal prosecutions of SGBV in eastern DRC, and arguably also to their legal quality in so far as the latter is similar to international law and human rights agendas, this development nonetheless raises several normative questions pertaining to relationships of sovereignty, criminal justice, and international human rights interventions.

Besides being identified as the world's rape capital, DRC is also considered emblematic of the 'absent', 'collapsed', 'limited', 'weak', or altogether 'failed' state—from a view of statehood as conceptualized in the Westphalian model of the global North (see Aas, 2012). It is within the spaces of limited, missing or failing statehood that external actors—including international NGOs—come to play a role 'imitating' functions of state governance; or, as regards penal governance, in spaces of 'failed justice'.

One example is the 'mobile gender justice courts' set up by international NGOs. Kelly Askin (2011), programme initiator and senior legal officer for international justice at the Open

Society Justice Initiative explains: 'My idea was to design a mobile court that would travel to very remote areas and provide recourse for victims without access to a formal justice process. The mobile court would focus on sexual violence but have discretion to hear other crimes and have both civilian and military jurisdiction.' Alongside the UN and EU, the Open Society Justice Initiative has, since 2009, financed mobile court programmes in eastern DRC, which are implemented by international organizations such as *Avocats sans Frontières* and the American Bar Association's Rule of Law Initiative. In the 'landmark' trial of Lieutenant Colonel Kibibi and his officers for mass rape near Fizi town, in which the decision 'broke new ground, arriving at an innovative and sophisticated judgement that combined elements of Congolese civil, criminal, and military law with the most up-to-date international human rights protections regarding SGBV' (Lake, 2014: 3), a tent was set up as a temporary courthouse:

> Legal representatives or outreach coordinators from the respective international organizations travelled with Congolese jurists to the trial location ahead of time to publicise the court, explain its purpose and mandate, and compile evidence on behalf of the civil parties. NGOs assist civilian or military jurists (depending on the nature of the crime) in identifying and detaining indictees, facilitating trial logistics, and recruiting witnesses. Once all witnesses and evidence are procured, trials begin. (Lake, 2014: 7–8)

In an Open Society blog post, Kelly Askin (2011) reflects further on the mobile court proceedings:

> This afternoon, we were allowed to observe the closed session hearing with the sex crime survivors. We heard heart-wrenching testimonies from young girls and elderly women who had their lives and families shattered by horrific violence. Often rejected by their husbands and shunned by their communities, they were extremely traumatized, and in both physical and emotional pain. They fretted over basic survival needs, including how to feed themselves and their children, and whether other soldiers would retaliate against them or their families. Despite all these concerns, one woman said that even though she'd never seen a trial before, she thought it was a necessary ingredient to bring peace to her country. I felt like a proud mother, listening to someone praise her baby.

In Askin's narrative, the faith in the transformative potential of criminal trials is presented as natural and innate, as indeed a universal. Rather than being an institution embedded in culture and history, the criminal trial becomes as a universal 'remedy'—a 'necessary ingredient' to 'bring peace'. It is also worth noting how the narrator narrates her own positionality as the 'mother'; signifying a benevolent and caring authority figure whose efforts, in return, are praised. By comparing the criminal trial to her 'baby', she also strengthens the notion that the criminal trial is *her* product—she is the producer of the universal good.

Sources of moral authority

Victims' issues are of course at the heart of many human rights institutions and organizations, and this is what our Coalition is made up of, so there is a much greater focus on victims' issues, to ensure that the best interests of victims are met ... At the end of the day, it's the victimhood, the victimized—that's what we're here for and working on.

A Coalition representative explained concern for victims as the reason for their engagement with international criminal justice. In so doing, she shows how victims have an importance for global justice-making beyond their material recognition as regards rights and provisions, illustrating the dominant narrative portraying victims as international criminal justice's *raison d'etre*. While the claim to represent the figure of the victim is invoked by activists, diplomats, and legal practitioners in international criminal justice alike (Kendall and Nouwen, 2014), the imperative to 'speak for', 'give voice to', and 're-present' the interests of absent victims are part and parcel of the practice of human rights NGOs. Thus, an important aspect of how imaginations about victims drive international criminal justice is the way in which the figure of the victim legitimates the participation of human rights NGOs in the first place. Victims are the 'giant engine' of international criminal justice and human rights NGOs alike, as '[w]ithout the victim there is no savage or savior, and the entire human rights enterprise collapses' (Mutua, 2001: 227). Human rights NGOs role as 'carriers' of victim imageries thus enable them to claim moral authority as participants in global justice-making through the ICC. To understand the processes through which moral authority travels, I will return to issues of representation.

Representation is one of the most widespread practices in criminal justice, exemplified by legal representation of the defendant and the state in domestic criminal justice, or the 'international community' in international criminal justice. Importantly, it is this act of representation that Christie (1977) identifies as appropriation of conflict in his critique of the criminal justice system. In its place, proponents of restorative justice emphasize the direct participation of those otherwise referred to as 'victims' and 'defendants'. By discarding the practice of legal representation, principles of restorative justice stress the *direct* participation of conflict owners in the resolution of conflict. While previous discussions were concerned with representation from the outset of political theory, here I am interested in further examining the sociological *meanings* of representation.

Representation means, literally, re-presentation—'a making present again' (Pitkin, 1967: 9):

> Except in its earliest use, however, this has always meant more than a literal bringing into presence, as one might bring a book into the room. Rather, representation, taken generally, means the making present *in some sense* of something which is nevertheless *not* present literally or in fact. Now, to say that something is simultaneously both present and not present is to utter a paradox, and thus a fundamental dualism is built into the meaning of representation ... But there is no need to make mysteries here; we can simply say that in representation something not literally present is considered as present in a nonliteral sense.

By 'standing for' or 'acting for' someone or something, another entity makes present what or who is missing, creating a discursive space of claims made on behalf of the absent. Drawing on what Bourdieu (1991: 211) calls the '*oracle effect*, thanks to which the spokesperson gives voice to the group in whose name he speaks, thereby speaking with all the authority of that elusive, absent phenomenon' Kendall and Nouwen (2014: 236) suggest that

> speaking on behalf of others thus entails an appropriation or 'usurpation' of the voices (and indeed authority) of the represented ... When the prosecutor prosecutes or the judges adjudicate international crimes—whether they do so on behalf of states that have ratified the Rome Statute, or on behalf of member states of the United Nations, or even on behalf of 'the victims' of international crimes—these actors simultaneously 'give voice to' and appropriate the voices and authority of those they claim to represent.

Yet, as representation brings into being what or who is being represented, the act of representation also constitutes the representative, or that or those which carry out the act of making present what is not. In the words of Bourdieu (1991: 204):

It is because the representative exists, because he *represents* (symbolic action), that the group that is represented and symbolized exists and that in return it gives existence to its representative as the representative of the group. One can see in this circular relation the root of the illusion which results in the fact that, ultimately, the spokesperson may appear, even in his own eyes, as *causa sui,* since he is the cause of that which produces his power, since the group which makes of him someone invested with powers would not exist—or at least, would not exist fully, as a represented group—if he were not there to incarnate it.

The relationship between the representative and the represented is in other words mutually constitutive. Following this conceptualization, notions of 'victims', 'global civil society', or even 'humanity' are constituted in part by those that claim to speak on behalf of them: here, human rights NGOs. It is notions of 'victims', 'global civil society', and 'humanity' that enable human rights NGOs to speak at all—it is the authority of the former that is transferred to the latter.

Unlike State Parties to the ICC, who enjoy more or less political authority through political representation of their state and citizens, the authority of human rights NGOs is *moral.* They speak not on behalf of a political constituency, but for and about a social constituency of victims. This endows them with a 'unique moral legitimacy' which makes them 'hard to ignore, politically' (Williams and Goodman, 2007: 250). Mindful of this 'deeply paradoxical strength of the weak' (Fassin, 2011: xii), the figure of the victim reflects those who speak in her place: In drawing attention to global violence and suffering, and in fighting for justice for victims, human rights NGOs are seen as 'virtuous' and 'moral' organizations. Thus, here too human rights NGOs have a role as *mediators,* going between the moral force of 'victims' and the ICC. However, as discussed previously, the role of 'mediator' is one of power: victims' advocates speak the cause of victims as a means to an end. As such, the figure of the victim is ultimately instrumentalized to serve a cause.

If only to 'see them smiling'

The invocation of victims' suffering in rhetoric and imagery is pervasive in international criminal justice, as if adding 'flesh' to deliberations on how to administer global justice. Rhetorically, meetings on international criminal justice—whether the ASP meeting or conferences and seminars in The Hague—were typically opened and closed with narratives of suffering, and a confirmation of 'our dedication to justice for victims'. Photographic images of victimized African bodies, some with their limbs chopped off, surrounded the entry into the ASP meeting rooms. These added to a 'sense of purpose', as a reminder of 'what it is all about', albeit it was less apparent why survivors of international crimes were made present in words and images but not in being. If anything, spectacles of suffering are alienating; reflecting a 'disembodied universalism' when seen from the position of an onlooker as a moral subject 'who is not of the landscape he is surveying' (Razack, 2007: 378). There is distance in humanitarianism.

While the distance between the Court and its victim constituency is what human rights NGOs aspire to 'bridge', the distance also opens up a space for their engagement and participation, and with that, their claim to moral legitimacy. Moreover, I also observed an interesting dynamic related to scale and distance as regards personal motivations, and specifically regarding perceived acknowledgement of their work vis-à-vis a constituency of victims. Personal and first-hand connection with victims was recognized as motivation for those who work in the field—a confirmation of their moral work. For example, an NGO representative who travelled to situation countries explained that—in contrast to *not* being in direct contact with victims—'It is very rewarding because when you work directly with the victims and with the groups on the ground you get reminded what it is that you do at work. These people matter!' For her, first-hand contact with victims of international criminal justice served as a reminder of the importance of her work, and of this being recognized. Similarly, *not* being in direct contact with victims seemed to disconnect some of this recognition and reward for one's efforts. Another NGO representative talked about his frustrations with international criminal justice, and with lobbying for victims' rights, revealing that 'At times I have felt like I just want to step out and go do grassroots human rights work where I can really work with victims and see them smiling.' In his work in The Hague, the immediate and imagined gratitude of victims—along with their physicality—is absent, indicating that physical proximity to victims plays a part in justice advocates' imaginations of recognition from victim constituencies. It was assumed that, the closer one is to victims; the greater will be the reward in the form of 'seeing' the implications of one's work. By contrast, when physically distant from them, one can only *imagine* the rewards of victims, in the way described here by an informant:

> Sometimes it is difficult—especially when you are here in The Hague and working on language in resolutions for example—to see if indeed for that one victim in DRC that it makes a difference. That is what it is all about in the end, you know. Sometimes you just don't see the link any more, and then it is good that we have this structure in our organizations where we are in touch ... [Yet] you still don't hear from that one woman who got raped by the rebels.

Despite not 'hearing' from her, the 'woman who got raped by the rebels' still features as a powerful image of who she is really working for, who is—and should be—the 'true' motivation for her work. In fact, there is a strong normative positioning of the victim as the *bona fide* motivation for embracing international criminal justice altogether. Even for a person who does not work *directly* with victims but through other NGOs, the victim *should be* the motivation in international criminal justice advocacy. Another informant said:

> If you meet people who work with victims all the time, if you work with people who are from DRC, if you work with former child soldiers who we meet, if you work with people that have been falsely imprisoned, or rape victims—those are the people that the whole thing stands for, in my opinion. But if you view it as an institution that is there to get convictions, hold a few trials—good for you, (but) then maybe your interest or motivation is not—(You don't) wholeheartedly believe in it.

While it is interesting to note the explicit invocation of emotions as a driving engine for working in international criminal justice—of 'believing' in the Court—and likewise the dismissal of the ICC as 'merely' an institution to 'hold a few trials', the response of victims to their work was generally imagined as positive and grateful. Although NGOs had complaints about the processes by which victims' rights are implemented at the ICC, the interests of victims were never presented as being antithetical to international criminal justice. These narratives thus inscribe themselves in the humanitarian imaginary of grateful recipients (see Mutua, 2001; Calhoun, 2010)—of 'justice for victims' as charity. The expressed desire to be close to victims does not necessarily transmute into a desire to be *accountable* to victims, that is, to be answerable to a constituency who has authorized the representative to speak in their name. After all, this authorization, 'the giving of authority to act' (Pitkin, 1967: 11), has not usually taken place when human rights NGOs speak on behalf of victims. Therefore, the question arises whether the desire to be closer to victims is more about imagining themselves 'standing for' victims' interests and confirming the humanitarian character of their efforts. Without undermining the convictions and reflexivity of those advocating for international criminal justice, Razack (2007: 376) reminds us of the 'slipperiness of empathy', and 'the ways in which the pain and suffering of Black people can become sources of moral authority and pleasure, obscuring in the process our own participation in the violence that is done to them.' Compassion for victims, and voicing of their suffering, does not translate to a realization of their rights as political subjects (Fassin, 2011). It does, however, reflect being in a position to help, constituting a 'relationship of dependency, not of equivalence' (Calhoun, 2010: 35).

Conclusions

This chapter has explored the victimological imagination of international criminal justice, both by probing the multiple conceptions of justice for victims ascribed to the ICC, and the cultural representation of victimhood as an animating force of victims for (international criminal) justice. I demonstrate how victims are a source of moral authority in the field, and one that is put to use by human rights NGOs in their claim to speak in their name.

There is, however, a conspicuous discrepancy between victims as the 'ethos' of international criminal justice, and the limited role of victims in legal proceedings at the Court. Still, despite the imbalances of ideologies and realities of justice delivery, this unsettlement of the retributive rationale to 'victims' justice', there appears to be 'a degree of conceptual misunderstanding about what their proper role should be, and how they should participate, and where the emphasis of the criminal trial should be' (McGonigle Leyh, 2012: 380). Hence, the chapter has challenged the notion that victim participation at the ICC necessarily indicates a turn to restorative justice, suggesting instead that the ICC represents a form of 'hybrid' justice (see also Hoyle and Ullrich, 2014). The question remains, however, whether the rhetorical embrace of 'alternative' conceptions of justice, such as 'restorative', 'reparative', 'transitional', and so forth, run the risk of being 'co-opted' by the retributive paradigm that dominates the Rome Statute system of justice. It therefore seems that, while rhetorically embracing justice as restorative through its provisions for victim participation, the ICC is indeed victim-*oriented—but within a retributive framework* (see also McGonigle Leyh, 2012). As McEvoy (2007) and others argue, the liberal legalist paradigm is by far the most dominant response in transitional justice processes.

As concerns cultural representations of victims of international crimes, they resonate but also significantly depart from victim imaginaries situated in the global North. In both aspects, the victim is universalized—in the global North by being a representational character of 'us all'; in international criminal justice also by representing 'us all', but in this case by being a symbol of humanity. Thus, rather than being a representational character, the image of the victim of international crimes is characterized by her essential 'otherness': she is part of the humanity that suffers.

Moving on from imaginations about the role of punishment, and about the victims, the next chapter deals with what can be thought of as the final corner of international criminal justice's triangle, namely imaginations about sovereignty and of 'humanity' as its embodiment.

7

Sovereignty and Solidarity

The Pursuit of Global Moral Order

The two previous chapters explored familiar constituents of criminal justice; on the one hand, ideas about the role of punishment; on the other, ideas about the role of victims. This chapter deals with a third component in the conceptual triangle of criminal justice, namely the punishing authority, which in domestic criminal justice is embodied by the State, but that in international criminal justice remains much more unsettled. The International Criminal Court (ICC), as the punishing authority, represents the international community, or, more concretely, the States Parties to the Rome Statute. Moving beyond such a politico-legal approach, a sociology of punishment for international criminal justice enables insight into the global power to punish by engaging the issue of how international criminal justice reflects *cultural* authority—bonds of common values and beliefs, tradition and interests on a global scale.

Critically, the idea of *crimes against humanity* underpins the development of international criminal justice. Albeit codified in the Rome Statute, it is considered the natural law for our time, with human rights as the basic normative principle against which all behaviour is judged. This chapter argues that in lieu of the State, the 'sovereign' of international criminal justice can be understood through the idea of humanity as representative of the cosmopolitan order. Animated by work that is the legacy of Émile Durkheim, the 'villains' and 'victims' outlined in previous chapters serve as representational dichotomies for constituting the boundaries of cosmopolitan community (Sagan, 2010). As such, international criminal justice serves, in the name of humanity, to reinforce the humanitarian imaginary embedded in global order making. I situate human rights NGOs at the forefront of

Advocates of Humanity. Kjersti Lohne, Oxford University Press (2019). © Kjersti Lohne.
DOI: 10.1093/oso/9780198818748.003.0007

this way of thinking, and discuss how they, as advocates of humanity and therefore 'responsible' (to humanity) and 'representative' (of humanity), conflate moral and political authority in their lobbying strategies in The Hague. Moreover, I demonstrate how global justice-making through international criminal law is not the exclusive domain of the 'international', but is regarded as a multiscalar project in need of implementation at the local and national levels too. Using the Rome Statute as a crowbar for 'penal aid' (Brisson-Boivin and O'Connor, 2013) in the global South, the cosmopolitan penal imaginary—and, by extension, cosmopolitan values—are expected to expand through the notion of 'positive complementarity', that is, capacity-building and rule of law development. As such, the analysis shows how the ICC has not only become a vehicle for unleashing a variety of criminal justice exports, but also demonstrates the civilizing dynamic underlying the ICC project. The chapter thus offers insight into how the project of international criminal justice reflects global social changes. By getting away from the 'villains' and 'victims' of global violence, and how the 'international community' reacts to threats 'of concern to the international community as a whole' (the Rome Statute's Preamble), the aim is to address ways in which social and personal order is constituted in the first place.

Punishment and Society

In contrast to most thinkers on the sociology of law and punishment, who see these as instruments of governmental power, Durkheim viewed law as expression of social values, and of morality in particular. In *The Division of Labour in Society*, first published in 1893, Durkheim was concerned with how moral solidarity is maintained in modern 'organic' society despite the increased autonomy of the individual that resulted from the industrial revolution and its complex division of labour. For him, the materiality of law was an observable manifestation of a society's 'collective consciousness' (*conscience collective*); defined in *The Division* as the 'totality of beliefs and sentiments common to the average members of a society [which] forms a determinate system with a life of its own' (Durkheim, 1984: 38–9). In the modern 'organic' society, the hold of the collective consciousness over individuals is established by their distinct roles and contributions in society. In other words, social solidarity is maintained through differentiation.[1] Crimes violate the collective consciousness, 'as attacks upon something which is transcendent'; and criminal punishment is an act not of 'personal vengeance, but rather vengeance for something sacred which we vaguely feel is more or less outside and above us ... Thus by taking vengeance for them it is indeed society and not ourselves that we are avenging' (Durkheim, 1984: 56–7).

In Durkheim's later work, he sees a 'moral individualism', representing the autonomy and dignity of all human beings, to be the overarching and necessary system of beliefs that can ensure moral unity. The relevance of this 'cult of the individual' (*culte de l'individu)*, also referred to as a 'cult of man' or 'religion of humanity' (Durkheim and Lukes, 1969) seems particularly acute today. Besides the fact that many societies have become increasingly differentiated and 'organic' than in Durkheim's time, the cult of the individual offers sociological insight into the significance of human rights for modern legal development (Cotterrell, 1999; Elliott, 2007).

> The human person, whose definition serves as the touchstone according to which good must be distinguished from evil, is considered as sacred, in what one might call the ritual sense of the word. It has something of that transcendental majesty which the churches of all times have given to the Gods ... Such a morality is therefore not simply a hygienic discipline or a wise principle of economy. It is a religion of which man is, at the same time, both believer and God. (Durkheim and Lukes, 1969: 21–2)

As the 'prototype of universal human rights discourse' (Cotterrell, 2015: 21), the moral individualism put forward by Durkheim is one in which the 'religion of humanity' is not philosophical and transcendent, but rather 'a social institution like all known religions' (Durkheim and Lukes, 1969: 28). Echoing this view, Hopgood (2013: x) proposes that it is 'only as a strategy for coping with what Nietzsche called "the death of god" in the West that we can begin to understand the real social function of humanitarianism and human rights in the twentieth century.'

Durkheim's emphasis on how solidarity in modern society is based around the notion of individualism, and of law and punishment as modes of social integration and as material reflections

[1] In 'mechanic' societies, solidarity is achieved through similarity and collective practices.

of the 'internal state' of collective imaginations, make his insights particularly valuable for a sociology of punishment, including at the global level of analysis (see also Tallgren 2013). The criminal justice system is above all a communicative system, whose function is social integration, since punishment reinforces the collective consciousness and strengthens its moral bonds. Durkheim therefore sees punishment and the morality of society as operating in a self-energizing, organic, manner. In a healthy social corpus, punishment contributes to sustain society's moral and internal solidarity. 'Yet when some cherished belief of ours is at stake we do not allow, and cannot allow, violence to be done to it with impunity' (Durkheim, 1984: 54). Impunity, then, becomes a sign of weakness in the societal corpus. The collective consciousness is therefore key to understanding the meaning of punishment in society: it is the source of outrage and punitive sensibilities, and thus a determinant of what is and what is not morally deviant. As it is reinforced though punishment, the collective consciousness is also the beneficiary of punishment.

However, many of Durkheim's proponents today conceptualize punishment and society primarily within a nation state framework. One may therefore ask to what extent it makes sense to talk of a 'global' collective consciousness. Who are the onlookers of international criminal justice; that is, in a Durkheimian sense, the constituency reflected by global justice? Whereas Durkheim saw the cult of the individual as the 'only possible candidate' in an increasingly complex and fragmented society, where 'there remains nothing that men may love and honour in common, apart from man himself' (Durkheim and Lukes, 1969: 26), whether the cult of the individual is able to unify citizens morally in a *world* society remained unanswered by the end of his career.

International criminal justice elevates punishment beyond the nation state, and in doing so, fundamentally upsets the Weberian notion of sovereignty resting on the monopoly of legitimate violence. International justice thus unsettles the notion of sovereignty, punishment, *and the social,* leading Cotterrell (2015: 9) to suggest that the 'cultural authority (the authority of popular ideas arising in everyday social life) to shape the concept of crime may have new significance as the political authority to shape it becomes less clear.' Transnational networks of community, such as transnational networks of NGOs, may thus provide the necessary cultural authority to underpin ideas of crime and punishment in transnational contexts.

However, crucially, Durkheimian sociology has no place for conflict, power, and unpredictability—'they escape the grid of its conceptual structure' (Lukes, 1982: 23). The methodical neglect of politics in his writings disregards the way laws are established as part of the dominating political authorities' system of rules.[2] In *The Division* for example, Durkheim treats the collective consciousness as a 'social fact' and a point of departure for his analysis; not as a result of historical, political, and social struggles that are themselves worthy of critical attention. Instead of seeing the collective consciousness as a hallmark of society as a whole, Garland suggests that 'we ought to conceive of a dominant moral order which is historically established by particular social forces' (1990b: 53; see also Smith, 2008). In this way, the social forces constitutive of the dominant moral order become central to the study of punishment. Put to use on international criminal justice, the collective consciousness reflects a dominant moral order conceptualized in the notion of 'humanity'. The social function of international criminal justice is thus to reinforce the dominant 'global' collective consciousness.

There is, however, considerable conceptual ambiguity in Durkheim's writings as regards cause and effect, explanations and functions (e.g. Lukes, 1982). For example, he is unclear about the relationship between the State and law, seeing them both as embodiments of the collective consciousness, rather than the result of social conflict and power struggles. Due to their position in between individuals and the State, Durkheim sees experts and professional groups as necessary intermediaries between the State and civil society. Thus, along with a 'radicalization' of Durkheim's legal sociology follows a re-evaluation of his views on professional groups' regulatory functions (Deflem, 2008). In his reworking of the Durkheimian logic of punishment, Smith (2008: 25) draws on Mikhail Bakhtin to refine an understanding of punishment as a communicative and didactic process between the centre and the periphery, conceiving the centre as 'broadly equivalent to the state

[2] But see Durkheim (1915), written two years before his death, where he may be working towards a concept of State power. Thanks to Andy Aydın-Aitchison for making me aware of this.

or sources of legitimate authority' and the periphery to civil society and popular culture.

I therefore suggest understanding human rights NGOs in international criminal justice as being at the centre of its communicative and political power, while on the periphery are onlookers of humanitarian suffering. As advocates of humanity and the universal values of human rights, human rights NGOs are dependent on the 'production' of moral outrage, a commodity chain moving in one direction: the raw material of human suffering is gathered in the global South for 'consumption' in the global North. Moral outrage is the intended product, and the theory of change premised on the assumption that knowledge about suffering reshapes political responses. Because they generate knowledge about human suffering, and produce moral outrage, human rights NGOs have a particular role as shapers of the cosmopolitan moral order; and therefore, it would seem, as shapers of a cosmopolitan penal imaginary. This authority is not only normative and moral, that is, as regards the ideas they represent and advocate towards others, but also as regards who they are. Human rights NGOs in international criminal justice must be understood as both *being* transnational networks of community and simultaneously engaging in work to *create* such networks through their dissemination of moral values. Those advocating on behalf of humanity in international criminal justice are professionals—they are highly educated, draw on expert and legal authority and, at least to a certain extent, can be seen as part of international criminal justice's 'epistemic community' (Haas, 1992) (see Chapter 4).

This book has focused on the organization, practices, and sensibilities of these organizations vis-à-vis the ICC, and on the roles they have, given the moral authority they acquire by producing moral outrage. In what follows, I probe deeper into the mentalities and sensibilities involved. Whether the sentiments expressed are 'authentic' is irrelevant, as this makes no difference to their existence as a social force. The development of international justice must be interpreted as reflective of this force. As has also been observed by others, in international criminal justice, legalism is not enough: one also needs moral outrage (Bass, 2000; Dixon and Tenove, 2013). International justice taps into and is propelled by the humanitarian impetus to 'do something' about the suffering of others, and about crimes against what is considered the most sacred thing of all: humanity itself.

Durkheim recognized the notion of a 'universal consciousness', although he acknowledged that the 'dream of an ideal of human brotherhood "cannot be satisfied unless all men form part of one and the same society"' (Cotterrell, 1999: 195). Until then, the transnational values of moral individualism remained attached to the nation state, standing at the head of the cult and acting as a local agent vis-à-vis the idea of a united humanity. However, a global criminal court, like other international organizations, challenges the view of the nation state as the protector of the cult of humanity. Today it is often the international rather than the national that is viewed as the principal agent for acting out of humanitarian concern and governance.

Cosmopolitanism as global solidarity

The end of the Cold War witnessed a significant move away from a 'pluralist' international society built around the notion of mutual recognition of states and minimal interference with legal sovereignty towards the idea of a 'liberal solidarist' international society. This shift was both institutional, as evidenced by the creation of the ICC, and normative, as demonstrated by appeals to an 'international community' suited to fulfil an expanding range of moral and political goals. It is a view of a state system seen not only to work better, but to reduce the gap between power and law on the one hand, and morality and law on the other. It is this way of thinking about moral solidarity that leads to an increase in international institutionalization as a reflection of shared norms and values. It is also this way of thinking that laid the ground for humanitarianism as a transnational concern for distant others. As such, it indicated a shift towards the individual, rather than the state, as the referent subject, reflecting a normative view of international society as constituted by individuals rather than by states (Hurrell, 2007). An NGO representative formulated it like this: 'I think solidarity with people doesn't stop at borders, and if you take ideas of racial inequality and so on to their natural conclusions, that means that a person in Syria for example has the same rights as person living next door to me.' Articulated as 'solidarity doesn't stop at borders', cosmopolitanism—the ethical, philosophical, and scientific world view transcending a nation-state outlook on society and society—prevails in international criminal justice advocacy. Within cosmopolitan thought, human rights have become the dominant normative language, as they epitomize a cosmopolitan worldview by drawing attention to the innate entitlements of humans, irrespective of state citizenship. The power of human rights is precisely their claim to universality—to global solidarity with the plights and rights of everyone. Against a background of transnational encounters and mobilization, the human rights movement has drawn on the cosmopolitan vision when it addresses issues 'as a matter of common responsibility in a perceived shared space of humanitarian consciousness' (Aas 2013: 219).

As a court transcending the Weberian notion of state sovereignty, the ICC is routinely referred to as a cosmopolitan court and a critical milestone on the way to the realization of the cosmopolitan project of global order. International criminal law is 'regarded as an integral part of the great transition to a cosmopolitan world, one of the microcosms of the proposed cosmos whereby Enlightenment ideals and legal principles will bring about the required state of humanitarian morality' (Brants, 2011: 53). Rather than by invoking democracy and popular sovereignty, cosmopolitanism claims legitimacy on the grounds of universality. As such, the universal is often identified with the 'international', with the international gaining supremacy as being morally superior to the national—along with the cosmopolitan vision of 'an unbounded, virtually deterritorialized common moral community in which the principle of sovereignty is subordinated to that of humanity' (Adelman, 2011: 11).

In material form, it is the community of states that has given rise to international punishment through the creation and ratification of the Rome Statute, thereby giving the ICC jurisdiction over its territories and peoples. However, the moral order reflected by international penalty is not state-centric; quite the contrary, the moral order invoked by international criminal justice is a cosmopolitan one where values of a common humanity, universal rights, and solidarity that transcend nation state borders are expressed. Thus, materially bound by the community of states, the image of the ICC is one of humanity, as was at once discernible in the Rome Statute's Preamble, with its references to 'common bonds', 'shared heritage', and the 'conscience of humanity'. As the 'global constituency' of global justice-making, humanity is put forward 'as the source and *telos* of the ICC's normative legitimacy' (Corrias and Gordon, 2015: 103). However, the cosmopolitan vision of global order has a structural problem:

> [R]ights are overwhelmingly contingent upon membership, i.e. citizenship of states whose sovereignty rests on what Weber acutely described as the monopoly of legitimate violence. On the one horn of the dilemma confronting cosmopolitanism is whether the effective enforcement of global citizenship requires a global state with a similar monopoly. On the other is the possibility that retention of this monopoly by nation-states will hole the project below the waterline. (Adelman, 2011: 14–15)

The catch-22 of the cosmopolitan project is certainly an issue for the ICC; the Court does not operate in a cosmopolitan vacuum beyond the interests of states and politics—far from it. Sovereignty is recognized as the biggest challenge to the realization of the 'ICC project'. This encompasses not only universal ratification and Court jurisdiction, but fundamentally the *enforcement* of international criminal justice itself: The ICC, like human rights, is dependent on implementation and enforcement by states. The ICC is thereby characterized by a critical, arguably inevitable, tension: that between the reality of the international order based on the state system, and the ideals and ideology of cosmopolitanism. At the same time, this tension might be seen as useful, as it is precisely the cosmopolitan and humanitarian imaginary that gives force to the implementation of international criminal justice in the first place—ensuring that solidarity should indeed *not* stop at borders. It is within this landscape that the role of human rights NGOs is pivotal, as embodiments and global 'avant-gardes' (see Ypi, 2012) of the cosmopolitan imaginary.

Within the fabric of the Westphalian international order, human rights NGOs claim allegiance to values superior to state interests and politics. Unlike states, which enjoy more or less political authority according to the political representation of their citizens, the authority of human rights NGOs is moral rather than political. As has been a central theme throughout this book, human rights NGOs do not speak on behalf of a political constituency, but for and about a social constituency encompassing victims, global civil society, 'the people': in short, for the *values* embedded in what is seen as the progression of humanity. Structurally, this involves curtailing the power of state sovereignty; ideologically, it has to do with human rights and humanitarian sensibilities. 'Above' politics and local interests, they plead the cause for everyone, everywhere, always—insisting on universal standards of human dignity, rights, and justice. While states are seen to represent state interests, human rights NGOs reject the importance of singularity and celebrate the good of all. Through their transnational networks of 2,500 organizations, the Coalition for the International Criminal Court (CICC) bypasses state borders and state sovereigns and other limitations and obstructions inherent in the state system—connecting the global with the local, the particular with the general, and the victim with the saviour. They represent cosmopolitanism and advocate on behalf of humanity. Thus, while the ICC consists materially of a community of states, imaginatively, it consists of humanity. This is at once the tragedy and the paradox of the ICC project. At the same time, it makes the role of the NGOs essential as embodiments of the Court's normative aspiration for global justice.

Reframing sovereignty

When I began this research project, I assumed NGOs would mainly lobby the ICC, rather than state representatives. The role of NGOs vis-à-vis the ICC was, after all, what animated the research project. I believed I was looking at two types of non-state international actors: one *supra*national and another, taking various forms, which were *non*-governmental and *trans*national. I would be researching the 'global' and, my assumption was, leaving the national scale behind. However, in the course of my research on the formation of 'global solutions to global problems', the nation state has been far from absent; on the contrary, it is still very much there. The ICC operates under the aegis of states; it is they that legally and legitimately govern the project of individual criminal accountability for mass violence. As the legislative body of the ICC, the Assembly of States Parties (ASP) oversees the Court's progress and development, partly by staking out its policies but also, importantly, by determining the Court's budget. Ideas about the nation state and of sovereignty thus feature prominently in the field, and in the cosmopolitan *mentalité*.

In advocacy on international criminal justice, the nation state is generally depicted as powerful yet lacking expertise. This combination—a mismatch of power and knowledge—is viewed as threatening both the realization of international criminal justice as a cosmopolitan project, and the global citizenry of humanity.

Compared to the state, that which is 'above' the state becomes better, safer, and more benign—more representative of humanity's alleged essence. The ICC project, the universal implementation of the Rome Statute system of justice, is essential manifestation of this cosmopolitan and humanitarian imaginary.

As discussed in previous chapters (especially Chapters 3 and 4), NGOs contribute information and expertise to the ICC project. NGO representatives that have been in the game for a long time, such as the Coalition's William (Bill) Pace, or Richard Dicker of Human Rights Watch, are not just NGO representatives, or human rights activists, but also, crucially, *experts* in international criminal justice. Although there is a difference between being an expert and claiming expertise, the latter is part of the normative legitimacy of the NGOs' seat at the table in international criminal justice. Their representatives often work exclusively on the ICC, sometimes on particular aspects of the ICC project, such as victims' rights or gender-based crimes. Through their networks and their visits to situation countries, they 'bring the voice of the ground to the court', as put by one of my informants.

State representatives, on the other hand, have many interests to pursue in The Hague, of which the ICC project may only be one; they do not have the same apparatus in situation countries, may not have the same legal expertise, and if they do, may not necessarily have that expertise represented in The Hague. Yet, when it comes to their relation to the *inter*national criminal court, they still have power. While this 'mismatch' between power and knowledge is, arguably, what has made possible the role of NGOs in the first place, it is also said to obstruct the progress of the ICC project, as the following statement from an NGO representative in The Hague made clear:

> Out of all the actors, they (states) are the ones with least expertise on the issues. They're becoming little spokes in the wheel. They come back like 'what's an intermediary? We don't know, we don't understand.' I don't blame the poor legal advisors, there's a new one every time, but I've been to conferences where the level of knowledge and expertise they have is very low—and they're the ones that make the most significant decisions! Once you decide about the budget, you decide what the Court is going to be doing.

The fact that states retain as much power as they do, without the same level of expertise and dedication to the 'project', seems not only to be a great source of frustration among advocates but also to be an *impediment* to the realization of global justice altogether—'spokes in the wheel' of the humanitarian advance across state borders. State sovereignty remains the bugbear of cosmopolitanism.

Consequently, a lot of work goes into reframing sovereignty as *responsibility,* to the extent that subordination to the ICC's jurisdiction through ratification of the Rome Statute becomes indicative of an 'appropriate' form of sovereignty—a far cry from absolute sovereignty; the underlying premise being that this is always a potential threat to human beings. In The Hague I talked to an NGO representative about his motivations for working in the sector. He told me that his motivation was not so much about international justice as about 'battering down the walls of sovereignty'. What interested him, he explained, is how people can have a say in the formation of international laws in the same way they do at the national level, thus likening citizens in liberal democracies to 'global civil society', and states in international relations to politicians in the domestic discourse. I asked whether state sovereignty is always 'bad':

> No, and you can't ignore the fact that people elect their governments. That's the first consideration in any of this. But certain people don't elect their governments but states still use the same arguments of sovereignty and so on. I don't think sovereignty is bad, but that there should be a limit to its power … I think the more oversight the better.

What is reflected here is an assumption that sovereignty is legitimate only insofar as it is democratic, and further, that it is in need of external oversight. However, by whom, one may ask, and according to which standards? It reflects a view of sovereignty that is far from being absolute power, or 'freedom to promote their own ends subject to minimal constraints' (Hurrell, 2007: 4). Instead, the view of legitimate sovereignty put forward is not only one of democratically elected sovereignty, but also one of *responsible* sovereignty that, if the situation demanded, would give way for the benefit of its demos (Anderson, 2005).

The view of sovereignty as responsibility surfaced at the beginning of the 21st century as a common discourse in the international arena; it was expressed in terms of norms and policy doctrines such as 'human security' and 'responsibility to protect'. What underlies this view of sovereignty is the notion that a sovereign state is legally and morally responsible for protecting (citizens from core international crimes as identified in the R2P doctrine) and ensuring the rights (as spelled out in the human security doctrine) of its citizens. If 'unable or unwilling' to fulfil its responsibility as a State, then the 'international community' is morally (not legally) obliged to intervene and carry out the state's unmet responsibilities vis-à-vis its citizens. In such a view, a State's sovereignty is perceived as 'better' if it becomes a signatory of the Court, as it underlines its commitment to ensure the protection of its citizens. Allowing an international institution jurisdiction over state territory, and giving it the power to prosecute and punish current heads of state, is not to be seen as 'giving up' sovereignty; instead, ratifying the Rome Statute is reframed as a symbol of responsible sovereignty.

> When you sign up for the Rome Statute, yes you give up some of your sovereignty, but what you're actually saying is: 'we're so committed to the protection of our people and the ability of our people to have recourse to an institution if we were to commit these crimes, that we don't mind an external—it will ensure that our citizens are protected'... It (the ICC) is actually an extension of your sovereignty: 'we will protect our people to the extent that we actually take it out of our hands' ... There's no greater expression of state sovereignty than actually being able to sign up to the Rome Statute.

This is a particularly interesting way of thinking about the State and of the idea of sovereignty. Human rights law and international tribunals alike have eroded the 'traditional' power of a State over its citizens. From a position of controller and supervisor of criminal justice processes, the State is now rendered a subject or participant in these processes through the very idea of state crimes and the criminal state—at times a victim or offender, obstructer or promoter of criminal justice (Cotterrell, 2015: 13). The view expressed by my informant above reflects this relocation of how the State is imagined, including its shifting role as the principal actor of social order.

> Within the pluralist world, states could be understood as 'agents' simply in the sense of those acting or exerting power and of doing so for themselves ... But the expanding normative agenda of solidarism has opened up a second and different meaning of agency—the idea of an agent as someone who acts for, or on behalf of, another. Within the solidarist order, states are no longer to act for themselves as sovereigns; but rather,

first, as agents for the individuals, groups, and national communities that they are supposed to represent; and second, as agents or interpreters of some notion of an international public good and some set of core norms against which state behaviour should be judged and evaluated. One of the most important aspects of solidarism is the idea that the norms that constitute what the state is, and what it is supposed to represent, become a formal part of the normative and legal order. (Hurrell, 2007: 65–6)

Before exploring further how the normative agenda is implemented into imaginations of the State, this reframing of agency into representation enables the participation of other actors, including non-state actors such as human rights NGOs.

Representing humanity

Above, I have described a view of the State as being threatening and a cause for concern. Part of this perception relates to a view of the State as standing for *its own inherent interests*—as an entity in itself—rather than protecting the interests of its citizens and constituency. This perception therefore explains how my informants saw the pluralist global order as an undesirable benchmark for global justice-making, compared to their cosmopolitan solidarity. It is therefore interesting to note how human rights NGOs sometimes frame themselves in opposition to the image of states' failure to act on behalf of their citizens; while states stand for their 'own' state interests, NGOs stand for 'the people'. For example, a Coalition representative asserted that, 'I'm not saying governments don't represent their people but they also have that side to them—they also represent state interests—whereas perhaps we don't have state interests as such.' Rather than state interests, NGOs claim to have the interests of 'people' in mind, not the citizenry of one particular state (which not even states are claimed to have) but an abstract notion of the world's people, the global citizenry. This perception of representing 'the people'—the global civil society—is fundamental to their moral authority. States may claim political authority, and to speak for their citizens because they have been elected, but human rights NGOs claim normative legitimacy on the grounds they are speaking for *all* peoples—beyond the political worldly and the universal interests of the human.

Occasionally however, this claim to moral authority and normative legitimacy was presented in a way that seems rather *like* political authority, especially in regards to their lobbying strategies (see also Lohne, 2017). A Coalition representative explained their strategy vis-a-vis The Hague Working Group meetings: 'It is something that we've worked very hard towards ... that when we go to these meetings that they (states) view us as parties, like complete and respected parties to the discussion.' This supports previous accounts of how Coalition representatives attempt to 'act like' diplomats in their advocacy, and it is reasonable to ask on what representational grounds they should be viewed as parties on a par with states in diplomatic deliberations. The perspective of another Secretariat staff member offers insights: 'They (state representatives) are all individuals, they're all regular Joes, and technically, they're all part of civil society—they're all people. One diplomat once said to me: "You're representing me! You're the people, and I'm one of them, so we're on the same page".' I ask if state representatives do not represent the people: 'Well, they represent governments more, don't they?'

In this way, claims to moral and political authority become entangled in the name of cosmopolitan solidarity and human rights. Whilst states are seen as representing some innate features of the State, which are neither necessarily benevolent nor concerned with the best interests of its citizen constituency, human rights NGOs view themselves as beyond the infection of self-interest and singularity. Wanting to be seen as 'political' delegations, they position themselves as better equipped to speak for 'the people'—the citizens of humanity—than elected governments and their officials. One of my informants provided an example of this as regarding the ongoing political situation in the Netherlands, and the political leverage of Geert Wilders's Party for Freedom in the Dutch Parliament. She said: 'If you work for the government, who do you really work for? We don't have this ... Like two million people of my fellow human beings in the Netherlands vote for him! ... At least our masters are these grand principles.'

The idea of 'humanity' is the idea of a cosmopolitan moral community. 'Humanity' implies that human kind belongs to one single moral realm, that there is an 'essence' of the human species that is transcendental and universal. A crime against humanity is thus a crime against this imagined moral community of humanity (see also Malkki, 1994), a desecration of the sacred self. Victims, in their representation of desecrated human life, represent a desecration of the self. A crime against humanity not only violates the values of the moral order of humanity but also produces individualized outrage in the face of this destruction of the sacred. It is the moral outrage of the onlookers, the participants in the field of international criminal justice, and, critically, the international audiences of humanitarian spectacles that lead to international punishment. I therefore suggest a reading of international criminal justice, with all its inadequacies and shortcomings, as a reinforcement of the moral community of 'humanity'.

According to a Durkheimean interpretation of international criminal justice, humanity is 'reconstituted' through the international penal process and its punishment of crimes. Impunity for international crimes becomes, by contrast, reflective of humanity's degeneration, reflecting a sign of weakness in the legal and moral order. This adds theoretical depth to the discussion of amnesty in Chapter 5, the notion of amnesty becoming a symbol of weakness and a threat to the dominant moral order. Similarly, it offers insights into how we can understand why Amnesty International (AI) insists on the importance of criminal prosecution, in spite of opposition from local civil society and 'individual victims' in northern Uganda.

> Even if it is individuals who are victims of crime, the seriousness of the crime has to be judged ultimately by its consequences in that network as a whole. If criminal punishment rather than individual redress is required it is because the wrong is viewed as sufficiently serious to threaten the order or security of the entire communal network, the general ideas about justice widely presumed within it, or the basic conditions of trust and interdependence (solidarity) that underpin it. (Cotterrell, 2015: 19)

The fight against impunity therefore becomes a fight *for* humanity. In other words, criminal punishment for international crimes comes to constitute a shared common morality in which 'humanity' is sacred. This collective moral order is necessarily the overriding concern of human rights NGOs. The ICC is thus the manifestation of humanity's protection, the *conscience collective* or the dominant moral order, which is in need of preservation. '[P]ursuing global justice by means of international criminal law suggests a *common* goal insofar as it is something "we, humanity" are understood to pursue together' (Corrias and Gordon, 2015: 104). In what follows however, I explore how contemporary manifestations of global solidarity also have 'coercive' characteristics, showing not only how the cosmopolitan penal imaginary is implemented as a deliberate process beyond The Hague, but also, critically, raises questions about the nature of state consent and penal power.

International Crimes and Local Justice: The ICC as a Multiscalar Project

International criminal justice is not conceptualized exclusively as a 'global' project, meaning something applied on a global scale, but is rather seen as a *multiscalar* project in need of implementation at the global, regional, and local levels. Mindful of the reconceptualization of the collective consciousness as the *dominant* moral order, this section turns its attention to 'the ideological work that has to be done to maintain a particular moral order in dominance' (Garland, 1990b: 53). Having situated human rights NGOs at the centre of this moral order, it is their role as carriers of values within the cosmopolitan imaginary that will be explored here. I argue that the exporting of what has become cosmopolitan values takes place in the name of 'positive complementarity', and that this development is not only a deliberate and engaged process, but also something that demonstrates the civilizing dynamic underlying the ICC project. Riding on the back of positive complementarity, the ICC has become a vehicle for unleashing a variety of criminal justice 'exports', what Aas (2011: 411) refers to as 'penal cosmopolitanism':

> Aspiring to universality beyond the mere core of human rights, this type of intervention captures a broader set of conditions, such as police practice, prison conditions, criminal law legislation, as well as the agendas of the war on drugs, terror and trafficking. Crime control and criminal justice reform are becoming increasingly popular modes of so-called political capacity building.

'King on the hill, forcing down'

According to the Principle of Complementarity, the ICC is a court of last resort. What this implies is that a case is only admissible to the Court where the 'State is unwilling or unable genuinely to carry out the investigation or prosecution' (Article 17, the Rome Statute). An often repeated mantra during interviews were 'complementarity is the future'. Along with this, the concept of *positive* complementarity has emerged and become a core principle in the field; it is mentioned and recognized, for example, in the official records and resolutions from the ICC review conference in Kampala in 2010 (ICC, 2010b; ICC, 2010a). However, what is meant by positive complementarity—what does it mean for the NGOs—and if this is the future, where is the future headed?

In The Hague, I asked a Coalition representative if she thinks universal jurisdiction will eventually evolve beyond the four core international crimes to include general criminal law:

Yes, absolutely! This is one of the things we're using the Rome Statute and the ICC for. It's not only a tool to fight impunity in itself, but also to—and this is positive complementarity, as we call it here in The Hague—but a tool to strengthen national jurisdictions. This is one of our main focuses as a coalition, to ensure that the Rome Statute and all the laws it has are implemented in national proceedings and jurisdictions. Then, in Ethiopia (for example), in fifty years or so, you won't even need the ICC ... That will never happen of course, but that is the idea. Once we finally manage to have the whole 193 states ratify—we only have 71 to go ... so we still have work to do—once we manage that, we'll then work towards global change and we'll gear our efforts into building—which we already do—national proceedings. That will help, it does help, and it helps already. Following the ratification of the Rome Statute; in most countries it's being implemented into national law, and that is fantastic if you think about it. On a national level, these crimes can now be prosecuted. That is a huge achievement already! And that is why we often call it the 'Rome Statute system of justice'. It's not only the ICC—it's the whole system! It's also the Trust Fund for Victims, it's having all of this on the agenda of the UN, of states, of ministries of foreign affairs, of academics—it's a system and the whole thing is boosting!

A senior NGO representative told me that most NGOs opposed the inclusion of the Principle of Complementarity in the Rome Statute under the treaty negotiations in 1998, seeing it as a sovereign shield for impunity. 'But we were wrong, and we realized it after Rome. I mean, I realized it before, but Amnesty and Human Rights Watch realized it after Rome: "Oh my God, that was genius!" ... King on the hill, forcing down.' What is alluded to is a view of the ICC as sovereign (King), as it is the Court that inevitably rules on its admissibility of cases and situations, and thus, on whether a domestic criminal justice system is 'able or willing'. In other words, the ICC has the final word in 'adjudicating' domestic criminal justice systems. This may be seen as an example of what Hurrell (2007: 65) identifies as 'part of a broader move towards coercive solidarism', with the 'expansion of different forms of conditionality'.

At the centre of this normative agenda are human rights NGOs, whose embrace of 'positive complementarity' can be interpreted as a result of two interrelated processes, one discursive and the other structural. First, reframing international criminal justice as rule of law development and capacity building fundamentally widens the field, and thus the areas of expertise, from an exclusive focus on *international* justice to that of *domestic* justice in states around the world. This also widens the job market for transnational justice experts (see Chapter 4): one of my informants talked about 'switching fields': 'Some of the positions I'm thinking of are more rule of law related—what's called in this field complementarity, but in essence are support for law reform and justice reform.' Moreover, the spread of international criminal justice through 'domestication', that is, implementation of 'international standards' in domestic systems is perceived as going in tandem with the overall agenda of the NGOs, namely the diffusion of human rights norms and the spread of cosmopolitan sensibilities. Several of the NGO representatives emphasized the need to 'mainstream' international criminal justice—in the name of positive complementarity—with development programmes on the rule of law, because, as one NGO representative put it: 'Criminal justice is part of the wider rule of law progress.' The underlying presumption is that the fight against impunity cannot be carried on at the international level exclusively, but has to be implemented—mainstreamed—at the domestic level as well.

> If you want to prevent—if you want to strengthen the rule of law—it's not all going to happen with the ICC in The Hague. You need some work to be done at the national level. So call it complementarity, call it rule of law, call it, you know, states taking up their own responsibilities—it has to happen.

As the 'king on the hill, forcing down', implementing legislation from the Rome Statute in domestic systems is also assumed to have trickle-down effects on the domestic system of justice generally, and, almost as if by magic, *morally appropriate* trickle-down effects. An NGO representative explained: 'By eliminating the death penalty for these crimes, eventually you may be able to eliminate it for ordinary crimes because it doesn't make sense. Working on enhancing domestic prosecutions and their capabilities—of course that has a spill-over to any other crime!' As discussed in Chapter 5, the type of punishment imposed by international criminal justice institutions, from prison conditions to sentence length, seems disproportionately 'lenient' considering the heinous acts offenders are convicted of. I noted there how this reflects a 'hybrid' form of justice compared to western domestic justice systems, one in which human rights are at the same time both a punitive and 'civilizing', or humanitarian, force. The death penalty, for example, is not in accord with the values of human rights. Looking at punishment and sentencing of international criminals within a Durkheimian frame of analysis, it seems natural that, when the function of international criminal justice is to strengthen the social bonds, morals, and values within global society—and these values place the sacredness of universal human rights at its core—one cannot use punishments that weaken the very values one wishes to reinforce.

Working for universal ratification and domestication of the Rome Statute in national legal systems is one of the NGO Coalition's main objectives. Out of the major NGOs, Parliamentarians for Global Action (PGA) and Open Society Justice Initiative (OSJI) are particularly active on issues of positive complementarity. A representative from OSJI explained:

> Now our approach on complementarity—which is something that we've advocated very strongly for—is to ensure that complementarity is integrated into broader rule of law programs ... The ICC, it should impact the domestic system. See the challenges the ICC is facing with witness protection. If the Court goes into a conflict in Kenya where there is a national witness protection agency, the Court should have a relationship with the national witness protection agency—help strengthen it! Because the Court is not going to be able to deal with its witnesses all by itself, the Court is going to need that national witness protection agency. But when the Court finally steps out of the situation—you know, that's the case we're in—the national witness protection agency will continue doing an excellent job—a job of a high standard.

This endeavour is confirmed by their publications on the topic. 'International Crimes, Local Justice', for example, is described as a 'complementarity toolkit' to ensure that criminal accountability for crimes that are so categorized internationally is enforced locally, that is, at the national level (OSJI, 2011). Part of this effort and one of their complementarity pilot projects is the aforementioned 'mobile courts' in the Democratic Republic of the Congo (DRC) (Chapter 6).

Advocacy efforts were also believed to be increasingly geared towards capitals instead of exclusively at international levels. In view of the increasing resistance towards the ICC's meddling in the internal affairs of African states, one possible explanation is that positive complementarity has been framed as a means to keep the ICC at a distance, as the ICC only intervenes in situations where it does not consider state efforts 'genuine'. For example, the issue of complementarity became central to the situation in Uganda when the government realized (albeit a little late perhaps) that the only way to reclaim ownership of the conflict was to challenge the ICC's admissibility of cases based on whether or not the Ugandan state was unable or unwilling to proceed with investigations and prosecutions themselves (Nouwen, 2012).

Positive complementarity in Uganda

Among the rule of law developments prompted by the ICC intervention in Uganda is the establishment of the 'International Crimes Division', or the 'Special Division of the High Court',[3] and the implementation of the 'ICC Act', that is, domestication of the ICC in Uganda's penal code. According to the International Crimes Division's websites:

> While originally meant to be part of a comprehensive peace agreement with the LRA, the International Crimes Division has come to be viewed as a court of 'complementarity' with respect to the International Criminal Court, thus fulfilling the principle of complementarity stipulated in the preamble and Article 1 of the Rome Statute.[4]

As part of these efforts, the ICD began its first case in 2011 against former LRA colonel Thomas Kwoyelo. During my interviews

[3] The War Crimes Commission originally developed out of the Juba peace talks, spelled out in the Agreement on Accountability and Reconciliation between the Government of the Republic of Uganda and the Lord's Resistance Army (LRA)/Movement (Juba, June 2007), and the Annexure to the Agreement of Accountability and Reconciliation (Juba, February 2008). Nouwen (2012) interprets this as a compromise reached as a result of the impending arrest warrants against the LRA.

[4] See http://www.judiciary.go.ug/data/smenu/18/International%20Crimes%20Division.html (accessed 14 November 2018).

in Gulu, the ICD and its case against Kwoyelo were broadly dismissed:

> This is a court established to serve someone else's interest—it's just for show! 'Let us establish this court so that ICC won't come after more of our people.' This special court, it is just symbolic, it was only established as a legal structure—nothing happens with it, it's just sham. And one may also ask: who is it that is tried before the court here? Kwoyelo—he was kidnapped as a child! And now he is to be punished because the government didn't manage to protect him? Because the international community didn't manage to protect him? Is this right? Where is the responsibility for those that do not manage to protect our children?

Located in the up-scale district of Nakasero, the International Crimes Commission occupies a conspicuous location in Kampala's expat area. The case against Kwoyelo immediately faced problems, as the Constitutional Court ruled to cease proceedings against him in 2011 on grounds that he was applicable for amnesty under the Amnesty Act (see Chapter 5). The ruling was not acted upon however, and Kwoyelo has remained in prison throughout a legal quagmire that resulted in a Supreme Court decision in 2015 denying him amnesty, effectively setting 'precedent [which] removes the legal security that amnesty provided to thousands of people' (Bradfield, 2017: 853), many of whose atrocious acts were committed under coercive circumstances, including the threat of death. On the one hand, this seems like complementarity in practice (and on paper). On the other, these are some of the tensions embedded in the system, whereby international criminal justice as a universalizing 'global design' (Mignolo, 2000) traverse local and national conceptualization of justice and reconciliation.

Nouwen (2013) is one of the few who have conducted empirical research on complementarity in the setting of Uganda (see also Clarke, 2009). She is highly critical of the way complementarity is used by international NGOs as a way to promote their agendas, notwithstanding their moral intentions to develop rule of law and human rights. While the Rome Statute is silent on criteria for domestic procedures, international NGOs have been working with and for an interpretation suggesting that domestic processes should 'mirror' that of the ICC, thereby taking advantage of conceptual ambiguities between 'ratification' and 'domestication' of the Rome Statute in their work. Mindful of their aim to promote human rights agendas and the ICC, and prior to the adoption of the ICC Act in Ugandan law, international NGOs had been working diligently to create parliamentary support, writing legal drafts and commentaries, and organizing events with parliamentarians and others.

> Instead of explaining what the Statute actually requires, they explained what, in their view, the Statue should require. Thus, whereas the Rome Statute requires states to adopt legislation only for cooperation, these NGOs argued that a state must domesticate the Rome Statute crimes; whereas the Rome Statute explicitly leaves states to determine the penalties applicable in their domestic proceedings, these NGOs contended that there can be no death penalty for international crimes because the Rome Statute does not apply it ... Some NGOs come with entire draft ICC Acts, stating that their draft amounts to a 'state-of-the-art ICC act, better than in many western countries. (Nouwen, 2012: 15)

This illustrates how 'complementarity' in the Rome Statute system of justice is used as a vehicle for universalizing a set of ideas, having become an instrument of rule of law promotion for *under*developed domestic systems of justice.

Parliamentarians for Global Action

One of the organizations that work specifically on creating momentum for the implementation of the ICC in domestic legislation is Parliamentarians for Global Action (PGA). Only sitting parliamentarians from democracies can become members of the network, but as pointed out by its Secretariat staff members, individuals that have left parliament continue to be important resources, especially in terms of establishing contacts. PGA describe themselves as non-partisan, and say they recruit to ensure multipartisan membership, and work to attract members from opposition parties as well as sitting governments. They do so claiming that their aims and objectives are *beyond* politics and that support for and promotion of the ICC and its 'domestication' in national legislation is in the interest of all, independent of political affiliations. 'We work with all parties—we cannot be seen as supporting a particular candidate. We need to maintain our nonpartisanship because we need to engage everybody.' Nonetheless, their strategy makes it clear that they are well aware of the fact that, even though they represent their objectives as above politics, they are dependent on politics to achieve them—their aims need to be implemented *through* politics, and importantly, through state politics. Political strategy is therefore central to how they run the network.

PGA navigates on the margins of politics. Because of their claim to non-partisanship, they cannot be seen to engage too closely with political outcomes, even where these are favourable. Their strategy is to *facilitate* politics that work in favour of their overall goals—a rule-based order with the Rome Statute at its core. At the same time, they act as a type of agenda-setter by bringing both causes and funds to the table. Implementation however, is dependent on 'traditional' legislators and state structures. Yet the Secretariat in The Hague explains that they have indeed contributed directly to drafting processes in implementing legislation in national jurisdictions, and claim to have drafted entire deals and bills, and amended adopted legislations, including incorporating the ICC into national constitutions.[5] In some circumstances, governments have officially requested their technical expertise to help do so; in other cases, governments 'officially' draft legislation, and the PGA Secretariat acts as their staff.

Although the organization does not provide a list of its members, they do chart their members' geographical locations. One of their biggest networks of parliamentarians is in the DRC, where they claim to have more than fifty members; likewise, in Uganda and Kenya, their membership is so large that they have hired local staff to coordinate them. As explained by their Secretariat staff, they have more members in the global South because incentives for joining and being affiliated with the network are more attractive to non-European parliamentarians:

> In Europe, many of them don't need a network like PGA because they have the structure, they have the money to go wherever they want, they have the connections in the European Parliament—they don't even have time ... it's definitely more useful for other countries than Europeans ... it also gives legitimacy, even to their own government.

On the one hand, this reflects the recurring notion of the 'international' or 'global' as status leverage: that just being affiliated to global networks and organizations somehow confers importance.

[5] The countries in which they claim to have done so are withheld by the request of informants.

At the same time PGA illustrate how the global is fundamentally constituted within the national (Sassen, 2001; Sassen, 2007). On a less abstract level however, are the 'perks' involved with being affiliated with these networks. As a Secretariat member explains when I asked her why she thinks parliamentarians join the network:

Some think they can travel, some want to go to conferences because they're genuinely interested, some want to work on the issues, some believe in the cause, some wants to have a share of power in an organization and they get on board and try to rule. You know, this is the world. There are so many reasons. I wouldn't be able to pin it down; each parliamentarian has a different reason, and different moments. We just try to exploit to the best whatever reasons and put them to use for the objectives of the program.

At the same time, this notion of the superiority of the 'international' and 'global' is strengthened by the parallel perception of the 'rule of law' as a valuable *in and of itself* (Humphreys, 2010), as if more law equals more justice. In previous chapters, I have addressed the 'force of law' (Bourdieu 1986) in the fight against impunity. The PGA is a prime example of how an NGO can draw on legal capital to create legitimacy for both the organization itself and importantly, its vision of a rule-based global moral order.

An implication of this, however, is that law triumphs over politics; in the same way that human rights are elevated above the political, so is law, which is seen as representing the universal 'right'. While politics may be subject to criticism and contestation, the rule of law, coupled with human rights law, becomes sacrosanct—beyond reach. Like humanitarianism, international criminal law becomes a moral force, as something inevitable and 'natural', of something that is already out there.

In a way, we are a political organization, so we have certain principles. We do not issue opinions on judicial decisions. Even if our staff may have sophisticated legal views on the validity of the decisions, we do not do it, because we won't interfere with the rule of law, and we want to teach that parliamentarians adopt a stance that judicial decisions are implemented, not argued against: you don't nitpick which judicial decisions you want to support or not.

What is striking about the quotation is how they claim not to interfere with the rule of law, which of course on the one hand goes along with judicial independence. On the other hand, however, judicial interference is the *raison d'être* of the organization, *albeit at the national level.* It is the *international* rule of law that is held sacred. Yet, what guarantees are there that the international is better than the national? What if a rules-based order is a *bad* rules-based order, a world government a despotic one? What underlies the cosmopolitan imagination are not only assumptions of what 'better' means, but also the idea that this has been determined once and for all, so that 'international' and 'rule of law' become values in and of themselves.

Whose Cosmopolitanism? Whose Humanity?

So far, this chapter has dealt with the mentalities and sensibilities of cosmopolitanism as they play out in global criminal justice-making. I have situated human rights NGOs at the centre of this imaginary, as providers of cultural authority in its implementation. By calling forth the moral outrage of one part of humanity at the crimes committed against another, human rights NGOs mediate the makings of a global moral order. The ICC, in its ability to punish irrespective of state sovereignty (albeit more in theory than in practice), and with a conception of humanity as its global constituency, is a materiality of an as yet unfinished ideal of world solidarity based on universal cosmopolitan values, and the cult of the individual—human rights for citizens of humanity. I have shown how this is implemented as a normative and deliberate project of progress, and that as a universal project, it aspires to expand (Tsing, 2005). However, whereas the above has focused on expressions of cosmopolitanism—its objectives and means—this final part will turn to the tacit assumptions underlying the cosmopolitan project of global justice-making through international criminal law.

In The Hague, I talked to an NGO representative about the ICC and its multiscalar ambitions. She brings up the notion of whether one can really talk about a difference between rule of law at the national and international levels; 'they're so interlinked,' she said, and continued: 'It's mind-blowing, and I love that! I just really love that idea, that feeling on a very personal basis, but, you know, that we're all linked.' I asked her to explain the feeling, why she thinks she loves it so much.

I don't know. It's emotional, I don't know. I've never really sought to answer that question for myself, (but) like I said, even since I was a pre-teenager, I loved it ... the international, how much I loved that when I was small. Like the European Union, I was following it since I was really, really small. It's an emotional thing; I don't know why I love it so much. I just love the fact you're breaking out of your own thing ...

She explained that she loves anything international, that when growing up, 'as long as it had the prefix international, I would be interested.' I asked her whether she thinks it is related to her growing up in a different European country than that of her parents and citizenship.

I think so. I grew up thinking I was such a foreigner. Since I was 18 I got the (European state X) nationality as well, which is good. But maybe that's it. I was so foreign until I realized that beyond Western Europe, there are other cultures. And then: 'Oh, pretty much the same as (European state Y).' And I grew up in a town which is very white, and I had no different cultural influences whatsoever. So maybe that's the reason why I find it so interesting. Growing up I had this feeling of being between two countries, two cultures—differences—and I loved that. And I just find it fascinating as well, and that's the reason why I studied law: this idea that we're all individuals and then we connect with one another and we relinquish those individual mind-sets that we have, and then all together as a community we set up these rules. I found that fascinating. And then at another level as nations we do that as well. It's really an emotional thing I think, but that's why I love working here as well.

Her narrative offers interesting insights into conceptions of the universal essentials of both the international, and of law: 'breaking out of', 'relinquishing individual mind-sets' in order to 'connect with one another' informs her representation of the potential of both the international and of law. Rather than addressing 'authenticity', such narratives and sensibilities inform social imaginaries of justice in today's world, and particularly imaginaries of those that advocate for justice to be done when dealing with global violence.

However, as Koskenniemi (2002b: 486) has forewarned, the 'great danger in cosmopolitan thought is that its cosmopolitanism will show itself to be false—a façade for particular interests'. My approach to humanity as the collective consciousness is animated by a reconfiguration of the concept as reflective of the dominant moral order, or 'ruling morality'; as an expression of the *dominant* moral order rather than as an 'authentic', or universal, conscience.

This does not undermine the 'realness' of collective sentiments, nor their social force—quite the contrary. As much as sensibilities and mentalities are rooted in individuals, in their emotional and moral dispositions, they are also outcomes of historical, political, and social processes. 'Laws and state actions do not simply "express" such sentiments—they also seek to transform and reshape them in accordance with a particular vision of society' (Garland, 1990b: 54).

Conclusions

In examining parts of what can be referred to as a cosmopolitan penal imaginary, this book has been concerned with the representatives of this imaginary and with human rights NGOs in particular. I have shown how there is an important dimension of class and situatedness in global justice-making that is much less articulated than its universal claims. A spatial inquiry makes clear that the view of global justice is a view from The Hague (see Chapter 2). This is also reflected in the dominant position of the Coalition for the ICC, and its core members of predominantly international human rights NGOs. These are very much part of the knowledge-based networks of international criminal justice, and by extension, the interpretive community of global justice-making (see Chapter 3). The idea of a 'global consciousness' as a foundation of a universal cultural authority for criminalization is a fantasy, it seems, paralleling the notion of a global 'international community' as a universal politico-legal authority (Cotterrell, 2015). Rather, this research has demonstrated how, instead, limited transnational networks of power animate cultural authority for global criminalization, relying on various forms of authority and relations. The book has shown how these networks are dominated by people with European, visa-friendly passports (see Chapter 5), and as such, serves as an indicator of how the 'transformationist rhetoric about "post-Westphalia" substantially overstates the degree to which we have in fact moved beyond a state- and sovereignty-based order' (Hurrell, 2007: 9). There is a particular lifestyle associated with those empowered to mediate the dominant moral order, to act and speak in the name of humanity. This lifestyle is characterized by transnational encounters and, as one of my informants described it, an 'Erasmus vibe'. Rather than seeing a global collective consciousness bearing down on individuals, I therefore, following a radicalization of Durkheim's view on law and society, suggest that individuals, coming together to share ideas and sentiments alike, develop collective beliefs and convictions that direct their lives (Cotterrell, 1999). Cosmopolitanism is not merely a philosophical worldview, but is profoundly social. It also, crucially, appears to be 'the class consciousness of frequent travellers' (Calhoun, 2002): Advocates of humanity propose a claim to being without recognition of their situatedness in materialities and determining social bases. 'In offering a seeming "view from nowhere" … [c]osmopolitanism is a discourse centered in a Western view of the world' (Calhoun, 2002: 873). Despite its claims to universality, cosmopolitanism emerges as a classed phenomenon; and despite its claims to universality, the 'global' collective consciousness is situated in particular segments of 'humanity' in a way uncomfortably reminiscent of colonialism and its civilizing mission. Through the objectification of the violent landscape as 'crimes against humanity', 'we, humanity' situate ourselves as part of this landscape—as moral subjects. From a position as onlookers of humanitarian suffering—as witnesses—we 'mark out the terrain of what is good and what is evil' (Razack, 2007: 381). In this manner, it demonstrates how humanity is split, how it breaks up into parts—into victims and saviours, good and evil.

> One part is the humanity that suffers, the human as victim; the other is the humanity that saves, the human as rescuer. Humanity's goodness depends on its suffering but without goodness suffering would not be recognized … Humanity suffers because parts of it are evil, degenerate, cruel and inflict indescribable horrors upon the rest. There can be no redemption without sin, no gift without deprivation, no Band Aid without famine. (Douzinas, 2007b: 12)

Recognition of—moral outrage at—humanity's suffering thus becomes a way of constituting humanity's 'essence'; the assumption of a common global morality materializes through recognition of crimes committed against it. The representational dichotomy between victims needing to be saved by international criminal justice and villains whose impunity makes international criminal justice necessary, is thus fundamental to the narrative purpose of global criminal justice-making (Sagan, 2010). International criminal punishment demonstrates a recognition that the 'delicate mosaic' of humanity has been desacralized through crimes committed against it (the Rome Statute's Preamble). If 'we, humanity' remain silent and do nothing, 'the collective beliefs and sentiments fade, endangering the existence of an audible "we"' (Tallgren, 2015: 148). Crimes against humanity, and efforts to punish them, therefore serve to reinforce the notion of 'humanity', and with that, the humanitarian imaginary of a global moral order.

While the two previous chapters dealt with the role and perceptions of victims and criminals, retribution and restoration, as well as humanitarian and penal sensibilities, this chapter discussed the inevitable third part in the adjudication of conflict—the judge, the punisher, the sovereign. Engaging with 'the voice of the international' (Tallgren, 2015), it is shown how international criminal justice punishes in the name of humanity, the same humanity that human rights NGOs advocate on behalf of. However, I have argued for a view of 'humanity' as reflecting a dominant global moral order, and one which, albeit solidarist, is coercively and deliberatively implemented. Through the notion of 'positive complementarity', global justice-making through international criminal law is a multiscalar project, associated with rule of law promotion and penal aid in situations of 'failed' justice. Bringing ideas and structures, imaginations and materialities together, I have argued that 'humanity' is split, and that the cosmopolitan vision is a vision associated with a particular group of people, speaking from a particular place. In my concluding chapter, I will situate some of the implications of this discrepancy for the understanding of current resistance towards international criminal justice, and for a sociology of punishment for international criminal justice.

8

Towards a Sociology of Punishment for International Criminal Justice

'Today is a dark day for international criminal justice,' said the International Criminal Court's Chief Prosecutor Fatou Bensouda on 4 December 4 2014. She had just announced the withdrawal of the charges against Kenya's President Uhuru Kenyatta, on grounds that 'the Kenyan Government's non-compliance compromised the Prosecution's ability to thoroughly investigate the charges' (ICC, 2014). Besides demonstrating the ICC's impotence vis-à-vis state power, the Kenya situation is significant because the two previous political adversaries President Kenyatta and Vice President William Ruto rose to power *after* their indictments. By electing individuals who were indicted by the ICC, supporters of the current Kenyan government protested against the Court and its administration of justice. It raises questions about the ICC's legitimacy, as a large portion of the Court's anticipated beneficiaries rejected it by voting against it.

Following their entry into office, the Kenyan government mobilized support against the ICC nationally as well as regionally through a deliberate charge of neo-colonialism. Following the ICC indictments, Kenya engaged in shuttle diplomacy regionally and internationally (De Hoon and Lohne, 2019). They used a variety of means to gain control over the legal process, such as asking the Security Council for a deferral, challenging the ICC's admissibility of the cases, and mobilizing regional legal processes such as the East African Court of Justice and the African Court of Justice and Human Rights (Mueller, 2014). In the run up to the October 2012 African Union (AU) extraordinary summit called to discuss the ICC proceedings against the Sudanese and Kenyan heads of state, there were many rumours about the prospect of a mass

Advocates of Humanity. Kjersti Lohne, Oxford University Press (2019). © Kjersti Lohne.
DOI: 10.1093/oso/9780198818748.003.0008

withdrawal from the ICC by African states. In early July 2014, the AU voted to grant heads of state immunity in proceedings at the African Court for Justice and Human Rights. This rejection of the absolute view of sovereignty, to the extent that the 'international community' can hold state leaders criminally accountable for violence against their citizens, is heralded as the *sine qua non* of the international criminal justice project. The withdrawal and vacation of charges against Kenyatta and Ruto, and the AU vote to grant heads of state immunity in the regional court, thus represent serious threats to the realization of the penal imaginary outlined in this book.

However, there is nothing inevitable about the global. While the analysis in this book has been concerned with the nature of the relationship between 'global civil society' and global justice-making, focusing on mobilizations and networks, connections and disconnections, there is now more pushback against the project of international criminal justice than ever before (Madsen et al., 2018). While several African countries expressed their intentions to leave the Court, Burundi (and the Philippines) so far are the only states to have done so (in attempts to escape legal accountability, as the situations are under ICC investigation and preliminary examination, respectively). The road ahead will be no less difficult, with the OTP's investigatory moves into the situation of Georgia and in relation to the armed conflict in Afghanistan, potentially implicating big powers, most notably Russia and the US.

The political turmoil facing the ICC must be seen alongside a changing geopolitical landscape. This book has dealt with global justice-making as it developed in the post-Cold War 1990s with ad hoc tribunals, the creation of the Rome Statute system of justice, and the parallel transnational justice movement founded upon notions of universal human rights. This period was not only the end of the Cold War, but represented, as Fukuyama famously claimed, the 'end of history', by which he meant 'the end point of mankind's ideological evolution and the universalization of Western liberal democracy as the final form of human government' (Fukuyama, 1989). In the newfound unipolar world order, universalism replaced ideology, and human rights went from being David's weapon against Goliath to becoming the *lingua franca* of the new world order. US power, market-based democratic liberalism, and a European legacy of secular religiosity subsumed human rights as part of its work to shape a 'plausible metanarrative of impartiality'

(Hopgood, 2013: 171). This was the golden age of international humanism, law making, and institutionalization. Now, however, the 'transformationist rhetoric about "post-Westphalia"'(Hurrell, 2007: 9) is declining in response to the emergence of a multipolar world order. The world today is one of revived sovereignty, and of stagnation and pushback against universal norms about human rights (Hopgood, 2013). With the rise of great powers such as China and India and the renewed cooling of relations between Russia and the West, global justice-making appears increasingly impotent, the lack of intervention in Syria being the paradigmatic example.

An equal if not more critical challenge to the international criminal justice project is its frequent rejection and disdain from those in whose name justice is done. For survivors of violence coded as international crimes, international criminal justice has been accused of being too little too late, to destabilize and disrupt peace negotiations, and to crowd out alternative paths towards peace, justice, and reconciliation in the aftermath of mass violence. There is thus fundamental friction in the relationship between those advocating and representing international criminal law and its institutions and ideas in international politics, and the societies most affected by its practices (Tallgren, 2015).

Thus there are grounds for reiterating the NGOs' mantra in international criminal justice advocacy that justice must not only be done but must also be *seen* to be done. While it is generally used when advocating for outreach and communications with a court constituency (e.g. HRW, 2009), this watchword recalls the importance of appearances.[1] Representations and images matter. The legitimacy of the ICC cannot just be assessed in terms of rationally defensible principles, such as those justifying the ICC's selective 'targeting' of Africa as a result of African states' self-referrals to the Court, or the Court's limited jurisdiction over violence committed in other territories, such as Palestine, Syria, and so forth. Legitimacy is also contingent on relevant social actors recognizing the court as rightful, including its staff and representatives, those subject to its power, and other third-party actors (Beetham, 2013). Social legitimacy is an ongoing dialogue between power-holders' claims to legitimacy, audience response,

[1] It originates from the English case *R* v. *Sussex Justices, Ex parte McCarthy* ([1924] 1 KB 256, All ER 233).

and—if they are receptive—power-holders' adjustment of their legitimacy claims (Bottoms and Tankebe, 2012). This means that international criminal justice must culturally embed itself within societies, securing 'grounding in populations that can culturally "own" this law' (Cotterrell, 2015: 22). Yet, it appears contemporary resistance towards the ICC precisely mobilizes on the lack of ownership, on the lack of its cultural embeddedness; it challenges the ICC's authority to represent 'the global', as its claim to universality is interpreted as a façade for particularist interest. The shadow of winner's justice that has followed international criminal justice since Nuremberg is now transformed into a suspicion that international criminal justice is a tool employed by certain states to impose a system of global criminal justice upon less powerful ones (Cotterrell, 2015). In this process, notions of crime, punishment, and justice have become instruments of power and governance beyond the national domain to control foreign populations.

This book has attempted sociological explanation to the legitimacy challenge that global justice-making is currently experiencing. The situatedness of global criminal justice-making—its trends, characteristics, and dynamics—point to a deeper lack of authority at the level of global criminal justice-making. Exacerbated by geopolitical shifts, 'universality' is starting to break apart (Lohne 2018c), along with international criminal justice and its supporting structure of human rights NGOs' claiming to represent it. In what follows, I will briefly revisit some of the major findings of this research, before elaborating on what this might mean for the need to globalize the penal research imagination in the study of punishment and society.

The Situatedness of the Global

The analysis put forward in this book is the result of an ethnographic approach to the field of international criminal justice, with a particular focus on how the role of NGOs yield analytical insight in the meaning of punishment at the global level of analysis. In approaching the field, I was guided by three sets of inquiries, namely what are the roles of NGOs in international criminal justice, what characterizes punishment 'gone global', and how is international criminal justice constituted by and of 'the global'. A sociology of punishment perspective enabled attention to the norms, morals, and values at play in the motivational dynamics of penal developments. As such, the research has taken seriously the humanitarian sensibilities embedded in human rights, and the imperative to 'do something' about the suffering of distant others. It has paid attention to both the punitive and non-punitive forces involved in the shaping of global justice: in short, to the merging of humanitarian and penal sensibilities (Lohne, 2018b). At the same time, these cultural forces have been analysed against the background of social organization and structure, to that which have enabled people to feel and think in certain ways, and to act and promote policies in accordance with their sensibilities. As revealed, 'sentiments and sensibilities sometimes neatly coincide with interests of a political, economic, or ideological kind' (Garland, 1990b: 197–8).

In spite of international criminal law's claim to be cosmopolitan, global, and universal, it is a situated practice. Indeed, given the nature of the spaces in which global justice-making takes place, the networks by which sites and ideas are connected and the individuals positioned to advocate their views, the analysis put forward casts doubt on the use of 'global' to describe the type of criminal justice expressed through the international criminal justice project. Nonetheless, there is power in words, and 'global justice' expresses a normative ambition rather than being an empirical observation. Importantly, *being able* to call it global justice also implies *being in position* to do so.

> [U]niversal reason, of course, was best articulated by the colonizers. In contrast, the colonized were characterized by particularistic cultures; here, the particular is that which cannot grow. The universal, however, opens the way to constantly improving truths and even, in its utilitarian forms, to a better life for all humanity. (Tsing, 2005: 9)

The examination of the situatedness of the global in global justice-making indicates that these distinctions still structure global asymmetries. As part of this, and to properly recognize the global force of humanitarianism, imaginations of global justice cannot be seen in isolation from its materialities. Norms and values, morals and sensibilities are situated within the framework of social interests, positions, and global power inequalities to reflect the complex existence of lived, social, cultural, and political life.

Thus, in setting out to make sense of cosmopolitan penality, I have shown how international criminal justice is perceived as a form of social justice that is however informed by a cosmopolitan rather than a nation state perspective. At the same time, the ICC and the project of international criminal justice demonstrate the popular and transnational aspiration to the realization of humanitarian values, and to shape the world so that it better reflects the interests of humanity. The ICC has become part of the global human rights regime, along with other international interventions such as humanitarian aid, human rights promotion, and humanitarian military interventions (Hopgood, 2013). Cultural representations of victims of international crimes reinforce the international linking of criminal justice with the humanitarian imaginary: instead of resembling the victim in western domestic crime discourses, the victim of international crimes is portrayed as the distant, powerless 'other'. Their suffering represents humanity's suffering, and therefore codes as human rights violations, humanitarian emergencies, and crimes against humanity (Branch, 2011). As ingrained in the Principle of Complementarity, the 'international' or 'global'—in the form of the ICC—is supposed to provide recourse when national criminal justice fails, thus identifying the international rather than the nation state as the principle humanitarian actor (Clarke, 2007). There is a dual moral claim to international criminal justice's legitimacy, to protect actual, mostly African, victims, while also protecting abstract humanity, and thus, to present itself as beyond politics. Law is in itself the most dominant language of political legitimacy (Kahn, 2001); invoking law and legal punishment in the name of humanity—as *humanity's law* (Teitel, 2011)—makes it sacrosanct. This is the religion of humanity, in which 'man has become a god for man' (Durkheim and Lukes, 1969: 26), creating a 'fantasy of a global moral community that may still be viable and the expectation that solidarity may have redeeming powers' (Fassin, 2011: xii).

However, while the association of international criminal justice and global justice is espoused by 'global civil society', the ICC, and the UN alike,[2] the 'claim of international criminal justice to global

[2] For example, the Coalition's new blog is called #globaljustice, the former ICC Chief Prosecutor wrote on 'The International Criminal Court: Seeking Global Justice' (Moreno-Ocampo, 2007), and the Secretary General of the United Nations Ban Ki-Moon has referred to the ICC as the 'keystone of a growing system of global justice' (see Nouwen and Werner, 2015a).

justice appears to be taken much more seriously by its practitioners than by those routinely thinking about global justice' (Mégret, 2015: 78). Global justice literature rarely gives much attention to international criminal justice (for an exception, see Roach, 2009). Scholarship on global justice is rather mostly concerned with distributive, not retributive, justice, and as part of this, the need to rethink political communities of justice (Fraser, 2008).

Yet, as the Westphalian mapping of political space has been 'denaturalized', the imaginary of states as the geographically and territorially bound units of political communities has been challenged—also as concerns criminal law, justice, and punishment. This research has therefore pointed to a lack of a clear and discernible constituency as regards international criminal justice too, and argued that international human rights NGOs play an important role in constituting one. For example, through their transnational advocacy networks, they seek to 'bridge' and 'mediate' between the local and the global, becoming central to a re-imagination of political space when it is disembedded from the nation state.

As part of this re-imagination of communities of justice, direct victims of international crimes, and a more abstract notion of humanity, are likewise invoked to justify global justice-making. Questions may however be asked about the hierarchy of these different 'scales' of victimhood, and about the extent to which international criminal justice is more concerned with 'humanity' than with individual victims of mass violence, and similarly, about whether the ICC is more dependent on the support of international human rights NGOs than that of local civil society—in northern Uganda and elsewhere. What have emerged into view are disconnections and tensions between 'doing' justice in the name of victims of international crimes, and their recognition as *subjects* of justice. By intervening in contexts of failed justice, international criminal justice bypasses the Westphalian frame. This is the point of global justice. However, crucially, the Westphalian frame remains the only frame that, at least theoretically and conceptually, recognizes individuals as political subjects—as citizens and as therefore legal subjects of a bounded community of justice. Even though individual victims are eligible for legal representation at the ICC, and human rights NGOs claim to speak on their behalf, this should not be mistaken for *political* representation—their right to dispute the *substance* of justice. Rather—and in spite of international criminal justice's claims to providing 'justice for victims'—it appears that victims of international crimes are *objects* of global justice-making. As Clarke observes, the 'failure to treat Ugandans and other Africans as political agents creates, again, the conditions for seeing Africans as in need of salvation by a benevolent "West"' (2009: 120). The disconnect between the handing down of global justice and the lack of recognition of political subjectivity easily inscribes itself within the post-colonial narrative of the 'civilizing mission' in Africa.

Similarly, global disconnections are also apparent in the participation of 'global civil society'. A central topic throughout this research is the claim by human rights NGOs to moral authority. I have argued that the participation of human rights NGOs in international criminal justice is contingent on this claim, and that human rights NGOs transfer moral authority to the ICC itself through their ideational support of the project generally, and the Court in particular. However, the book has made clear how embedded human rights NGOs are in the making of global criminal justice: they are materially and ideationally deeply entrenched in the field of international criminal justice. Beyond their elaborate functions in the everyday operation of international criminal justice, this is also manifested in, for example, the social position of people who advocate for global justice in The Hague: generally, they belong to a class of transnational western professionals. The embeddedness of global justice in The Hague and the EU also makes it more difficult for non-EU citizens to work in the field—to work 'on' making global justice. Moreover, the close relationship between the ICC and the CICC is occasionally confused to the extent that the latter is perceived as part of the former, perhaps an understandable mistake, when the NGO coalition holds joint outreach events with the Court. People in the field call the relationship between the ICC and the NGOs 'synergetic'—they have a joint mission, striving together to end impunity and build global criminal justice.

The ICC and the human rights NGOs thus both represent the same imaginations of global justice. For both, the notion of humanity is the utopic authority of global order, to be imposed by the judges at the Court. However, the quality the cosmopolitan activists have to build on is that of detachment—of *not belonging:* 'Their possession of no material identities with those they seek to advise and judge gives them the authority of neutrality, impartiality, independence' (Hopgood, 2009: 238). Accordingly, the embeddedness of NGOs in international criminal justice brings about significant dualities and tensions, in particular as regards their claim to moral authority. Notwithstanding their worthy intentions, human rights NGOs have become part of the material power structures of global social order.

The Need to Globalize the Penal Research Imagination

This raises new and important questions about the legitimacy of punishment. International criminal justice does not only represent novel 'functions' of punishment, but is also associated with new sets of actors we are relatively unfamiliar with in the domestic terrain. Crucially, while the power to punish has traditionally been embedded in the nation state, this book shows how this power is not only curtailed and shaped by international actors such as the ICC, but also by human rights NGOs and their transnational networks. Imagined as part of the move towards a 'humanity's law' (Teitel, 2011), international criminal justice inscribes itself in a narrative of civilization and progress, adding another layer to the penal histories of modern punishment as a result of enlightened progress (Garland, 1990b).

While this book has been concerned with the development and dynamics embedded in international criminal justice, this empirical study is but a fraction of the plethora of ongoing developments suggesting a disconnection between crime, punishment, and the nation state (Franko, 2017; Bosworth et al., 2018). At the global level, 'world politics is increasingly concerned with setting up regulations that define and redefine criminal activities … with a worldwide reach' (Jakobi, 2013: 2). This relates to common criminalization through 'global prohibition regimes' (Nadelmann, 1990) as well as global policing, information sharing, and standard-setting (see e.g. UNODC, 2016; Goldsmith and Sheptycki, 2007). International prisons are emerging not only for those convicted by international criminal courts (van Zyl Smit, 2005; see also Abels, 2012), but also for those found guilty of piracy in domestic courts—the oldest and original universal jurisdiction crime (Dutton, 2010). After being brought before trial in the Seychelles, Somali pirates are now transferred to a newly built prison in Somaliland, funded by the UN.[3] At the regional level, there has been a significant increase in transborder police cooperation (Aas and Gundhus, 2015) and the growth of regional (criminal) courts and judicial fora (Slaughter, 2004). Developments are underway to establish an African Criminal Court (Werle and Vormbaum, 2017) as well as a joint EU prosecutorial office for 'EU crimes' (Ligeti and Simonato, 2013). At the transnational level, it appears a market for bilateral prison deals is emerging, with states such as Norway and Belgium renting prison cells in the Netherlands, transferring prison population and jurisdictions alike into foreign nation-state territory. This commodification of 'the transnational prisoner' (Pakes and Holt, 2015) somewhat parallels the UK's efforts to transfer its Jamaican prison population to a newly built prison in Jamaica, funded under the auspices of the UK's foreign aid budget (Bosworth, 2017). While not only generating new empirical fields of study, these developments necessitate a reconsideration of the relationship between punishment and society as defined through the nation-state framework.

While this might entail letting go of the epistemological and ontological privilege of the national, it is not tantamount to scaling 'upwards' and 'above'—nor necessarily 'bigger'. Rather, it may entail the pursuit of a defiant research imagination—one in which established and specified research techniques are not uncritically accepted as the only path to producing new knowledge (see Kenway and Fahey, 2008). Disciplines are also epistemologies; they are situated, provisional, incomplete, and above all constitutive of the field, in a manner that may sometimes blur as much as clarify. To globalize the penal research imagination thus calls for an 'inter' or 'trans' disciplinary imagination, and to challenge the boundaries that hinder communication across disciplines in order to find points of intersection. This would continue the legacy of punishment and society as a *problematique*, as a complex of questions in need of different approaches (Simon and Sparks, 2013). Methodological difficulties such as these, force the researcher into a space of humility, provoking her to keep an open

[3] http://www.un.org/apps/news/story.asp?NewsID=34601#.WHSyPv4zVaQ (accessed 28 July 2019); http://www.seychellesnewsagency.com/articles/3066/First+trial+starts+before+the+Seychelles+dedicated+court+for+piracy+and+maritime+crime+cases (accessed 28 July 2019); https://www.unodc.org/unodc/en/piracy/piracy-prisoner-transfer-programme.html (accessed 28 July 2019).

mind in following connections, forces, and imaginations rather than dwelling on the self-evident. For me, that entailed digging into the smooth surfaces of global justice-making, dirtying the beautiful-looking advocates of humanity. It entailed rejecting the equation of the global with the universal, the local with the particular, and the fight against impunity with global justice.

References

Aas KF. (2007) 'Analysing a World in Motion', *Theoretical Criminology* 11: 283–303.

Aas KF. (2011) 'Visions of Global Control: Cosmopolitan Aspirations in a World of Friction', in Hoyle C and Bosworth M (eds) *What is Criminology?* Oxford: Oxford University Press.

Aas KF. (2012) '"The Earth is One but the World is Not": Criminological Theory and its Geopolitical Divisions', *Theoretical Criminology* 16: 5–20.

Aas KF. (2013) *Globalization and Crime*, London: Sage Publications Limited.

Aas KF and Gundhus HOI. (2015) 'Policing Humanitarian Borderlands: Frontex, Human Rights and the Precariousness of Life', *The British Journal of Criminology* 55: 1–18.

Abels D. (2012) *Prisoners of the International Community: The Legal Position of Persons Detained at International Criminal Tribunals*, Berlin: Springer Science & Business Media.

Adelman S. (2011) 'Cosmopolitan Sovereignty', in Baillet CM and Aas KF (eds) *Cosmopolitan Justice and Its Discontents*. Abingdon: Routledge.

Adler E. (1997) 'Seizing the Middle Ground: Constructivism in World Politics', *European Journal of International Relations* 3: 319–63.

Agger K. (2012) The End of Amnesty in Uganda: Implications for LRA Defections. The Enough Project.

Agozino B. (2003) *Counter-colonial Criminology: A Critique of Imperialist Reason*, London: Pluto Press.

AI. (1999) Uganda: Breaking the Circle: Protecting Human Rights in the Northern War Zone. *AFR59/001/2004*. Amnesty International.

AI. (2004a) Uganda: First Steps to Investigate Crimes must be Part of Comprehensive Plan to End Impunity. *AFR 59/001/2004*. Amnesty International.

AI. (2004b) Uganda: International Criminal Court Investigation an Important Step toward Ending Impunity. *AFR 59/006/2004*. Amnesty International.

AI. (2005) Open Letter to the Chief Prosecutor of the International Criminal Court: Comments on the Concept of the Interests of Justice. *IOR 40/023/2005*. Amnesty International.

AI. (2006) Uganda: Amnesty International Calls for an Effective Alternative to Impunity. *AFR 59/004/2006*. Amnesty International.

AI. (2008) Agreement and Annex on Accountability and Reconciliation falls short of a Comprehensive Plan to End Impunity. *AFR 59/001/2008*. Amnesty International.

Akhavan P. (1996) 'The International Criminal Tribunal for Rwanda: The Politics and Pragmatics of Punishment', *The American Journal of International Law* 90: 501–10.

Akhavan P. (1998) 'Justice in the Hague, Peace in the Former Yugoslavia? A Commentary on the United Nations War Crimes Tribunal', *Human Rights Quarterly* 20: 737–816.

Allen T. (2006) *Trial Justice: The International Criminal Court and the Lord's Resistance Army*, London: Zed Books.

Allen T and Vlassenroot K. (2010) *The Lord's Resistance Army: Myth and Reality*, London: Zed Books.

Anders G. (2007) 'Follow the Trial', *Anthropology Today* 23: 23–6.

Anderson K. (2005) 'Squaring the Circle? Reconciling Sovereignty and Global Governance Through Global Government Networks', *Harvard Law Review* 118: 1255–312.

Anderson K and Rieff D. (2005) '"Global Civil Society": A Sceptical View', in Glasius M, Kaldor M, and Anheier HK (eds) *Global Civil Society*. Thousand Oaks: Sage Publications.

Arendt H. (2006) *Eichmann in Jerusalem*, London: Penguin.

ARLPI/Snowdon W. (2008) *Quest for Reconciliation: The Acholi Religious Leaders Peace Initiative's Pursuit of Sustainable Peace*, Gulu, Uganda: The Acholi Religious Leaders Peace Initiative.

Ashworth A. (1986) 'Punishment and Compensation: Victims, Offenders and the State', *Oxford Journal of Legal Studies* 6: 86–122.

Askin K. (2011) Fizi Diary: Mobile Court Tries Landmark Rape Case. *Voices*. Open Society Foundations.

AU. (2013) Africa to Request Deferment of Indictments against Kenyan President and Vice President. *Press Release No 177/2013*. Addis Ababa: African Union.

Autesserre S. (2012) 'Dangerous Tales: Dominant Narratives on the Congo and their Unintended Consequences', *African Affairs* 111: 202–22.

Avocats sans Frontières, Center for Justice and Reconciliation, Coalition Nationale pour la Cour Pénale Internationale – RCD, et al. (2006) DR Congo: ICC Charges Raise Concern *Joint letter to the Chief Prosecutor of the International Criminal Court*.

Baines EK. (2009) 'Complex Political Perpetrators: Reflections on Dominic Ongwen', *The Journal of Modern African Studies* 47: 163–91.

Barberá P, Godzimirska Z, and Mayoral JA. (2018) Courting the Public? The Strategic Use of Social Media by International Courts. *ECPR General Conference*. Hamburg.

Barrow K. (2004) 'The Role of NGOs in the Establishment of the International Criminal Court', *Dialogue* 2: 11–22.

Bass GJ. (2000) *Stay the Hand of Vengeance: The Politics of War Crimes Tribunals*, Princeton, New Jersey: Princeton University Press.

Bassiouni MC. (1998) *The Statute of the International Criminal Court: A Documentary History*, Ardsley, NY: Transnational Publishers.

Bassiouni MC. (2006) 'International Recognition of Victims' Rights', *Human Rights Law Review* 6: 203–79.

Baylis E. (2009) 'Outsourcing Investigations', *UCLA Journal of International Law and Foreign Affairs* 14: 121–49.

BBC News. (2010) UN official calls DR Congo 'rape capital of the world' *BBC News*. BBC.

Beck U. (1992) *Risk Society: Towards a New Modernity*, London: Sage.

Becker H. (1991 [1963]) *Outsiders: Studies in the Sociology of Deviance*, New York: The Free Press.

Beckett C. (2012) *Communicating for Change: Media and Agency in the Networked Public Sphere*, London: POLIS, London School of Economics and Political Science.

Beetham D. (2013) 'Revisiting Legitimacy, Twenty Years On', in Tankebe J and Liebing A (eds) *Legitimacy and Criminal Justice*. Oxford: Oxford University Press.

Benedetti F, Bonneau K, and Washburn JL. (2014) *Negotiating the International Criminal Court: New York to Rome, 1994–1998*, Leiden: Nijhoff.

Bergsmo M. (2012) *Thematic Prosecution of International Sex Crimes: FICHL Publication Series*, Beijing: Torkel Opsahl Academic EPublisher.

Bergsmo M, Ling CW, and Ping Y. (2014) *Historical Origins of International Criminal Law*, Brussels: Torkel Opsahl Academic EPublisher.

Boltanski L. (1999) *Distant Suffering: Morality, Media and Politics*, Cambridge: Cambridge University Press.

Bosco D. (2013) *Rough Justice: The International Criminal Court in a World of Power Politics*, Oxford: Oxford University Press.

Bosworth, M. (2012) 'Subjectivity and Identity in Detention: Punishment and Society in a Global Age', *Theoretical Criminology* 16.2: 123–140.

Bosworth M. (2017) 'Penal Humanitarianism? Sovereign Power in an Era of Mass Migration', *New Criminal Law Review: An International and Interdisciplinary Journal* 20: 39–65.

Bosworth M, Franko K, and Pickering S. (2018) 'Punishment, Globalization and Migration Control: "Get them the hell out of here"', *Punishment & Society* 20: 34–53.

Bosworth M and Hoyle C. (2011) *What is Criminology?* Oxford: Oxford University Press.

Bottoms A and Tankebe J. (2012) 'Beyond Procedural Justice: A Dialogic Approach to Legitimacy in Criminal Justice', *Journal of Criminal Law & Criminology* 102: 119.

Bourdieu, P. (1986) 'The Force of Law: Toward a Sociology of the Juridical Field', *Hatings Law Journal,* vol. 38.

Bourdieu P. (1991) *Language and Symbolic Power*, Cambridge: Polity Press.

Bradfield P. (2017) 'Reshaping Amnesty in Uganda: The Case of Thomas Kwoyelo', *Journal of International Criminal Justice* 15: 827–55.

Branch A. (2007) 'Uganda's Civil War and the Politics of ICC Intervention', *Ethics & International Affairs* 21: 179–98.

Branch A. (2011) *Displacing Human Rights: War and Intervention in Northern Uganda*, Oxford: Oxford University Press.

Branch A. (2013) 'Gulu in War … and Peace? The Town as Camp in Northern Uganda', *Urban Studies* 50: 3152–67.

Brants C. (2011) 'Universal Crimes, Universal Justice? The Legitimacy of the International Response to Genocide, Crimes against Humanity and War Crimes', in Crawford A (ed) *International and Comparative Criminal Justice and Urban Governance: Convergence and Divergence in Global, National and Local Settings*. Cambridge: Cambridge University Press.

Brisson-Boivin K and O'Connor D. (2013) 'The Rule of Law, Security-development and Penal Aid: The Case of Detention in Haiti', *Punishment & Society* 15: 515–33.

Bunch C. (1990) 'Women's Rights as Human Rights: Toward a Re-Vision of Human Rights', *Human Rights Quarterly* 12: 486–98.

Burawoy M. (2000) *Global Ethnography: Forces, Connections, and Imaginations in a Postmodern World*, Berkeley: University of California Press.

Burawoy M. (2001) 'Manufacturing the Global', *Ethnography* 2: 147–59.

Cakmak C. (2008) 'Transnational Activism in World Politics and Effectiveness of a Loosely Organised Principled Global Network: The Case of the NGO Coalition for an International Criminal Court', *The International Journal of Human Rights* 12: 373–93.

Calhoun C. (2010) 'The Idea of Emergency: Humanitarian Action and Global (Dis)Order', in Fassin D and Pandolfi M (eds) *Contemporary States of Emergency: The Politics of Military and Humanitarian Interventions*. New York: Zone Books.

Calhoun CJ. (2002) 'The Class Consciousness of Frequent Travelers: Toward a Critique of Actually Existing Cosmopolitanism', *The South Atlantic Quarterly* 101: 869–97.

Carothers T. (2010) 'The Continuing Backlash against Democracy Promotion', in Burnell P and Youngs R (eds) *New Challenges to Democratization*. Abingdon: Routledge.

Carpenter RC. (2007) 'Setting the Advocacy Agenda: Theorizing Issue Emergence and Nonemergence in Transnational Advocacy Networks', *International Studies Quarterly* 51: 99–120.

Carrington K, Hogg R, and Sozzo M. (2015) 'Southern Criminology', *British Journal of Criminology* 56: 1–20.

Cassese A. (1998) 'On the Current Trends towards Criminal Prosecution and Punishment of Breaches of International Humanitarian Law', *European Journal of International Law* 9: 2–17.

Castells M. (1996) *The Rise of the Networked Society*, Oxford: Blackwell Publishers.

Castells M. (2012) *Networks of Outrage and Hope*, Cambridge: Polity Press.

Cavadino M and Dignan J. (2006) 'Penal Policy and Political Economy', *Criminology and Criminal Justice* 6: 435–56.

CEPEJ. (2014) Report on 'European judicial systems—Edition 2014 (2012 data): Efficiency and Quality of Justice'. The European Commission for the Efficiency of Justice.

Chouliaraki L. (2013) *The Ironic Spectator: Solidarity in the Age of Post-Humanitarianism*, Cambridge: Polity.

Christensen MJ. (2015a) 'The Emerging Sociology of International Criminal Courts: Between Global Restructurings and Scientific Innovations', *Current Sociology* 63: 825–49.

Christensen MJ. (2015b) 'From Symbolic Surge to Closing Courts: The Transformation of International Criminal Justice and its Professional Practices', *International Journal of Law, Crime and Justice* 43: 609–25.

Christie N. (1977) 'Conflicts as Property', *British Journal of Criminology* 17: 1.

Christie N. (1986) 'The Ideal Victim', in Fattah E (ed) *From Crime Policy to Victim Policy.* London: MacMillan.

Christie N. (2000) *Crime Control as Industry: Towards Gulags, Western Style*, London: Routledge.

Christie N. (2004) *A Suitable Amount of Crime*, London: Routledge.

CICC. (2010) Letter to CICC Members announcing Steering Committee Expansion.

CICC. (2012) ASIA–PACIFIC Update. Coalition for the International Criminal Court.

City of The Hague. (2011) *The Hague International City of Peace and Justice* The Hague: Department of Information and External Relations.

City of The Hague. (2012) NGO Roadmap: Starting an NGO in The Hague. The Hague: Department of International Affairs (BIZ).

City of The Hague. (2013) *Guide to International Organisations in The Hague*. The Hague: Bruikman Reclame.

City of The Hague and Decisio. (2011) *The Hague international city of peace and justice: Economic impact international organizations, English summary of the Decisio report 2010*. The Hague: Department of Information and External Relations.

Clark AM. (2010) *Diplomacy of Conscience: Amnesty International and Changing Human Rights Norms*, Princeton, New Jersey: Princeton University Press.

Clarke KM. (2007) 'Global Justice, Local Controversies: The International Criminal Court and the Sovereignty of Victims', in Dembour M-B and Kelly T (eds) *Paths to International Justice: Social and Legal Perspectives.* Cambridge: Cambridge University Press.

Clarke KM. (2009) *Fictions of Justice: The International Criminal Court and the Challenge of Legal Pluralism in Sub-Saharan Africa*, Cambridge: Cambridge University Press.

Clarke KM, Knottnerus AS, and De Volder E. (2016) *Africa and the ICC*, Cambridge: Cambridge University Press.

Cohen S. (1985) *Visions of Social Control: Crime, Punishment, and Classification*, Cambridge: Polity.

Connell R. (2007) *Southern Theory: The Global Dynamics of Knowledge in Social Science*, Cambridge: Polity Press.

Corrias LDA and Gordon GM. (2015) 'Judging in the Name of Humanity: International Criminal Tribunals and the Representation of a Global Public', *Journal of International Criminal Justice* 13: 97–112.

Cotterrell R. (1999) *Émile Durkheim: Law in a Moral Domain*, Edinburgh: Edinburgh University Press.

Cotterrell R. (2015) 'The Concept of Crime and Transnational Networks of Community', in Alldridge P, Cheliotis L, and Mitsilegal V (eds) *Globalisation, Criminal Law and Criminal Justice: Theoretical, Comparative and Transnational Perspectives*. Oxford: Hart.

Cottle S. (2001) 'Contingency, Blunders and Serendipity in News Research: Tales from the Field', *Communications* 26: 149–67.

Davenport D. (2002) 'The New Diplomacy', *Policy Review* 116: 17–30.

De Hoon M and Lohne K. (2019) '"All the World's a Stage": Constituting International Justice at the Assembly of States Parties Meeting', in Boer LJM and Stolk S (eds) *Backstage Practices of Transnational Law*. Abingdon: Routledge.

De Silva N. (2017) 'Intermediary Complexity in Regulatory Governance: The International Criminal Court's use of NGOs in Regulating International Crimes', *The ANNALS of the American Academy of Political and Social Science* 670: 170–88.

de Souza e Silva A. (2006) 'From Cyber to Hybrid Mobile Technologies as Interfaces of Hybrid Spaces', *Space and Culture* 9: 261–78.

De Waal A. (2003) 'Human Rights Organizations and the Political Imagination: How the West and Africa have Diverged', *Journal of Human Rights* 2: 475–94.

Deflem M. (2008) *Sociology of Law: Visions of a Scholarly Tradition*, Cambridge: Cambridge University Press.

Della Porta D. (2007) *The Global Justice Movement: Cross-national and Transnational Perspectives*, London: Paradigm Publishers.

Della Porta D and Diani M. (2006) *Social Movements: An Introduction*, Malden, MA: Blackwell.

Dezalay Y and Garth B. (2006) 'From the Cold War to Kosovo: The Rise and Renewal of the Field of International Human Rights', *Annual Review of Law and Social Science* 2: 231–55.

Dezalay Y and Garth BG. (1998) *Dealing in Virtue: International Commercial Arbitration and the Construction of a Transnational Legal Order*, Chicago: University of Chicago Press.

Dixon P and Tenove C. (2013) 'International Criminal Justice as a Transnational Field: Rules, Authority and Victims', *International Journal of Transitional Justice* 7: 393–412.

Douzinas C. (2007a) *Human Rights and Empire: The Political Philosophy of Cosmopolitanism*, Abingdon: Routledge-Cavendish.

Douzinas C. (2007b) 'The Many Faces of Humanitarianism', *Parrhesia* 2: 1–28.

Drumbl MA. (1997) 'Rule of Law Amid Lawlessness: Counseling the Accused in Rwanda's Domestic Genocide Trials', *Columbia Human Rights Law Review* 29: 545.

Drumbl MA. (2000) 'Sclerosis: Retributive Justice and the Rwandan Genocide', *Punishment & Society* 2: 287–307.

Drumbl MA. (2003) 'Toward a Criminology of International Crime', *Ohio State Journal on Dispute Resolution* 19: 263.

Drumbl MA. (2007) *Atrocity, Punishment and International law*, Cambridge: Cambridge University Press.

Dudai R. (2006) 'Advocacy with Footnotes: The Human Rights Report as a Literary Genre', *Human Rights Quarterly* 28: 783–95.

Duffield M. (2001) 'Governing the Borderlands: Decoding the Power of Aid', *Disasters* 25: 308–20.

Duffield M. (2010) 'Risk-management and the Fortified Aid Compound: Everyday Life in Post-Interventionary Society', *Journal of Intervention and Statebuilding* 4: 453–74.

Durkheim É. (1915) *'Germany above all': German Mentality and War*, Paris: A. Colin.

Durkheim É. (1984) *The Division of Labour in Society*, London: Macmillan.

Durkheim É and Lukes S. (1969) 'Durkheim's "Individualism and the Intellectuals"', *Political Studies* 17: 14–30.

Dutton YM. (2010) 'Bringing Pirates to Justice: A Case for Including Piracy within the Jurisdiction of the International Criminal Court', *Chicago Journal of International Law* 11: 197.

Elias N. (1978 [1939]) *The Civilizing Process*, Oxford: Basil Blackwell.

Elliott MA. (2007) 'Human Rights and the Triumph of the Individual in World Culture', *Cultural Sociology* 1: 343–63.

Engle K. (2012) 'Self-critique, (Anti)politics and Criminalization: Reflections on the History and Trajectory of the Human Rights Movement', in Beneyto JM and Kennedy D (eds) *New Approaches to International Law.* The Hague: T.M.C Asser Press.

Engle K, Miller Z, and Davis DM. (2016) *Anti-impunity and the Human Rights Agenda*, Cambridge: Cambridge University Press.

Ericsson K. (2007) 'Kriminologisk kjønnsforskning mellom faderhuset og moderhuset', *Tidsskrift for kjønnsforskning* 2: 71–88.

Eriksson Baaz M and Stern M. (2013) *Sexual Violence as a Weapon of War? Perceptions, Prescriptions, Problems in the Congo and Beyond*, London: Zed Books.

Eslava L. (2015) *Local Space, Global Life*, Cambridge: Cambridge University Press.

Fassin D. (2011) *Humanitarian Reason: A Moral History of the Present*, Berkeley: University of California Press.

Fassin D and Pandolfi M. (2010) *Contemporary States of Emergency: The Politics of Military and Humanitarian Interventions*, New York: Zone Books New York.

Faubion JD and Marcus GE. (2009) *Fieldwork is Not what it Used to be: Learning Anthropology's Method in a Time of Transition*, Ithaca: Cornell University Press.

Feeley MM and Simon J. (1992) 'The New Penology: Notes on the Emerging Strategy of Correction and its Implications', *Criminology* 30: 449–74.

Ferstman C. (2012) 'Limited Charges and Limited Judgments by the International Criminal Court—who bears the greatest responsibility? ' *The International Journal of Human Rights* 16: 796–813.

FIDH. (2006) Supporting the Participation of Victims from DRC before the International Criminal Court. *Report of the FIDH Legal Action Group*. FIDH-International Federation for Human Rights.

FIDH and Carboni M. (2012) Cutting the Weakest Link: Budget Discussions and their Impact on Victims Rights to Participate in the Proceedings. *Position Paper, 11th Session of the Assembly of States Parties to the Rome Statute*. FIDH-International Federation for Human Rights.

FIHD. (2006) First Victims Recognised by the International Criminal Court. FIDH-International Federation for Human Rights.

Findlay M. (2011) 'Locating Victim Communities within Global Justice and Governance', in Crawford A (ed) *International and Comparative Criminal Justice and Urban Governance: Convergence and Divergence in Global, National and Local Settings*. Cambridge: Cambridge University Press.

Finnström S. (2008) *Living with Bad Surroundings: War, History, and Everyday Moments in Northern Uganda*, Durham: Duke University Press.

Fisher J. (2013) 'The Limits–and Limiters–of External Influence: Donors, the Ugandan Electoral Commission and the 2011 Elections', *Journal of Eastern African Studies* 7: 471–91.

Fletcher LE and Weinstein HM. (2002) 'Violence and Social Repair: Rethinking the Contribution of Justice to Reconciliation', *Human Rights Quarterly* 24: 573.

Foucault M. (2005) *The Order of Things*, Abingdon: Routledge.
Franko K. (2017) 'Criminology, Punishment, and the State in A Globalized Society', in Liebling A, Maruna S, and McAra L (eds) *The Oxford Handbook of Criminology.* Oxford: Oxford University Press.
Fraser N. (2008) *Scales of Justice: Reimagining Political Space in a Globalizing World*, Cambridge: Polity.
Fukuyama F. (1989) 'The End of History', *The National Interest* 16.
Furedi F. (2002) *Culture of Fear. Revised Edition*, London: Continuum.
Galtung J. (1964) 'An Editorial', *Journal of Peace Research* 1: 1–4.
Garland D. (1990a) 'Frameworks of Inquiry in the Sociology of Punishment', *British Journal of Sociology*: 1–15.
Garland D. (1990b) *Punishment and Modern Society: A Study in Social Theory*, Chicago: University of Chicago Press.
Garland D. (2001) *The Culture of Control: Crime and Social Order in Contemporary Society*, Chicago: University of Chicago Press.
Garland D. (2006) 'Concepts of Culture in the Sociology of Punishment', *Theoretical Criminology* 10: 419–47.
Garland D. (2013) 'Penality and the Penal State', *Criminology* 51: 475–517.
Gibson JL. (2005) 'The Truth About Truth and Reconciliation in South Africa', *International Political Science Review* 26: 341–61.
Giddens A. (1990) *The Consequences of Modernity*, Cambridge: Polity Press.
Gille Z and Riain SÓ. (2002) 'Global Ethnography', *Annual Review of Sociology* 28: 271–95.
Givoni M. (2014) 'The Ethics of Witnessing and the Politics of the Governed', *Theory, Culture & Society* 31: 123–42.
Glasius M. (2002) 'Expertise in the Cause of Justice: Global Civil Society Influence on the Statute for an International Criminal Court', in Glasius M, Kaldor M, and Anheier HK (eds) *Global Civil Society.* Oxford: Oxford University Press.
Glasius M. (2005) 'Who is the Real Civil Society? Women's Groups versus Pro-Family Groups at the International Criminal Court Negotiations', in Howell J and Mulligan D (eds) *Gender and Civil Society.* London: Routledge.
Glasius M. (2006) *The International Criminal Court: A Global Civil Society Achievement*, London: Routledge.
Glasius M. (2010) 'Expertise in the Cause of Justice: Global Civil Society Influence on the Statute for an International Criminal Court', in Glasius M, Kaldor M, and Anheier HK (eds) *Global Civil Society Yearbook 2002.* Oxford: Oxford University Press.
Goldsmith A and Sheptycki J. (2007) *Crafting Transnational Policing: Police Capacity-building and Global Policing Reform*, London: Bloomsbury Publishing.

Griffin L and Blacker K. (2010) 'Megan's Law and Sarah's Law: A Comparative Study of Sex Offender Community Notification Schemes in the United States and the United Kingdom', *Criminal Law Bulletin* 46: 987.

Guo C and Saxton GD. (2014) 'Tweeting Social Change: How Social Media Are Changing Nonprofit Advocacy', *Nonprofit and Voluntary Sector Quarterly* 43: 57–79.

Haas PM. (1992) 'Introduction: Epistemic Communities and International Policy Coordination', *International Organization* 46: 1–35.

Haddad HN. (2011) 'Mobilizing the Will to Prosecute: Crimes of Rape at the Yugoslav and Rwandan Tribunals', *Human Rights Review* 12: 109–32.

Haddad HN. (2012) 'Judicial Institution Builders: NGOs and International Human Rights Courts', *Journal of Human Rights* 11: 126–49.

Haddad HN. (2013) 'After the Norm Cascade: NGO Mission Expansion and the Coalition for the International Criminal Court', *Global Governance: A Review of Multilateralism and International Organizations* 19: 187–206.

Hagan J. (2010) *Justice in the Balkans: Prosecuting War Crimes in the Hague Tribunal*, Chicago: University of Chicago Press.

Hayner PB. (2002) *Unspeakable Truths: Facing the Challenge of Truth Commissions*, New York: Routledge.

Hayward KJ. (2012) 'Five Spaces of Cultural Criminology', *British Journal of Criminology* 52: 441–62.

Heller KJ. (2008) 'What Happens to the Acquitted?', *Leiden Journal of International Law* 21: 663–80.

Henry B. (2005) 'The Acquitted Accused, a Forgotten Party of the ICTR', *New England Journal of International and Comparative Law.* 12: 81.

Holá B and van Wijk J. (2014) 'Life after Conviction at International Criminal Tribunals: An Empirical Overview', *Journal of International Criminal Justice* 12: 109–32.

Hopgood S. (2006) *Keepers of the Flame: Understanding Amnesty International*, Ithaca: Cornell University Press.

Hopgood S. (2009) 'Moral Authority, Modernity and the Politics of the Sacred',. *European Journal of International Relations* 15: 229–55.

Hopgood S. (2013) *The Endtimes of Human Rights*, Ithaca: Cornell University Press.

Houge AB and Lohne K. (2017) 'End Impunity! Reducing Conflict-Related Sexual Violence to a Problem of Law', *Law & Society Review* 51: 755–89.

Houge AB, Lohne K, and Skilbrei M-L. (2015) 'Gender and Crime Revisited: Criminological Gender Research on International and Transnational Crime and Crime Control', *Journal of Scandinavian Studies in Criminology and Crime Prevention* 16: 160–74.

Hoyle C. (2011) 'Can International Justice be Restorative Justice? The Role of Reparations', in Palmer N, Clark P, and Granville D (eds) *Critical Perspectives in Transitional Justice*. Cambridge: Intersentia Press.

Hoyle C and Ullrich L. (2014) 'New Court, New Justice?: The Evolution of 'Justice for Victims' at Domestic Courts and at the International Criminal Court', *Journal of International Criminal Justice* 12: 681–703.

HRW. (1997) *Human Rights Watch Condemns Abduction and Killing of Children by Ugandan Rebel Group*, New York: Human Rights Watch.

HRW. (2009) The International Criminal Court Trial of Thomas Lubanga. Human Rights Watch.

Human Rights Watch. (2010) Letter to Obama on Targeted Killings and Drones. Human Rights Watch.

Humphreys S. (2010) *Theatre of the Rule of Law: Transnational Legal Intervention in Theory and Practice*, Cambridge: Cambridge University Press.

Hurrell A. (2007) *On Global Order: Power, Values, and the Constitution of International Society*, Oxford: Oxford Universisty Press.

Hurwitz DR. (2003) 'Lawyering for Justice and the Inevitablity of International Human Rights Clinics', *Yale Journal of International Law* 28: 505.

ICC-ASP. (2013) Report of the Committee on Budget and Finance on the work of its twentieth session. *ICC-ASP/12/5/Rev.1*. The Hague: International Criminal Court—Assembly of States Parties.

ICC-ASP. (2014) 'Report of the Court on Human Resources Management', in International Criminal Court—Assembly of States Parties (ed) *Thirteenth session*. New York: International Criminal Court.

ICC-OTP. (2013) Strategic plan June 2012–2015. The Hague: International Criminal Court—Office of the Prosecutor.

ICC-OTP. (2014) Policy Paper on Sexual and Gender-Based Crimes. The Hague: International Criminal Court—Office of the Prosecutor.

ICC-PRES/02-01-06. (2006) Agreement between the International Criminal Court and the International Committee of the Red Cross on Visits to Persons deprived of Liberty Pursuant to the Jurisdiction of the International Criminal Court *ICC-PRES/02-01-06*.

ICC-Registry. (2013) *Figures from Registry*, The Hague: International Criminal Court.

ICC. (2004) *President of Uganda refers situation concerning the Lord's Resistance Army (LRA) to the ICC*, The Hague: International Criminal Court.

ICC. (2009) 'Victims before the Court', in Registry (ed) *ICC-PIDS-FS-02-001/09_Eng*. The Hague: International Criminal Court.

ICC. (2010a) Complementarity *RC/Res.1*. International Criminal Court.

ICC. (2010b) Resolutions and Declarations adopted by the Review Conference: Annexes. *RC/11*. International Criminal Court.

ICC. (2013) ICC holds Groundbreaking Ceremony for Permanent Premises Construction. *ICC-ASP-20130416-PR898*. The Hague.

ICC. (2014) Statement of the Prosecutor of the International Criminal Court, Fatou Bensouda, on the withdrawal of charges against Mr. Uhuru Muigai Kenyatta. The Hague: International Criminal Court, 5 December.

Intelmann T. (2013) Annual Session of States Parties to the Statute of the International Criminal Court. The World Post: TheHuffingtonPost.com.

Jakobi AP. (2013) *Common Goods and Evils?: The Formation of Global Crime Governance*, Oxford: Oxford University Press.

Jewkes Y. (2011) *Media & Crime*, London: Sage.

Johnson R. (2013) The Travesty of Human Rights Watch on Rwanda. http://travesty-of-hrw-on-rwanda.blogspot.com/ (accessed 25 September 2019).

JRP and Ederu O. (2013) TJ Monitor: The Ugandan draft Transitional Justice Policy 2013. Justice and Reconciliation Project. http://justiceandreconciliation.com/2013/06/tj-monitor-the-ugandan-draft-transitional-justice-policy-2013/.

Kahn PW. (2001) 'Freedom, Autonomy, and the Cultural Study of Law', *Yale Journal of Law & the Humanities* 13: 141–74.

Kaldor M, Moore HL, and Selchow S. (2012) *Global Civil Society 2012: Ten Years of Critical Reflection. Global Civil Society Yearbook*, Basingstoke: Palgrave Macmillan.

Karstedt S. (2002) 'Emotions and Criminal Justice', *Theoretical Criminology* 6: 299–317.

Karstedt S. (2007) 'Explorations into the Sociology of Criminal Justice and Punishment Leaving the Modernist Project Behind', *History of the Human Sciences* 20: 51–70.

Karstedt S. (2011) 'Handle with Care: Emotions, Crime and Justice', in Karstedt S and Strang H (eds) *Emotions, Crime and Justice*. Oxford: Hard Publishing.

Karstedt S and Farrall S. (2006) 'The Moral Economy of Everyday Crime: Markets, Consumers and Citizens', *British Journal of Criminology* 46: 1011–36.

Karstedt S, Loader I, and Strang H. (2011) *Emotions, Crime and Justice*, London: Bloomsbury Publishing.

Kauppi N and Madsen MR. (2013) *Transnational Power Elites: The New Professionals of Governance, Law and Security*, Abingdon: Routledge.

Keck ME and Sikkink K. (1998) *Activists Beyond Borders: Advocacy Networks in International Politics*, Ithaca: Cornell University Press.

Kendall S and Nouwen S. (2014) 'Representational Practices at the International Criminal Court: The Gap between Juridified and Abstract Victimhood', *Law and Contemporary Problems* 76: 235–62.

Kendall S and Nouwen S. (2018) International Criminal Justice and Humanitarianism. *University of Cambridge Faculty of Law Research Paper* 69.

Kenway J and Fahey J. (2008) *Globalizing the Research Imagination*, London: Routledge.

Kersten M. (2016) *Justice in Conflict: The Effects of the International Criminal Court's Interventions on Ending Wars and Building Peace*, Oxford: Oxford University Press.

Knepper P. (2010) *The Invention of International Crime: A Global Issue in the Making, 1881–1914*, Basingstoke: Palgrave Macmillan.

Knepper P. (2011) *International Crime in the 20th Century: The League of Nations Era, 1919–1939*, Basingstoke: Palgrave Macmillan.

Koskenniemi M. (2001) *The Gentle Civilizer of Nations: The Rise and Fall of International Law 1870–1960*, Cambridge: Cambridge University Press.

Koskenniemi M. (2002a) 'Between Impunity and Show Trials', *Max Planck Yearbook of United Nations Law Online* 6: 1–32.

Koskenniemi M. (2002b) 'Legal Cosmopolitanism: Tom Franck's Massianic World', *New York University Journal of International Law and Politics* 35: 471–86.

Koskenniemi M. (2005) *From Apology to Utopia: The Structure of International Legal Argument*, Cambridge: Cambridge University Press.

Krause M. (2014) *The Good Project: Humanitarian Relief NGOs and the Fragmentation of Reason*, Chicago: University of Chicago Press.

Kreß C. (2018) 'On the Activation of ICC Jurisdiction over the Crime of Aggression', *Journal of International Criminal Justice* 16: 1–17.

Lacey N. (1988) *State Punishment: Political Principles and Community Values*, London: Routledge.

Lake M. (2014) 'Organizing Hypocrisy: Providing Legal Accountability for Human Rights Violations in Areas of Limited Statehood', *International Studies Quarterly* 58: 515–26.

Latour B. (2005) *Reassembling the Social: An Introduction to Actor-Network-Theory*, Oxford: Clarendon.

Lie JHS. (2014) 'The Humanitarian–Development Nexus: Lessons from Northern Uganda', in Mirshahi M (ed) *Norwegian Centre for Humanitarian Studies*. Oslo: Norwegian Centre for Humanitarian Studies.

Ligeti K and Simonato M. (2013) 'The European Public Prosecutor's Office: Towards a Truly European Prosecution Service', *New Journal of European Criminal Law* 4: 7.

Lingsma, T. (2014) 'Aqcuitted by the ICC, but still not free', *International Justice Tribune,* (The Hague, 4 April 2014) 4.

Loader I and Percy S. (2012) 'Bringing the 'outside' in and the 'inside' out: Crossing the Criminology/IR divide', *Global Crime* 13: 213–18.

Lohne K. (2017) 'Global Civil Society, the ICC, and Legitimacy in International Criminal Justice', in Hayashi N and Bailliet C (eds) *The Legitimacy of International Criminal Tribunals*. Cambridge: Cambridge University Press.

Lohne K. (2018a) 'NGOs for International Justice: Criminal or Victims' Justice', in Ulfstein G and Føllesdal A (eds) *The Judicalization of International Law—A Mixed Blessing?* Oxford: Oxford University Press.

Lohne K. (2018b) 'Penal Humanitarianism beyond the Nation State: An Analysis of International Criminal Justice', *Theoretical Criminology* online first.

Lohne, K. (2018c) 'As the Universal Breaks: Moments of Awkwardness in International Justice', *New Perspectives: Interdisciplinary Journal of Central & East European Politics and International Relations* 26: 135–141.

Lohne, K. (forthcoming) 'Toward a Sociology of International Criminal Justice', in Bergsmo M, Klamberg M, Lohne K, and C Mahony (eds) *Power in International Criminal Justice: Towards a Sociology of International Justice*. Brussels: Torkel Opsahl Academic EPublisher.

Lohne K and Sandvik KB. (2017) 'Bringing Law into the Political Sociology of Humanitarianism', *Oslo Law Review* 4: 4–27.

Low S. (2003) *Behind the Gates*, New York and London: Routledge.

Lukes S. (1982) 'Introduction', in Lukes S (ed) *The Rules of Sociological Method by Emile Durkheim*. New York: The Free Press.

MacKenzie D and Wajcman J. (1999) *The Social Shaping of Technology*, Buckingham: Open University Press.

Madsen MR. (2006) 'Transnational Fields: Elements of a Reflexive Sociology of the Internationalisation of Law', *Retfærd. Nordisk Juridisk Tidsskrift* 29: 34–41.

Madsen MR. (2011) 'Reflexivity and the Construction of the International Object: The Case of Human Rights', *International Political Sociology* 5: 259–75.

Madsen MR. (2014a) 'The International Judiciary as Transnational Power Elite', *International Political Sociology* 8: 332–4.

Madsen MR. (2014b) 'Unpacking Legal Network Power: The Structural Construction of Transnational Legal Expert Networks', in Fenwick M, Uytsel SV, and Wrbka S (eds) *Networked Governance, Transnational Business and the Law*, Heidelberg: Springer.

Madsen MR, Cebulak P, and Wiebusch M. (2018) 'Special Issue—Resistance to International Courts: Introduction and Conclusion', *International Journal of Law in Context* 14: 193–6.

Malkki L. (1994) 'Citizens of Humanity: Internationalism and the Imagined Community of Nations', *Diaspora: A Journal of Transnational Studies* 3: 41–68.

Mamdani M. (2010) 'Responsibility to Protect or Right to Punish?', *Journal of Intervention Statebuilding* 4: 53–67.
Massey D. (1992) 'Politics and Space/Time', *New Left Review*: 65–84.
Massey D. (1994) *Space, Place and Gender*, Cambridge: Polity Press.
Massey D. (2006) 'Space, Time and Political Responsibility in the Midst of Global Inequality', *Erdkunde* 60: 89–95.
Massey D. (2007) *World City*, Cambridge: Polity Press.
Mathiesen T. (1986) 'FN-konferansen som kultur', *Nordisk Tidsskrift for Kriminalvidenskap* 73: 157.
Matthews R. (2005) 'The Myth of Punitiveness', *Theoretical Criminology* 9: 175–201.
McEvoy K. (2007) 'Beyond Legalism: Towards a Thicker Understanding of Transitional Justice', *Journal of Law and Society* 34: 411–40.
McEvoy K and Mallinder L. (2012) 'Amnesties in Transition: Punishment, Restoration, and the Governance of Mercy', *Journal of Law and Society* 39: 410–40.
McGarry R and Walklate S. (2015) *Victims: Trauma, Testimony and Justice*, Abingdon: Routledge.
McGonigle Leyh B. (2012) 'Victim-Oriented Measures at International Criminal Institutions: Participation and its Pitfalls', *International Criminal Law Review* 12: 375–408.
McMillan N. (2016) 'Imagining the International: The Constitution of the International as a Site of Crime, Justice and Community', *Social & Legal Studies* 25: 163–80.
Mégret F. (2010) 'Justifying Compensation by the International Criminal Court's Victims Trust Fund: Lessons from Domestic Compensation Schemes', *Brooklyn Journal of International Law* 36: 123–204.
Mégret F. (2015) 'What Sort of Global Justice is "International Criminal Justice"?', *Journal of International Criminal Justice* 13: 77–96.
Mégret F. (2016a) 'The Anxieties of International Criminal Justice', *Leiden Journal of International Law* 29: 197–221.
Mégret F. (2016b) 'International Criminal Justice as a Juridical Field', *Champ pénal/Penal field* 13: 13.
Mignolo W. (2000) 'The Many Faces of Cosmo-polis: Border Thinking and Critical Cosmopolitanism', *Public Culture* 12: 721–48.
Mills CW. (1959) *The Sociological Imagination*, New York: Grove Press.
Minow M. (1998) *Between Vengeance and Forgiveness: Facing History after Genocide and Mass Violence*, Boston: Beacon Press.
Moreno-Ocampo L. (2007) 'The International Criminal Court: Seeking Global Justice', *Case Western Reserve Journal of International Law* 40: 215.
Morrison W. (2005) 'Rethinking Narratives of Penal Change in Global Context', in Pratt J, Brown D, Brown M, et al. (eds) *New Punitiveness: Trends, Theories, Perspectives*. Cullompton: Willan.

Mueller SD. (2014) 'Kenya and the International Criminal Court (ICC): Politics, the Election and the Law', *Journal of Eastern African Studies* 8: 25–42.

Murdie A and Davis DR. (2012) 'Looking in the Mirror: Comparing INGO Networks across Issue Areas', *The Review of International Organizations* 7: 177–202.

Murphy T and Whitty N. (2013) 'Making History: Academic Criminology and Human Rights', *British Journal of Criminology* 53: 568–87.

Mutua M. (2001) 'Savages, Victims, and Saviors: The Metaphor of Human Rights', *Harvard International Law Journal* 42: 201–45.

Mutua M. (2009a) 'Defining Challenges to Civil Society in Africa', in Mutua M (ed) *Human Rights NGOs in East Africa*. Philadelphia: University Pennsylvania Press.

Mutua M. (2009b) *Human Rights NGOs in East Africa: Political and Normative Tensions*, Philadelphia: University of Pennsylvania Press.

Mythen G. (2007) 'Cultural Victimology: Are We all Victims Now?' in Walklate S (ed) *Handbook of Victims and Victimology.* Cullompton: Willan Publishing.

Nadelmann EA. (1990) 'Global Prohibition Regimes: The Evolution of Norms in International Society', *International Organization* 44: 479–526.

Ndanyi M. (2013) Kenya's NGOs almost defeated Uhuru in Hague, *The Star*: The Star.

Nelson PJ and Dorsey E. (2008) *New Rights Advocacy: Changing Strategies of Development and Human Rights NGOs*, Washington DC: Georgetown University Press.

Nielsen N. (2013) Brussels interns to protest over poor work conditions. eu*observer*. http://euobserver.com/social/120872

Nouwen S. (2012) The ICC's Intervention in Uganda: Which Rule of Law Does it Promote? University of Cambridge Faculty of Law Research Paper No. 22/2012. Available at SSRN: https://ssrn.com/abstract=2139311 or http://dx.doi.org/10.2139/ssrn.2139311

Nouwen S. (2013) *Complementarity in the Line of Fire: The Catalysing Effect of the International Criminal Court in Uganda and Sudan*, Cambridge: Cambridge University Press.

Nouwen SM. (2014) '"As You Set out for Ithaka": Practical, Epistemological, Ethical, and Existential Questions about Socio-Legal Empirical Research in Conflict', *Leiden Journal of International Law* 27: 227–60.

Nouwen SMH and Werner WG. (2010) 'Doing Justice to the Political: The International Criminal Court in Uganda and Sudan', *European Journal of International Law* 21: 941–65.

Nouwen SMH and Werner WG. (2015a) 'Foreword', *Journal of International Criminal Justice* 13: 73–5.

Nouwen SMH and Werner WG. (2015b) 'Monopolizing Global Justice: International Criminal Law as Challenge to Human Diversity', *Journal of International Criminal Justice* 13: 157–76.

O'Malley P. (1999) 'Volatile and Contradictory Punishment', *Theoretical Criminology* 3: 175–96.

Okello M. (2007) The False Polarisation of Peace and Justice in Uganda. *Paper delivered at the International Conference on Peace and Justice.* 25–7.

OSJI. (2011) *International Crimes, Local Justice: A Handbook for Rule-of-Law Policymakers, Donors, and Implementers*, New York: Open Society Foundations.

Pace WR. (2013) Statement by William R. Pace, Convenor, The Coalition for the International Criminal Court at the 12th Session of the Assembly of States Parties to the Rome Statute of the International Criminal Court, in Coalition for the International Criminal Court. The Hague.

Pace WR and Schense J. (2001) 'Coalition for the International Criminal Court at the Preparatory Commission', in Lee RS (ed) *The International Criminal Court: Elements of Crimes and Rules of Procedure and Evidence.* Ardsley, New York: Transnational Publishers.

Pakes F and Holt K. (2015) 'The Transnational Prisoner: Exploring Themes and Trends Involving a Prison Deal with the Netherlands and Norway', *British Journal of Criminology* 57: 79–93.

Park RE and Burgess EW. (1921) *Introduction to the Science of Sociology*, Chicago: University of Chicago Press.

Parmentier S. (2011) 'The Missing Link: Criminological Perspectives on Transitional Justice and International Crimes', in Hoyle C and Bosworth M (eds) *What is Criminology?* Oxford: Oxford University Press.

Pearson Z. (2006) 'Non-Governmental Organizations and the International Criminal Court: Changing Landscapes of International Law', *Cornell International Law Journal* 39: 243–84.

Pearson Z. (2008) 'Spaces of International Law', *Griffith Law Review* 17: 489–514.

Pena M. (2009) 'Victim Participation at the International Criminal Court: Achievements Made and Challenges Lying Ahead', *International Law Students Association Journal of International & Comparative Law* 16: 497–516.

Pena M and Carayon G. (2013) 'Is the ICC Making the Most of Victim Participation?', *International Journal of Transitional Justice* 7:518–535.

Perlin R. (2012) *Intern Nation: How to Earn Nothing and Learn Little in the Brave New Economy*, London, New York: Verso Books.

Philippopoulos-Mihalopoulos A. (2011) 'Law's Spatial Turn: Geography, Justice and a Certain Fear of Space', *Law, Culture and the Humanities* 7: 187–202.

Phillips A. (1995) *The Politics of Presence*, Oxford: Clarendon Press.

Pitkin HF. (1967) *The Concept of Representation*, Berkeley: University of California Press.

Pollock DC and Van Reken RE. (2001) *Third Culture Kids: The Experience of Growing up among Worlds*, London: Nicholas Brealey Publishing.

Posner EA and Vermeule A. (2004) 'Transitional Justice as Ordinary Justice', *Harvard Law Review* 117: 761–825.

Pratt J. (2000) 'Emotive and Ostentatious Punishment: Its Decline and Resurgence in Modern Society', *Punishment & Society* 2: 417–39.

Pratt J. (2007) *Penal Populism*, Abingdon: Routledge.

Pratt J. (2008) 'Scandinavian Exceptionalism in an Era of Penal Excess', *British Journal of Criminology* 48: 119–27.

Price R. (1998) 'Reversing the Gun Sights: Transnational Civil Society Targets Land Mines', *International Organization* 52: 613–44.

Price R. (2003) 'Transnational Civil Society and Advocacy in World Politics', *World Politics* 55: 579–606.

Razack SH. (2007) 'Stealing the Pain of Others: Reflections on Canadian humanitarian responses', *The Review of Education/Pedagogy/Cultural Studies* 29: 375–94.

Reijven J and van Wijk J. (2014) 'Caught in Limbo: How Alleged Perpetrators of International Crimes who Applied for Asylum in the Netherlands are Affected by a Fundamental System Error in International Law', *International Journal of Refugee Law* 26: 248–71.

Risse T, Risse-Kappen T, Ropp SC, et al. (2013) *The Persistent Power of Human Rights: From Commitment to Compliance*, Cambridge: Cambridge University Press.

Roach SC. (2009) *Governance, Order, and the International Criminal Court: Between Realpolitik and a Cosmopolitan Court*, Oxford: Oxford University Press.

Robinson D. (2003) 'Serving the Interests of Justice: Amnesties, Truth Commissions and the International Criminal Court', *European Journal of International Law* 14: 481–505.

Robinson D. (2008) 'The Identity Crisis of International Criminal Law', *Leiden Journal of International Law* 21: 925–63.

Rodley N. (2013) Christopher Keith Hall obituary. *The Guardian*. Guardian News and Media Limited.

Rosenau JN. (2002) 'Governance in a New Global Order', in Held D and McGrew A (eds) *Governing globalization: Power, Authority and Global Governance*. Cambridge: Policy Press, 70–86.

Roudometof V. (2005) 'Transnationalism, Cosmopolitanism and Glocalization', *Current Sociology* 53: 113–35.

Sagan A. (2010) 'African Criminals/African Victims: The Institutionalised Production of Cultural Narratives in International Criminal Law', *Millennium—Journal of International Studies* 39: 3–21.

Sander B. (2018) 'Unveiling the Historical Function of International Criminal Courts: Between Adjudicative and Sociopolitical Justice', *International Journal of Transitional Justice* 12: 334–355.

Sandvik KB. (2012) 'The Politics and Possibilities of Victim-Making in International Law', *Revista Da Faculdade De Direito Do Sul De Minas* 27: 237–58.

Sandvik KB, Jumbert MG, Karlsrud J, et al. (2014) 'Humanitarian Technology: A Critical Research Agenda', *International Review of the Red Cross* 96: 219–42.

Sarat A and Scheingold SA. (2005) *The Worlds Cause Lawyers Make: Structure and Agency in Legal Practice*, Standford: Stanford University Press.

Sassen S. (1994) *Global City*, Princeton, New Jersey: Princeton University Press.

Sassen S. (1998) *Globalization and its Discontents*, New York: New Press.

Sassen S. (2001) *The Global City: New York, London, Tokyo*, Princeton, New Jersey: Princeton University Press.

Sassen S. (2007) *Deciphering the Global: Its Scales, Spaces and Subjects*, New York: Routledge.

Sassen S. (2013) *The Global City: New York, London, Tokyo*, Princeton, New Jersey: Princeton University Press.

Savelsberg JJ. (2018) 'Punitive Turn and Justice Cascade: Mutual Inspiration from Punishment and Society and Human Rights Literatures', *Punishment & Society* 20: 73–91.

Schabas WA. (1996) 'Sentencing by International Tribunals: A Human Rights Approach', *Duke Journal of Comparative & International Law* 7: 461–508.

Schabas WA. (2011) *An Introduction to the International Criminal Court*, Cambridge: Cambridge University Press.

Scharf MP. (1999) 'The Amnesty Exception to the Jurisdiction of the International Criminal Court', *Cornell International Law Journal* 32: 507–28.

Scholte JA. (2018) 'Civil Cociety and NGOs', in Weiss TG and Wilkonson R (eds) *International Organization and Global Governance.* (2nd edn) Abingdon: Routledge.

Schonfeld Z. (2014) The Fight to Protect Unpaid Interns Against Sexual Harassment. *Newsweek*. NEWSWEEK LLC.

Schwöbel CEJ. (2014) *Critical Approaches to International Criminal Law: An Introduction*, Abingdon: Routledge.

Seabrooke L. (2014a) 'Epistemic Arbitrage: Transnational Professional Knowledge in Action', *Journal of Professions and Organization* 1: 49–64.

Seabrooke L. (2014b) 'Identity Switching from Transnational Professionals', *International Political Sociology* 8: 334–6.

Selwyn N. (2004) 'Reconsidering Political and Popular Understandings of the Digital Divide', *New Media & Society* 6: 341–62.

Sending OJ. (2015) *The Politics of Expertise: Competing for Authority in Global Governance*, Ann Arbor: University of Michigan Press.

Shklar JN. (1986) *Legalism: Law, Morals and Political Trials*, Cambridge: Harvard University Press.

Sikkink K. (2011) *The Justice Cascade: How Human Rights Prosecutions are Changing World Politics*, New York: W. W. Norton & Company.

Simon J. (2000) 'The "Society of Captives" in the Era of Hyper-incarceration', *Theoretical Criminology* 4: 285–308.

Simon J and Sparks R. (2013) 'Punishment and Society: The Emergence of an Academic Field', in Simon J and Sparks R (eds) *The Sage Handbook of Punishment and Society.* London: Sage.

Slaughter AM. (2004) *A New World Order*, Princeton, New Jersey: Princeton University Press.

Slosson M. (2012) ICC Prosecutor Courts Hollywood with Invisible Children. *Reuters.* http://www.reuters.com/article/2012/04/01/us-kony-campaign-hollywood-idUSBRE8300JZ20120401

Smeulers A and Haveman R. (2008) *Supranational Criminology: Towards a Criminology of International Crimes*, Antwerp: Intersentia.

Smeulers A, Hola B, and van den Berg T. (2013) 'Sixty-Five Years of International Criminal Justice: The Facts and Figures', *International Criminal Law Review* 13: 7–41.

Smith A. (2006) *The Theory of Moral Sentiments*, Mineola, New York: Dover Publications.

Smith P. (2008) *Punishment and Culture*, Chicago: University of Chicago Press.

Snyder SB. (2011) *Human Rights Activism and the End of the Cold War: A Transnational History of the Helsinki Network*, Cambridge: Cambridge University Press.

Song JS-H. (2014) 'Tribute to A.N.R. Robinson at State Ecumenical Service', in ICC-The Presidency (ed). Port-of-Spain, Trinidad and Tobago: International Criminal Court.

Spees P. (2003) 'Women's Advocacy in the Creation of the International Criminal Court: Changing the Landscapes of Justice and Power', *Signs* 28: 1233–54.

Steains C. (1999) 'Gender Issues', in Lee RS (ed) *The International Criminal Court: The Making of the Rome Statute.* The Hague: Kluwer Law International.

Tallgren I. (2002) 'The Sensibility and Sense of International Criminal Law', *European Journal of International Law* 13: 561–95.

Tallgren, I. (2013) 'The Durkheimean Spell of International Criminal Law?', *Revue interdisciplinaire d'etudes juridiques* 71: 137–169.

Tallgren I. (2015) 'The Voice of the International: Who is Speaking?', *Journal of International Criminal Justice* 13: 135–55.

Tangri R and Mwenda AM. (2006) 'Politics, Donors and the Ineffectiveness of Anti-corruption Institutions in Uganda', *The Journal of Modern African Studies* 44: 101–24.

Tarrow SG. (2005) *The New Transnational Activism*, Cambridge: Cambridge University Press.

Taub A. (2012) *Beyond #Kony2012: Atrocity, Awareness, & Activism in the Internet Age*. Lean Publishing.

Teitel RG. (2000) *Transitional Justice*, Oxford: Oxford University Press.

Teitel RG. (2011) *Humanity's Law*, Oxford: Oxford University Press.

TFV. (2014) *A Road to Recovery: Healing, Empowerment and Reconciliation. Programme Progress Report*, The Hague: The Trust Fund for Victims, International Criminal Court.

The Guardian. (2011) The worst places in the world for women: Congo. *The Guardian*. Guardian News and Media Limited.

The Hague Trials Kenya. (2014) Fergal Gaynor, the man who speaks for 20,000 Kenyatta case victims at the ICC. *The Hague Trials Kenya*. RNW-radionetherlandsworldwide.

The Observatory for the Protection of Human Rights Defenders. (2013) Violations of the right of NGOs to funding: from harassment to criminalisation. *Annual Report*. The World Organisation Against Torture, International Federation for Human Rights

Tomczak P. (2016) *The Penal Voluntary Sector*, London: Taylor & Francis.

Tsing AL. (2005) *Friction: An Ethnography of Global Connection*, Princeton, New Jersey: Princeton University Press.

Ugelvik T and Dullum J. (2011) *Penal Exceptionalism?: Nordic Prison Policy and Practice*, Abingdon: Routledge.

Ullrich L. (2016) 'Beyond the 'Global–Local Divide' Local Intermediaries, Victims and the Justice Contestations of the International Criminal Court', *Journal of International Criminal Justice* 14: 543–68.

UNODC. (2016) UNODC Annual Report Covering activities during 2016. United Nations Office of Drugs and Crime.

Urry J. (2002) 'The Global Complexities of September 11th', *Theory, Culture & Society* 19: 57–69.

Valverde M. (2012) 'Analyzing Punishment: Scope and Scale', *Theoretical Criminology* 16: 245–53.

Van den Wyngaert C. (2011) 'Victims before International Criminal Courts: Some Views and Concerns of an ICC Trial Judge', *Case Western Reserve Journal of International Law* 44: 475–96.

Van Schaack B and Slye R. (2010) *International Criminal Law and its Enforcement: Cases and Materials*, New York: Foundation Press.

van Wijk J. (2013) 'When International Criminal Justice Collides with Principles of International Protection: Assessing the Consequences of ICC Witnesses Seeking Asylum, Defendants Being Acquitted, and

Convicted Being Released', *Leiden Journal of International Law* 26: 173–91.

van Zyl Smit D. (2005) 'International Imprisonment', *International and Comparative Law Quarterly* 54: 357–86.

Vasiliev S. (2015) 'On Trajectories and Destinations of International Criminal Law Scholarship', *Leiden Journal of International Law* 28: 701–16.

Vauchez A. (2011) 'Interstitial Power in Fields of Limited Statehood: Introducing a "Weak Field" Approach to the Study of Transnational Settings', *International Political Sociology* 5: 340–5.

Verfuss T. (2004) 'Trying Poor Countries' Crimes in a Rich City: The Problems of the Press from the Former Yugoslavia', *Journal of International Criminal Justice* 2: 509–15.

Watkins AF and Welch CE. (2011) 'Extending Enforcement: The Coalition for the International Criminal Court', *Human Rights Quarterly* 33: 927–1031.

Welch CEJ. (2001) *NGOs and Human Rights: Promise and Performance*, Philadelphia: University of Pennsylvania Press.

Wemmers J-A. (2009) 'Victims and the International Criminal Court (ICC): Evaluating the Success of the ICC with Respect to Victims', *International Review of Victimology* 16: 211–27.

Wemmers J-A. (2010) 'Victims' Rights and the International Criminal Court: Perceptions within the Court Regarding the Victims' Right to Participate', *Leiden Journal of International Law* 23: 629–43.

Wemmers J-A and de Brouwer A-M. (2011) 'Globalization and Victims' Rights at the International Criminal Court', in Letschert R and van Dijk J (eds) *The New Faces of Victimhood*. Dordrecth: Springer.

Wendt A. (1999) *Social Theory of International Politics*, Cambridge: Cambridge University Press.

Werle G and Vormbaum M. (2017) *The African Criminal Court*, The Hague: TMC Asser Press.

Werner W, De Hoon M, and Galán A. (2017) *The Law of International Lawyers*, Cambridge: Cambridge University Press.

WIGJ. (2012) 'Gender Report Card on the International Criminal Court 2012', in Women's Initiatives for Gender Justice. The Hague: WIGJ.

Williams B and Goodman H. (2007) 'The Role of the Voluntary Sector', in Walklate S (ed) *Handbook of Victims and Victimology*. Cullompton: Willan Publishing.

Yanacopulos H. (2005) 'The Strategies that Bind: NGO Coalitions and their Influence', *Global Networks* 5: 93–110.

Young J. (2011) *The Criminological Imagination*, Cambridge: Polity Press.

Ypi L. (2012) *Global Justice and Avant-Garde Political Agency*, Oxford: Oxford University Press.

Zappalà S. (2010) 'The Rights of Victims v. the Rights of the Accused', *Journal of International Criminal Justice* 8: 137–64.

Zedner L. (2016) 'Penal Subversions: When is a Punishment not Punishment, who Decides and on what Grounds?', *Theoretical Criminology* 20: 3–20.

Zedner L. (1994) 'Reparation and Retribution: Are They Reconcilable?', *Modern Law Review* 57: 228–50.

Index

For the benefit of digital users, indexed terms that span two pages (e.g., 52–53) may, on occasion, appear on only one of those pages.